The New Significance of Learning

Should education be understood mainly as a practice in its own right, or is it essentially a subordinate affair to be shaped and controlled by a society's powers-that-be? What difference does it make if students are chiefly viewed as recipients of a set of skills and knowledge, or as active participants in their own learning? Does education have a responsibility in cultivating humanity's maturity, or are its purposes to be effectively matched to the functional requirements of a globalized age?

The New Significance of Learning explores these and other high-stakes questions. It challenges hierarchical and custodial conceptions of education that have been inherited as the 'natural order' of things. It discloses a more original and imaginative understanding of educational practice, illustrating this understanding with frequent practical examples.

Among the merits highlighted by this approach are:

- a recognition that education is first and foremost an invitation to join a renewed experience of quest and disclosure;
- a realization that taking up and pursuing such an invitation is a basic right, as distinct from a privilege to be bestowed or withheld;
- an awareness of the decisive importance of specific kinds of relationship in practices of teaching and learning;
- an emphasis on the human qualities as well as the intellectual achievements nourished by dedicated communities of learning;
- an acknowledgement of partiality – of incompleteness and bias – in even the best of humankind's learning efforts;
- the emergence of a distinctive ethical orientation for education as a practice in its own right.

Pádraig Hogan is Senior Lecturer in Education at the National University of Ireland, Maynooth and Assistant Editor of the *Journal of Philosophy of Education*.

The New Significance of Learning

Imagination's heartwork

Pádraig Hogan

Routledge
Taylor & Francis Group

LONDON AND NEW YORK

First published 2010
by Routledge
2 Park Square, Milton Park, Abingdon, Oxon OX14 4RN

Simultaneously published in the USA and Canada
by Routledge
270 Madison Avenue, New York, NY 10016

Routledge is an imprint of the Taylor & Francis Group, an informa business

© 2010 Pádraig Hogan

Typeset in Garamond by Pindar NZ, Auckland, New Zealand
Printed and bound in Great Britain by CPI Antony Rowe, Chippenham, Wiltshire

British Library Cataloguing in Publication Data
A catalogue record for this book is available from the British Library

Library of Congress Cataloging in Publication Data
Hogan, Pádraig.
The new significance of learning : imagination's heartwork / Pádraig Hogan.
   p. cm. — (Routledge international studies in the philosophy of education)
   Includes bibliographical references and index.
   1. Education—Philosophy. 2. Education—History. I. Title.
   LB14.7.H645 2010
   370.1—dc22   2009022259

ISBN 10: 0-415-54967-1 (hbk)
ISBN 10: 0-203-86448-4 (ebk)

ISBN 13: 978-0-415-54967-7 (hbk)
ISBN 13: 978-0-203- 86448-7 (ebk)

I ndíl chuimhne ar mo athair agus mo mháthair,
Micheál Ó hÓgáin agus Bríd Uí Ógáin

Contents

Acknowledgements

The contents of this book have been slowly gathering for more than a decade. I am indebted to authors that I've read and these authors are acknowledged in the text and endnotes, but here I'd like to mention a debt of a different source: to countless conversations with colleagues, students, teachers, and others, in Ireland and overseas, during this extended period. The insights, criticisms and affirmations yielded by these conversations have been invaluable. To do justice to the many people I would like to name would take many pages, so I'm confining myself to a wholehearted thank you to all. Also crucial in this connection has been the standing invitation by a Dublin post-primary school, which has enabled me to teach there in a part-time voluntary capacity from time to time, thus helping my research on educational practice to have a lively home, if sometimes a challenging one, at the heart of practice itself.

I want to record my gratitude to the National University of Ireland Maynooth for granting me a year's sabbatical leave in 2007–2008. This enabled me to converse more widely, to think less intermittently and to get a first complete draft committed to print.

I owe a special word of thanks to Rosemarie, my wife, whose support of my writing efforts has been unfailing and whose refreshing take on my studies has taught me more than once what it means to be surprised by joy.

Introduction

A loss of inspirations

Throughout its history, educational practice has regularly been harnessed to one or other large-scale body of interests. In earlier times, these interests were mainly ecclesiastical, especially in Western societies, although nowadays in the West they tend to be the interests of governments and other corporate bodies. Public arenas are invariably replete with influential groups who have designs of their own on the minds and hearts of the young, and who see public education as a vehicle for legitimately advancing such designs. In such circumstances, the fact that educational practice might have inherent purposes of its own – purposes that are educational *before* they are religious, or political, or anything else – becomes all too frequently obscured. Where this loss of vision of inherent purposes affects multitudes of practitioners themselves – as often happened historically when teachers had to conform to the demands of church or state – the practice atrophies. Atrophy can yield to disfigurement, however, as teachers' commitments to inherently educational purposes are replaced by an enforced acquiescence in government-imposed requirements for measurable performances. The 'effectiveness' sought by the international educational reform of the 1990s, especially in its initial forms, often made such disfigurement the practised norm. It did so by redefining the question of quality in education as one of indexed quantity (of grades, test results, etc.) and by an associated machinery of inspection that effectively sidelined educational purposes themselves.

In the early twenty-first century, effectiveness, as measured by performance indicators, remains a central priority in educational practice. In a post-reform era, things have settled down somewhat. Whole societies have become increasingly at home with such indicators, chiefly as devices that make the conduct of different practices more amenable to prompt public scrutiny. In practices that deal mainly with tangible products (e.g. financial accounting, industrial manufacturing), such devices seem appropriate enough. However, in practices where tangible outcomes bear a complex relationship to the enduring benefits of the practice (e.g. teaching and learning), such devices are deeply problematic if they purport to capture the heart of the matter. In the case of public education, funding is now commonly related to the measured performance of outcomes, so practitioners' energies become attracted by what is most likely to bring the greatest tangible reward. Where habituation in such exercises becomes a prevalent feature of practitioners' work, major changes occur in workplace cultures. The lore of the practice becomes progressively shorn of its best inspirations, with consequences that are particularly incapacitating for newcomers to the practice. Such workplace cultures have become increasingly common in schools, colleges and other learning environments over the past two decades, just as the more worthy ideals that draw people to teaching as a way of life have become increasingly marginalized.

Against this context of a new colonization of teaching and learning, and the longer context of earlier colonizations, there is a pressing necessity to ask anew about education as a practice: to explore the distinctive benefits for humanity and its prospects that arise from the promotion of learning as an undertaking in its own right. To speak of an undertaking in its own right here is not to suggest that education should enjoy an absolute form of independence. Practices that are supported by the public's monies must be properly answerable to the public for the resources and the public trust placed in them. Crucially however, this means being answerable, not for anything and everything, but for fruits *that are properly those of the practice in question*. Governments are now invariably the agencies through which this trust is mediated to educational practitioners. But governments also frequently mis-recognize the nature of this trust, or can't resist turning it to imperatives of their own and making educational practice more a subordinate than a substantive field of action. Subordinate conceptions of education have become so commonplace that it is difficult for many to understand what a substantive account of educational practice might look like. But such an understanding is just what this book is about, together with an elucidation of the possibilities it recovers for productive action. Let us start, then, with a brief thought experiment.

Suppose one were asked to capture, in a nutshell, a view of educational practice that could command public approval but that wasn't the preserve of one or other interest group. One might venture something like this: Educational practice attempts to uncover the potentials most native to each person, and to nourish these through forms of learning that bring benefits of mind and heart to others as much as to oneself. So far so good perhaps, allowing that one can hardly avoid being a bit general when trying to capture something big in a nutshell. Such attempts to uncover and nourish human potentials might count as initially credible candidates at least, for purposes that are distinctly educational. Each person's range of potentials is, of course, different from that of others. Many individuals are responsive to common influences, but often in different ways and in different degrees. Equally clearly, a topic or field of study that might evoke lasting enthusiasms in one person might find no response in another. Tailoring a curriculum to the best aptitudes and abilities of each is a demanding and discerning undertaking; indeed, a goal that remains desirable, but unachievable in a full sense, for most schools and colleges. Scarcely less demanding is the responsibility to ensure that the cultivation of each person's strengths contributes to, rather than takes from, the beneficial learning of all. Even where a single individual is concerned, it often occurs that a formal education that succeeds in cultivating some of a person's potentials to high levels of accomplishment leaves other potentials fallow, or undiscovered. High accomplishment itself sometimes becomes turned to avaricious or other dubious purposes. Also, for reasons that are sometimes clear but are often less so, some students remain untouched by or resistant to virtually everything their formal education seeks to offer. The challenges of educational practice are many, and are often intractable.

Reflections like these disclose the deliberate promotion of human learning, through practices described as educational, as a distinct undertaking, or more accurately, a distinct family of undertakings. Commitment to such practices involves a perceptive recognition of the individuality – both promise and limitations – of each human being. It also involves endeavouring to advance the capabilities of each person in shared environments, where efforts at learning become co-operative, venturesome, and mutually respectful. Where educational practice, thus understood and carried out, is largely successful in its formative stages, it contributes to the unforced disclosure of a vibrant sense of personal identity. It develops the capacities and fluencies required to be an open-minded and discerning learner as an adult. It enables an enduring sense of responsibility for one's continuing learning to take root. Consequences like these are possible where the integrity of educational practice – its distinctness and authenticity – is granted sufficient public recognition and support to make such consequences, themselves, realistic goals.

But every practice has a history: of advances, restrictions, flourishings, near-extinctions, and so on. Such histories reveal that prominent social practices – law, medicine, education – can rarely or ever be carried out independently of the dominant powers of particular times and places. To say this is to say that every practice is affected by politics, both internal and external. This distinction is a crucial one. The internal politics are largely concerned with debates among practitioners themselves over how the goals of the practice are best to be defined, organized and pursued. In addition, they frequently involve controversies over who is to be included or excluded from different forms and benefits of the practice. The external politics are normally concerned with the relations between the interests of a particular practice and those of the reigning powers in the society. They focus particularly on how a particular practice might be harnessed or aligned to what the interests of the reigning powers deem desirable, or just, or expedient. Sometimes there might be a substantial measure of agreement between practitioners and the reigning powers. For instance, medical practitioners might be in substantial agreement with a government Ministry of Health on a range of priorities for the promotion of public health. But there could be deep divisions between both parties on issues such as the ranking or the resourcing of such priorities. Where education is concerned, the long history of the practice in Western civilizations shows that such harnessing has been an ever-recurring, or even an ever-present, feature.

A landmark example from recent times lies in the indignation, then dismay, of teachers in many Western countries at government reforms of the 1990s that removed central discretionary powers from teachers' hands to those of newly powerful government agencies.

But interventions of this kind were so common in educational practice in previous centuries that they hardly counted as landmarks. Of course, in those earlier times, the reigning powers were more usually ecclesiastical than political. But the nature and reach of the interventions were such that whatever integrity the practice might seek to uphold was more often honoured in the breach than in the observance. An appreciation of this point is important to understand the context for the enquiry this book hopes to undertake. A few key historical observations will help to establish that context and also to identify some important themes for exploration in the chapters that follow.

Historical insights

Learning received a particular flavour and significance in Western civilization for more than 1,000 years, roughly from the year AD 800 (the coronation of Charlemagne) to the end of the eighteenth century (the aftermath of the American and French Revolutions). This was so mainly because of the association of learning itself with the patronage of the Christian church, and in later centuries the Christian churches. Monastery and cathedral schools grew up in many European locations during the early Middle Ages and these led, from the eleventh century onwards, to the rise of universities as places of advanced learning. From foundations such as Bologna (1088), Paris (c.1150), Oxford (c.1167) and Salamanca (1218), Christian universities became major centres of study throughout Europe in the following centuries. These historical developments helped to institutionalize the link between the interests of religion and those of education. This marked a widespread consecration of learning, which became a defining feature of European culture – to such an extent that it was difficult to conceive of education on any large scale outside of a religious context. However, this consecration of learning, as Chapter 1 will illustrate, was also a custodianship of learning. Custodianship here means a schooling of mind and heart that was often as restrictive as it was enabling, and that frequently associated virtue with vehemence in belief and action – even with violence towards contrasting outlooks. The notion of 'Christendom', which nowadays has a quaint ring to it, captures something of this fusion of religion with the conduct of learning. It also captures a certain deference towards religious authority on the part of monarchs and other political leaders. As a religious-cultural ethos, 'Christendom' was both a geographical and a historical reality. The word refers not only to the geographical regions where public life was pervaded by ecclesiastical influence,[1] but also to a long historical era. This stretched from the Middle Ages, through the denominational aftermath of the Reformation, up to the effective separation of church and state in many Western countries after the eighteenth-century Enlightenment.

Curiously, the dismantling of the link between religion and public life in one country after another rarely meant a new freedom for the conduct of learning in schools and colleges. Despite inspirations supplied by Rousseau, Pestalozzi and Froebel from the late eighteenth century onwards, custodial conceptions of educational practice invariably survived even the more radical forms of revolution. Where ecclesiastical authorities lost control of schooling, that control passed not to schools themselves, but to newly powerful secular interests, often of a utilitarian, or nationalist, or commercial tenor. To ask why the powers that were formerly in religious hands didn't now pass to the hands of educational practitioners, or to their representative leaders, is to ask what might seem an obvious question. Yet it is a question that has rarely been raised as an explicit theme by scholarly research in the field of education. It would seem that most scholars, and people more widely, accept as 'natural' the outlook that education is essentially a subordinate undertaking; that it must receive its primary cast and character from a class of superiors – political, religious, or otherwise.

The 'naturalness' of this view could have arisen, however, only by the displacement, over many centuries, of a more independent view of the purposes of human learning. Such an independent view, as exemplified (for instance) in the everyday actions of Socrates in ancient Athens, is home to many incisive insights that still remain under-explored. That is to say, Socrates' life and work identifies a particularly promising contribution to Western educational practice, not merely to Western philosophy. This *educational* legacy might subsequently have become a cherished tradition in teaching and learning in Europe and farther afield. That it didn't do so says much for the political power and influence of what displaced it. More subtly, however, it also beckons attention towards the potential of what became eclipsed.

Let us turn now to what can be gleaned from these brief historical observations. To begin with, they show that a fuller and more critical understanding is called for of the 'natural' view and of its enduring force. The same goes for the eclipsed potential of the more independent view. This fuller understanding will enable a searching appraisal of the appropriateness of interventions-from-above in educational practice, including both historical interventions and the major educational reforms of recent decades. It will help to illuminate both the underlying assumptions of reform orthodoxy and the possibilities that a less encumbered kind of educational thinking might reveal. Such a fuller understanding can be advanced, first, by critically investigating the 'natural' view, including its more contemporary secular forms. The fruits of this investigation should, in turn, cast in sharper relief the chief features of an independent view. They might thus disclose its more distinctive insights and illustrate its aptness to societies where learning is to be taken seriously as a life-enhancing, as well as a life-long, endeavour.

The case to be made

Uncovering such an original understanding and highlighting its more salient consequences for educational practice are the chief aims of this book. But to make a convincing case, it will be necessary to establish at an early stage at least the three following points: first, to show what is distinctive about educational purposes (i.e. taken in their own right) and what is lost by an abiding failure to appreciate their integrity; second, to show that such loss remains a decisive feature of today's changing landscapes of learning, not least in the international rise of a new set of goals for educational practice in recent decades; and third, to illustrate that in the democracies of the West, the newly ascendant goals of educational reform compound the loss in question, chiefly by promoting a coercive uniformity that goes largely unremarked behind the everyday faces of a wider pluralism.

I am aware that these three aims look like an overture to a large-scale critique. So it's important to say a few words here about how the enquiry might proceed, and about my own standpoint as author. To begin with, I should stress that, where social practices are concerned, I am unhappy with any investigation that undertakes a critique and then regards its work done. A critique of anything called a practice is less than fully intelligible unless one asks the question: critique in the name of what?, or more precisely, critique for the sake of what? Making such questions explicit puts the spotlight on the necessity for an enquiry into any practice to move beyond critique. This is a necessity not so much to provide a blueprint or grand design for action, but to use the fruits of the critique to identify some important inspirations and insights for advancing the practice concerned. More particularly, these would be inspirations that might be promising and defensible candidates for the commitments of those engaged in the practice. In other words, they would seek to be worthy of acceptance among practitioners as such (i.e. universally), albeit with a circumspect eye to cultural and social factors. The Hippocratic Oath for medical practitioners, including successive variants of it in the history of medicine as a practice, provides a rough example of what is involved here.[2] Such oaths are largely strangers, or are at best implicit, where education is concerned. Even where practitioners hold to something like them, they remain unvoiced. Had education gained something of the degree of independence achieved by medicine, its historical story would be interestingly different. So also would its present concerns and future expectations. These are issues that we will explore in some detail in later pages.

To venture beyond critique in the case of a practice such as teaching and learning, which is essentially a social one (as distinct from practices like medicine with a stronger basis in the natural sciences), is of course a fallible undertaking. It may also be a hazardous one, especially where some prominent currents in today's intellectual life insist on an insurmountable 'incommensurability' of human interests. An incommensurability stance gives priority to the identification and affirmation of differences, and is especially wary of 'consensualism' – namely, of socially engineered forms of consensus that marginalize or oppress those voices that prove intractable to such engineering. Watchful of the claims of any privileged 'we' in the conduct of public debates, upholders of the incommensurability stance would tend to view with deep scepticism any arguments that seek universal acceptance, whether those arguments are addressed to the practitioners of a particular practice or to the wider diversity of humanity. This scepticism, a capacity for which is essential for a proper working of democracy, has been a notable feature of recent writings in a post-modern vein – for example, those of influential authors such as Jean François Lyotard and Michel Foucault. Its insights have to be taken seriously, but its debilitating effects have to be reviewed with no less seriousness, particularly its effects on the kind of venturing needed to advance both the understanding and the conduct of important social practices.

To insist on the primacy of incommensurability is, in effect, to make a virtue of adversarial action. It is to view such action more as an end than as a sometimes necessary means. Such insistence can be described as a strong version of the incommensurability stance. But there is something odd about the logic of such a stance. For instance, if I am an upholder of a strong version of incommensurability, and I write a book advocating this stance, to whom is the book addressed? Just to those who might already be likely to agree with me? Or to that more diverse potential readership whom I would hope to influence, or persuade to my stance? If the latter, I have already abandoned a strong version of the incommensurability stance. In fact, it is difficult to see how any author who addresses a body of arguments to the public can hold a strong version of the incommensurability stance. To write a book or an article is to ask for a hearing. It is to hope to influence, in some degree, readers' thoughts and to prompt them to new pathways – even to encourage a change of outlook among some readers who might previously have thought and believed quite differently. In short, while it isn't possible to dissolve or overcome all human differences, incommensurability is not such a stumbling block to human thought and action as to preclude renewed efforts to learn from the perspectives of others.

As regards the style of the enquiry, I hope to make this conversational – not so much a dialogue as an invitation to readers to an investigation that is in some real measure a joint one. For the author, this involves cultivating a keen alertness to possible points of disagreement that readers might raise. Such an approach means that there will be frequent use of the first person, both singular and plural. Using 'we' can, of course, be seductive. Even employing as much critical vigilance as possible, it is still difficult to avoid using a privileged 'we' that hides its own exclusive character. For instance, what remains unspoken in 'we' is often something like: 'we educated Westerners', 'we defenders of high standards', 'we refined intellectuals', or other such self-designation. In keeping with the conversational approach just mentioned, it is important to ensure as far as possible that the use of 'we' remains alert to such self-regarding traps. In my own use of it, I hope to make it refer simply to the reader and myself; or more widely, my readers, *whoever they happen to be*, and myself. This use of 'we' acknowledges from the start that readers are differently predisposed; the more widely so, the larger the readership happens to be. But it also presupposes that whoever picks up a book with a readiness to read it is, in some degree, prepared to lend an ear, critical or sympathetic as the case may be, to what the author seeks to say.

Mapping the enquiry

The remainder of the Introduction will now identify in outline the structure of the book and the concerns of each chapter. Part I, 'The Identity of Education as a Practice', contains six chapters and seeks to reclaim the all-but-obscured idea that education is a practice with an integrity of its own. Chapter 1 investigates how it became natural in Western civilizations to view education less as an independent practice concerned with inherent purposes of learning, and more as a subordinate undertaking controlled by the powers-that-be in a particular society. Command of education by an external body would have been quite contrary to customary practice in ancient Athens, for instance.[3] The historical explorations in the opening chapter show how the growth of such control involved an effective conquest of practice, mainly by institutionalized religion in pre-modern times, but by a more worldly body of beliefs in an increasingly globalized age. Highlighting the point that historical influences remain active in every practice, efforts are made in the later part of the chapter to capture something definitive of education as a practice with an integrity of its own.

The second chapter reviews a widespread hesitancy among today's philosophers and other intellectuals to put visionary ideals for humanity's betterment, including its educational betterment, into the public arena. This hesitancy allows influence and initiative to become more concentrated in other hands – usually bureaucratic hands. There is no shortage, for instance, of schemes for a betterment understood in more technical terms: as effectiveness measured by performance indicators. The hesitancy among intellectuals is identified as a notable consequence of the dominance of post-modern currents of thinking in recent decades. Incisive critique has been conspicuously to the fore in such currents of thinking. But this critique's preoccupation with destabilizing newly emergent powers-on-the-rise before they get too dominant has made its own best efforts reluctant to venture further than critique itself. Meanwhile, a new and forceful uniformity in the domains of economy and working life pragmatically eschews the culture wars of post-modernism and continues to establish its dominion internationally. The later parts of the chapter argue that, where education is concerned, it is particularly necessary to press beyond critique and to elucidate the distinctiveness of the practice itself. This necessity springs first from imperatives that are inherently educational. But it also springs from a recognition that educational practice has shown itself to be particularly vulnerable to the reforming zeal of champions of the new uniformity.

The integrity of education as a practice is explored in some detail in

Chapter 3. The argument here highlights the point that historical influences are active in every practice, whether these influences are religious, political, cultural or otherwise. However, where such influences come to dominate the practice – as can happen in practices such as medicine and law, as well as in education – the inherent purposes of the practice become sidelined, or realigned to extrinsic goals or interests. Bearing such tendencies in mind, efforts are made to capture something definitive of education as a practice in its own right. Central features of the educational work of Socrates are examined, focusing on a range of striking pedagogical insights that underlie these features. But these imaginative Socratic insights never attained the status of a robust tradition in the world of learning. They were eclipsed as a particular form of Christianity – heavily Platonist in its theology and its educational stance – became institutionalized as the religion of the Roman Empire, and later of Western civilization. Few things were more unwelcome to empire or church than the Greek (but un-Platonist) idea of education as practice undertaken by practitioners with a strong sense of occupational identity who enjoyed a large measure of autonomy in their local settings.

Chapter 4 begins with a critical review of Alasdair MacIntyre's bold claim that teaching is not a practice, but a set of skills; that teaching is 'never more than a means'. After illustrating that a distinction between means and ends doesn't hold up in teaching, attention in this chapter focuses on a close consideration of the kinds of relationships that constitute teaching and learning. Four kinds of 'relationships of learning' are explored in turn: the teacher's relationship to students; to the subject or material being taught; to colleagues, parents and others; and finally the teacher's relationship to him/herself, within which the nature and significance of the other three relationships are decided. These relationships are each considered as active interplays, as is their mingling with each other. They invariably involve a wooing – fruitful, frustrated or other. In this wooing, there is, on the one hand, the voice of a subject that seeks to speak through the teacher's enactments. On the other, there are sensibilities (including abilities) of a diversity of learners. To show what this means in practice, and to highlight that teaching inescapably goes beyond skill and involves the teacher's self-understanding, the chapter concludes with a practical example of such wooing and its inherent benefits. This is presented as a fictional, although realistic, first-person account.

Chapter 5 examines the neglected importance of the teacher's imaginative capabilities, especially in his or her relationship with the subject or theme being studied. This begins with a review of George Steiner's exalted conception of pedagogical imagination in his *Lessons of the Masters*. I argue here that, although teaching remains in Steiner's debt for his many striking insights, his understanding of the central educational relationship as that between masters and disciples is too one-sided. It obscures much of what it had begun to open up. To explore this obscured landscape further, the chapter seeks to illuminate a conception of pedagogic imagination that is no less incisive, but notably less aristocratic, than Steiner's. This exploration discloses teaching as the

disciplined 'heartwork' of human imagination. It stresses the singular importance of originality, self-criticism and renewal in the teacher's own learning,
for as long as teaching remains his or her way of life.

Wooing of hearts and minds always involves care of one kind or another, and
sometimes of one kind *and* another. Chapter 6 examines the kinds of care that
are most appropriate and most fruitful in relationships of learning. Conceptions
that give a prominent place to the erotic in teaching and learning are analysed.
This analysis highlights the point that apart from the ever-present overtones of
sexual desire in the notion of *Eros*, even a 'purified' *Eros* remains problematic.
This is because *Eros* always chooses the object of its desire, to the exclusion of
others. Teachers, by contrast, invariably find themselves confronted by a more
differentiated humanity, from the most agreeable and appreciative to the most
difficult and resistant. The unerotic nature of relationships of learning lies in
the commitment that the teacher must make to one and all. The particular
nature of the ethics of educational practice – further probing of the 'heartwork'
theme – thus arise for investigation later in this chapter.

Part II of the book, 'Educational Forms of Understanding and Action', shifts
the emphasis of the enquiry. Exploration of the distinct features of education
as a practice yields to an investigation of *the forms of understanding* that are most
appropriate to the practice itself and its defensible conduct. If educational
practice is centrally concerned with developing human understanding and
its fruits among learners, its practitioners must themselves become fluent
in how understanding happens, and mis-happens, in human experience.
This sounds obvious enough, but it touches on something that is frequently
overlooked – something more fundamental and more sensitive, for instance,
than psychology's explanations of the development of different kinds of cognition. At issue here is nothing less than the *predisposed* character of all acts
of human understanding. But to claim that all understanding is coloured by
preconceptions that are bedded in one's history of experience is to fly in the
face of traditional theories of epistemology, from Descartes, Hume and Locke
to Kant, Russell and Husserl. Yet this is a claim that most teachers would find
intuitively convincing, despite the fact that a public avowal of its cogency
might invite a charge of relativism. It is a claim, moreover, that has found
substantial warrant in philosophical researches of recent times. This research
has yielded a bountiful harvest of insights, articulated in different ways in
pioneering works of writers such as Heidegger, Wittgenstein and Gadamer.
Despite these major investigations, the decisive import of such insights for
educational thinking and practice has received comparatively little attention
to date. Accordingly, Chapters 7, 8 and 9 critically explore different aspects
of this body of insights in some detail. In doing so, they also draw on the
enquiries of Part I and seek to reclaim the original freshness and incisiveness
of a Socratic educational legacy.

Chapter 7 investigates the heart of the argument that all experiences of
human understanding involve interpretation as an inherent feature, as distinct
from something added subsequently. It reviews the charge of relativism that

might be brought against this 'predisposed' conception of human understanding. It then examines how a pedagogical alertness might detect, and distinguish between, predisposing influences that are disabling and those that are enabling, for purposes of fruitful learning. The historical character of human understanding is probed further in Chapter 8, now in connection with the central place of cultural tradition in teaching and learning. The ever-active influences of tradition – including ancestral and contemporary – on human experiences of understanding are explored. This is done by reviewing the merits of conceptions of tradition that are sceptically adversarial (Lyotard), ones that are avowedly partisan (MacIntyre) and ones that are more openly oriented (Gadamer, Benhabib, Charles Taylor). The chapter concludes by outlining the main features of an *educational conception of tradition*. It links these features to insights from the Socratic legacy considered earlier, and reviews the generous promise that this confluence holds for educational practice. Chapter 9 examines further the merits of an educational conception of tradition. It investigates, in particular, what happens when texts are brought to life, and their contexts brought to light, in learning environments. It reviews the kinds of influences that come into play when learners experience new imaginative neighbourhoods. As the stakes are high in such venturing, some practical examples are given to illustrate the points at issue and to defend an educational conception of tradition from more custodial or partisan ones.

Chapter 10 is concerned with the education of teachers, not in any restricted sense of skill training, but with the formative pathways that teachers' experiences of learning need to travel if teachers themselves are to enable others to travel likewise. Approaches to teacher education that lack a self-critical dimension and a co-operative approach to the cultivation of pedagogical capability are critically reviewed. This review traces the progression from the hierarchical 'competences' approaches, enforced by the international reforms of the 1990s, to a different and more recent concern with competences among international policy bodies such as the OECD. The case is argued that while the former approaches were essentially part of an uncomprehending state machinery that regularly disfigured educational practice, the context for the latter is quite different. That context is informed mainly by a new international awareness that imaginative and committed teachers are a key asset for any country that hopes for sustained economic and social advancement in a globalized era. Competences are thus important, chiefly in the context of the mutual recognition of qualifications, to assist 'the free movement of labour and capital', including sophisticated labour and advanced intellectual capital. Clearly, the main concerns here are not those of educational practice itself and its own betterment. Pragmatically viewed, however, the new concerns of policy-makers mark a historic opportunity for educational practitioners and their leaders to gain a place at international policy-formation tables.

Chapter 11 attempts to sketch what education might newly signify in an era of globalization, if conceived as a practice in its own right. This would be a practice largely freed from the partisan purposes it has historically, or more recently, been compelled to promote. A long list of themes calls for attention from this specifically educational perspective. Rather than carrying out an exhaustive review of these, the chapter selects some salient ones – curriculum development and assessment, justice and equality in education, research and innovation – and brings to bear on these the kinds of insights yielded by earlier chapters: those springing from a tradition of thinking that is educational before it is anything else (e.g. political, religious, commercial).

Continuing in this vein, Chapter 12 explicitly joins the 'new significance of learning' in the book's main title with the 'imagination's heartwork' of the supplementary title. It suggests that this new significance lies less in being a strategic device for economic and technological advancement than in imaginatively cultivating a family of dispositions that are of major importance for the quality of human life, both as a personal and a shared experience. These are dispositions that combine an alert sense of the critical with a disciplining of adversarial and aggressive tendencies, especially where the understanding of human differences is concerned. Such aggressive tendencies are all too often aggravated by the unexamined practices, as distinct from the carefully prepared policies, of contemporary schooling. Benefits of such disciplining include a deeper understanding of humanity's inherent limitations, as well as its possibilities, and an appreciation that human differences must be seen more as a natural profusion than as an ensemble of acrimoniously disposed forces. These benefits might be called the qualities of humanity's maturity. Such qualities enable human learning to become more self-aware, more vibrant and more sustained in the different fields of study and research. But they also enable the advances wrought by learning, not least technological advances, to enhance rather than to diminish humankind's prospects for a peaceful and just co-existence on an increasingly volatile earth.

PART I

The identity of education as a practice

1 The harnessing of learning

Older and newer reins

The rise of corporate tutelage

The first question that calls for exploration in our enquiry is how a practice that was largely independent in its Greek origins lost that independence. How did it become subordinate, first of all to Church interests, and later to those of more secular powers? The decisive points in this transformation of education are closely linked to the historical fortunes of Christianity in Western civilization. In the brief historical overview that follows here, we will see how the seeds of the transformation were sown as early as the fourth and fifth centuries after Christ. But we will also see that changes didn't begin to affect practice on a wide scale until the ninth century or so. The major events of the transformation occurred only after the first millennium.

Revealing insights into the tenor and significance of learning in medieval Europe can be gleaned from a few of the historic conflicts over its conduct that arose between the twelfth century and the aftermath of the Reformation. How these conflicts were dealt with also discloses much about the nature and scope of church control of education. Three short opening examples will help to illustrate this point, and set the context for the larger enquiry. These examples are international landmarks, but the educational histories of individual countries provide abundant further such examples on a smaller scale. A search for counter examples, however – ones that might show a loosening of the ties between institutional religious interests and educational interests – turns up little of note, at least until the revolutionary period of the late eighteenth century.

The first of the three examples is the prolonged quarrel between Peter Abelard and Bernard, Abbot of Clairvaux, during the 1120s and 1130s. Abelard, an exceptionally able logician, was Master of Mont Sainte Geneviève School, to which students flocked from many countries and from which the University of Paris was later to grow. Around 1120, Abelard had published a work called *Sic et Non* (Yes and No), an investigation of 158 questions of Church doctrine on which there had grown up a conflicting body of interpretations. In *Sic et Non*, Abelard systematically assembled authoritative evidence for the arguments on either side of these questions, but he declined to take a conclusive position on them himself. On his own account, his aim here was to 'stimulate youthful readers to greater energy in the enquiry after truth, and make them more acute in their pursuit of it'.[1] In contrast to Abelard's propensity for raising challenging questions, Bernard was a mystic by temperament, for whom the teachings of Christian faith were incomparably beyond the powers of human reason to explore. To him, everything about Abelard's writings and educational approach was repugnant. In a series of vehement complaints to the pope, Bernard charged that in Abelard's work 'the mysteries of God are forced open, the deepest things bandied about in discussion without reverence'.[2] The eventual outcome of the very public row between Abelard and Bernard was that Abelard's work was condemned by the Council of Sens in 1140. The vigorous questioning of received teachings that he practised was not stopped in its tracks, but his hopes for its wider cultivation in the schools as a pedagogical style were sharply curtailed. When a more elaborate form of Abelard's approach was later carried out by Thomas Aquinas (1225–1274), his major work, *Summa Theologica*, provided detailed answers that were clearly intended to be orthodox and conclusive. Although these provoked some minor controversy in the short term, Thomas's work furnished lasting foundations for 'scholasticism'. Scholasticism was both a body of teachings and a pedagogical approach. It involved the raising, but also the authoritative answering, of intricate questions and was to become a prominent feature of European learning for many centuries. The philosophical venturings cultivated by Abelard's work became steered by the efforts of Aquinas into a labyrinth of mapped pathways for the pursuit of learning – but pathways that now carried the stamp of papal approval.

The second example comes, almost four centuries after the Abelard–Bernard controversy, from Martin Luther's break with Rome. Following the publication of his *Ninety-Five Theses* in Wittenberg in 1517, the next four years reveal a striking burst of creative energies on Luther's part. In his successive writings of these years, he severed, with startling daring, all of the ties that bound learning and scholarship to Rome's ecclesiastical authority. 'I wish to be free', he declared. 'I do not wish to become the slave of any authority, whether that of a council, or any other power, or of the University or the Pope.'[3] His eventual excommunication in 1521 would serve to ensure, in Rome's anticipation, that his work would henceforth be without influence in European centres of learning. Subsequent developments, even in the short term, showed Rome's anticipation here to be profoundly wrong. Prominent among these developments was the emergence of new forms of Christianity in various regions of Europe. In these, the pursuit of learning became, not free, but subject to the requirements of differing denominations of orthodoxy that were antagonistic to Rome, and often to each other.

The third example is the investigation of Galileo's work by the Vatican. Galileo was a product of a monastery school and of the University of Pisa. Like Copernicus before him, he became keenly aware that his researches might fall foul of theological orthodoxy. Many of his early experiments and inventions took place while he was a teacher, first in the University of Pisa (1589–1592) and then in the University of Padua (1592–1610). He had been prohibited by the Vatican in 1616 from writing anything further in support of the Copernican theory of astronomy, which he had been advocating for a number of years before then. Galileo's way around this ban was to compose his famous *Dialogue on the Two Great World Systems*, published in 1632. In this book, the arguments in favour of the Copernican system are placed in the mouth of a perceptive thinker called Salviati, whereas those for the Ptolemaic system are given to a character called Simplicio. This artful device did not protect Galileo, however, from the censure of the Inquisition. Threatened with torture, he was forced to recant and the *Dialogue* was placed on the church's Index of banned books.

These examples uncover a few crucial points. First, all three reveal a deep paternalism at the core of the church's stance towards education. Also evident here is an institutionalized, or corporate twist, given to the biblical warrant frequently invoked by church authorities for their educational mission: 'Go ye therefore and teach all nations.'[4] But a close study of the recurring teaching encounters involving Christ in the New Testament reveals that Christ's own teaching approach was conspicuously divorced from institutional power, whether that of 'Caesar', or of the 'scribes and Pharisees'. A Christian church that was based faithfully on the substance and manner of Christ's teachings could scarcely have developed the kind of rationale that came to inform the predominant pattern in Western education.

Second, all three examples also show the unresponsiveness that characteristically occurs when a particular outlook, paternalistic or other, becomes wedded to institutionalized power. As the history of Western education shows repeatedly, once it has been formally announced it is quite rare for a questionable decision to be reconsidered by those who hold corporate power over the conduct of learning. Even though Abelard knew that the outcome of the Council of Sens was procured by dubious means, he also knew that it would be futile to protest that outcome. In the case of Luther, the steadfast refusal by the Vatican to question the rightness of its own stance greatly raised the stakes in the conflict. This ensured that the break that followed would be irreparable, leading to the historic rise of new forms of learning, with their own forms of control, in various regions of Europe. In the case of Galileo, his *Dialogue* remained on the Index until 1835. The Vatican eventually made a formal apology to him in 1992.

Third, examples such as these reveal an insight that is too frequently overlooked – namely, the degree to which purposes that are educational in their own right can become colonized and redefined by the interests of a powerful institution, in this case the church. In the absence of this insight, what gets lost from sight is that the real significance of learning may lie elsewhere than where the macro interests of powerful institutions would place it. That is to say, this significance arises first and foremost from the *experienced quality of learning* by learners themselves – a point that we will explore in detail in the following chapters. And, of course, this experienced quality can vary greatly from one person to another. But where it is largely in conformity with the priorities that external powers can enforce through teachers, a view of education as a subordinate undertaking becomes perceived as the natural order of things. So much so, in fact, that even in the event of an upheaval leading to revolutionary changes, established priorities might be replaced by newer ones – but the order of hierarchy, or colonization, remains essentially unchanged. The subordinate standing of education as a practice becomes newly confirmed.

To argue like this is not to say that educational purposes are necessarily hostile to those of religion or of politics, or of economic activity, or indeed any other set of human purposes that have historically contributed to the shaping of culture and society. It is, however, to say that educational purposes are recognizably different from those other long-established kinds of human purpose, as these latter are from each other. It is also to maintain that the subsuming of educational purposes by other kinds of purpose effectively smothers key educational insights. This curtails what is most distinctive in educational experience itself, properly understood.

These arguments may look strange, indeed counter-intuitive, to minds that are accustomed to the 'natural order' described in the previous paragraphs. And that order could include a great majority of democratically minded people. A brief look at a few key developments in the ancestry of Western learning is necessary to show that the case I'm making is anything but an eccentric one. In particular, it is important to trace the origins of the view that education is part of the machinery of influence of the reigning powers-that-be, as distinct from a practice in its own right. These origins lie in decisive political events of the fourth century AD that changed the character and influence of Christianity, although their initial inspirations reach back to Plato's later writings. In summary, the essentials of the story are as follows.

Roman persecutions of Christians had ceased with the reign of Constantine I (306–324). Then, in a decree of Emperor Theodosius I in the year 381, a Christianity based on the Nicene Creed became officially embraced as the religion of the Roman Empire. In such a situation, it was probably inevitable that Christianity's educational mission would take on some of the authoritarian trappings of the empire itself. The decree of Theodosius I banned all pagan religions. This kind of prohibition was alien to Christianity as previously practised, however contrary its own teachings might be to the pagan religions. Had Christianity itself been developing a non-paternalistic educational emphasis in these early centuries, that emphasis might have become something of a tradition in its monasteries and in other early centres of learning. In this, it might have offered a counter-example to the authoritarianism of imperial rule, at least where educational practices were concerned. But developments of an opposite kind were already taking place within Christianity, perhaps mirroring the largely patriarchal nature of Western civilizations at that time.

These developments received a decisive new impetus from the work of Augustine of Hippo (354–430), not least from his multi-volume book, *The City of God (De Civitate Dei)*. This hugely influential work presented a dramatic and gripping contrast between a sublimely ordered Divine realm and an earthly realm heavily soiled by sinfulness. The sharp rift between the two realms reflected Augustine's underlying attraction to a decisive point in Plato's later philosophy – one which had received fresh emphasis in the writings of Neo-Platonists who were Augustine's mentors and contemporaries. This decisive point was the Platonist doctrine that depicted a higher, unseen world of truth and goodness on the one hand, and a lower world of sensual appetites and their gratification on the other. For Augustine, however, the lower world was now infused with the darker elements of St. Paul's teachings on sin, particularly as found in Paul's *Letter to the Romans*.[5] This confluence of Platonist and Pauline thinking eclipsed some of the brighter tidings of Christianity as it gave shape and force to Augustine's views on learning, authority and obedience. As well as underlying his writings, it also provided the background for his actions in public life, including his support for the primacy of the Roman papacy.[6]

These early events reveal the origins of a much longer historical sequence, through which custodial or colonizing conceptions of education came to prevail in European civilization. The institutionalizing of an Augustinian Christianity played a crucial part in this sequence. A detailed study of the sequence would show how and why it became common to view education as a high stakes undertaking where teaching and learning would be kept under surveillance.[7] Control of education would have a critical importance where education itself was primarily seen as a recurring struggle, even a battle between forces of good and evil, for the minds and hearts of the young. Such strategic control, as the examples reviewed earlier show, would be increasingly exerted throughout Western Christendom as the powers of the Vatican advanced and became more secure.

We have touched in this summary on themes – e.g. institutionalization, custodianship, eclipse – whose fuller impact will become clearer as the enquiry unfolds. It is now time, however, to turn our attentions to more recent forms of colonization in education, and then to exploring what both the older and newer versions obscure.

Takeover in new forms

Paternalism can sometimes be present in educational practice without enduring injury to the experience of learners. It is possible to imagine, for instance, an educational practice inspired by the ideals of Plato or Augustine where influences of an altruistic or a loving kind are experienced more strongly than are custodial or punitive ones. Likewise, with Aristotle's demand in his *Politics* Bk VIII, that education must be controlled by the *polis* rather than by private interests, and that all must be seen as 'belonging to the *polis*.'[8] This is not necessarily the police state it might seem to modern eyes, where extensive surveillance precludes the flowering of diverse forms of creativity. For Aristotle, the *ethos* of the *polis* was to be experienced as a vibrant one, with which citizens would want to identify and to which they would want to belong. Where this sense of vibrancy and voluntary identification is missing, paternalism becomes institutionalized and its effects on educational practice can hardly avoid becoming those of a colonizing force.

To illustrate the import of these points with two contrasting examples, let us consider first of all the case of an imaginary country: country X. Here, a revolution takes place that focuses its attention in a particular way on education. The incoming party, convinced that existing schools and colleges are continually leading people in a range of corrupting directions, closes all of them down. Henceforth, the direction of schooling will strictly follow the lines approved by the revolutionary party, with pride of place being given to the learning by heart of approved texts or scriptures. Recognizing that that this will take considerable time, the new rulers lay down an obligatory 12 years for such schooling for all males. Females are to be forbidden to attend school. The rulers also provide an inspection system to ensure that a deeper immersion in the approved texts is accomplished in each year of schooling and that no serious questioning of orthodoxy can arise among learners.

Consider now a contrasting country, Y. This is a democracy with a wide cultural diversity among the people. The Ministry of Education views itself not as an overlord of ranks of subordinates, but more as a leader – both responsive and innovative – in developing and sustaining a distinctive educational tradition. It also regards itself as a vigilant guarantor of educational rights. Within a democratically developed legislative framework, it seeks to keep tendencies towards bureaucratization to a minimum. It delegates not only the provision and support of schooling, but also much of policy-making, to a range of national and more local agencies. Decisions over what each learner will study in school or other learning centres are taken at the beginning of each school year. These decisions require the involvement of a teacher, the learner and, at least until the school leaving age of 16 years, the learner's parents or guardians. Learners are expected to be active and questioning participants in their own learning and there is a wide range of structures for review, feedback, complaints and appeals. There is also a range of schemes that enable people in their adult years to take further courses, including professional development courses and courses that meet emergent changes in personal expectations and needs. What sustains the system, more so than the regularly reviewed official policies, is a pride in the tradition itself – a widely shared conviction that learning is a lifelong undertaking with its own integrity. This conviction holds that the cultivation of learning is a responsibility and an entitlement, both for each person and for the society of which each is a member.

The first of these two examples, which recalls a recently familiar situation in some regions in the Middle East, reveals a stance where paternalism has hardened into totalitarianism among the powers-that-be. The characteristics of the second example would look quite utopian a generation ago, except perhaps in the most northern of European countries. Yet the educational systems of many countries today would embody both more *and* fewer – as we shall see – of such characteristics.

We have already observed that wherever a long-standing control of education by ecclesiastical authorities declined, this control usually passed into the hands of corporate bodies with interests of their own – invariably more secular interests than their predecessors. This major change marked the historical experience of many countries during the nineteenth century. In most cases, the newly ascendant power was the state, whether at a central or more local level. This, of course, didn't mean the disappearance of church control of education. But it meant its relegation, and thereafter its prolonged waning. Then, in the twentieth century, more than a few totalitarian administrations showed how pervasive and unyielding state control of education could be, and not just in the Eastern Bloc countries.[9] There were also instances, of course, especially during the late 1960s and the 1970s, of counter trends: where governments in more than a few Western countries attempted to promote initiatives that gave educators at a local and regional level more say in the provision and widening of educational opportunities. Most of these initiatives declined, however, after the first oil crisis (1974), and were consigned to the past in the 1990s by new waves of educational reforms internationally. These reforms were largely inspired by neo-liberal Reagan–Thatcher doctrines that had been gathering force during the 1980s. In any event, the fall of the Eastern communist administrations in the final decades of the twentieth century opened the way for a globalized economic order – one that had already been on the rise through an intensifying competition between the major trading blocs. Things like economic know-how, entrepreneurial capacity and technological expertise (including information and communications technology) received a new importance in the globalized order, and in political priorities that were soon to become manifest as educational ones.

The import for education of these developments can perhaps best be shown by drawing two comparisons with earlier eras. First, during the Middle Ages, theology was the most highly ranked form of study in centres of learning throughout Western civilization. The brightest students flocked from afar to the great European universities to obtain distinguished qualifications in this discipline. In an era of globalization, the rank once enjoyed by theology is now enjoyed by economic and scientific disciplines, and by forms of research that become ever more technologized. The qualifications increasingly sought by postgraduate students who now flock to prestigious universities in different parts of the world tend to be a Ph.D. in specialized science, or an M.B.A, not a Magister in theology. Second, following the transformations wrought by the Industrial Revolution, a particular importance was more widely given to natural resources such as coal, iron ore, copper, oil and mineral deposits. In a globalized era, often referred to as a 'post-industrial' age, a new category of resources has come to prominence, namely 'human resources'. Such resources at the more rudimentary level include a literate workforce capable of benefiting quickly from training and retraining. The ability to take initiatives and to work in teams is also becoming a sought-after quality in employees. At more advanced levels, highly valued human resources include: a supply of entrepreneurs and business leaders; a managerial corps that can efficiently monitor performance and either forestall or minimize industrial relations difficulties; and a body of advanced researchers capable of furnishing innovations that have important commercial applications.

In short, the dominance of ecclesiastical authorities in education in an earlier era has been replaced by that of commercially minded politicians and technocrats. The religious imperatives that were once central to the control of schooling in Christendom have progressively yielded to the material imperatives of international competition. Where these changes have been most pronounced, teachers have increasingly come to be ruled by a new set of masters, and their work has become subject to a range of recurring economic and social pressures. Many of these pressures are less blatant, although scarcely less paternalistic, than their historical predecessors. Some are in the form of inducements or sponsorships from business interests. More widely, however, they take the form of government policies that reflect a new international credo, more mercenary than theological in character. In such circumstances (which are prevalent but not universal in Western countries), the tenor of learning becomes regularly vulnerable to the demands of economic and social policy. Teachers thus become newly subordinate, with many state-imposed curtailments on their scope to be the authors of their own work.

These kinds of developments may appear unwelcome only to those who hold deep convictions that the promotion of learning has purposes of its own that are worthy of public recognition and respect. Nevertheless, few can deny the overt highhandedness that marked the first waves of educational reform that took place in the late 1980s and early 1990s. Governments in many Western countries proclaimed that schools were failing to produce what society expected of them and that strong medicine had to be used to remedy matters. The new powers that governments at that time gave themselves for reforming education produced some years of protest and turbulence in schools. These powers did much to raise the anxiety of school leaderships and to lower the morale of teachers. But they failed to bring about smoothly functioning systems yielding ever higher test results, as envisaged by the thrust of the reform movement.[10] After the height of the strong medicine phase had passed, however, governments realized that their new powers could be used in more ingenious ways, especially by giving rewards at least as much prominence as punitive measures. Schools, colleges and universities that actively embraced the priorities and schemes favoured by governments could, by these means, increase their own access to funds. By doing so successfully on a few occasions, the thrust of their teaching, learning and research might become realigned to the new official priorities. The corollary of this kind of policy was that other priorities, and particularly ones that were educational before being anything else, could not expect an entitlement to their own place in the sun – unless perchance a government Minister, or other substantial source of support, could be convinced that one or more of such priorities had some special importance.

It's difficult to assess the historical significance of events-of-change that occur in our own times. Still, this major recasting of educational priorities and actions in recent years seems to carry the marks of a revolution rather than an evolution. It may come to be seen by historians as an educational Reformation, largely accomplished in the final decade of the twentieth and the first decade of the twenty-first century. I believe it will. Unlike the religious Reformation of the sixteenth century, it does not announce new articles of belief in seminal documents such as the *Augsburg Confession*, or the *Institutes of the Christian Religion*, or the *Book of Common Prayer*. Its credo, if one can call it that, can be discerned in strong family resemblances among the educational policy documents of Western governments and international state-sponsored agencies in the last quarter-century. A particularly significant document in this connection is the European Commission's White Paper of 1996, *Teaching and Learning: Towards the Learning Society*,[11] which conspicuously dissolved for policy purposes the distinction between education and training. (EU publications thereafter use 'education and training' as if it were a single word). Among the chief themes of this document that also recur in others are: bringing education and industry closer together, using schools to combat social exclusion, treating investment in education in a similar way to investment in industry, promoting communicative proficiency in a few major languages, developing entrepreneurship through education, and promoting commercially oriented research in universities.[12]

This range of goals, largely neo-liberal ones, could not be called a credo in any religious sense. Perhaps the combating of social exclusion could be seen as semi-religious, but it also fits squarely in the economic scheme of things. For instance, the consequences of social exclusion (e.g. urban violence, organized crime, expanded prison service, increased social welfare bill) are disproportionately costly compared to the efforts that try to limit or minimize such exclusion. In any case, such goals serve as the most widely canvassed of aspirations in educational discourse internationally today, not merely the discourse of economic and social policy. They are repeatedly advanced as goals worthy of the convictions of educators, students and the public more generally. In this sense, they do indeed constitute a credo, more secular and somewhat more informal in character than the credos of the major religions. The international rise of such goals, moreover, concentrates thoughts and energies on economic activity as a major peace-time occupation – one that requires political stability and that helps to keep conflicts at bay, or at least at manageable levels. The success of the European Union is often pointed to in this connection.

What is worth stressing now is that this ever-growing order of economic goals is also a new international uniformity, notwithstanding the increasing diversity of cultures internationally or the increasing differentiation of identities within particular countries. In fact, the latter can hinder our awareness of the former. Also, paradoxically, the new uniformity becomes a more influential force for not being proclaimed as an explicit credo. For instance, its main goals are rarely defined in opposition to any religious beliefs. But to the extent that these goals win the effective commitments of individuals and larger groups, religious commitments (even in secularized form) are likely to rank lower, or even to drop out of the picture. More particularly, where education is concerned, the relegation of the more inherent goals of learning is accomplished not by any attack, frontal or otherwise, on these. Rather, the newer goals throng centre stage with such display and consequence that older ones get sidelined, or almost lost from view. An elaborate machinery of inducements and resourceful duress plays a crucial part here. A transfer to a new order of things thus advances a different kind of orthodoxy in places of learning. One might object to this by pointing, rightly, to an unprecedented diversity of pursuits in today's schools and colleges. Yet a critical look at the bigger picture reveals larger forces at play, and also something of the revolutionary character of what has recently been afoot. Where for many centuries of Western civilization, institutional educational efforts became harnessed on a grand scale to the interests of the church (denominational churches after the Reformation), such efforts have now become harnessed on a more global scale to the interests of economic and technological advance.

So thoroughly have newly controlling conceptions of education become the established pattern in most countries, that it is taken as normal to associate the goals of educational practice with the powers of political office. And this remains largely the case regardless of the ideological colour of the party in power. This explains why it may seem a bit odd to suggest that education is a practice in its own right, with inherent goals of its own that may or may not be compatible with those of the powers-that-be. Yet, as I hope to show in the following chapters, only by pursuing this suggestion does educational practice itself properly come into view. But in order to clarify what such an investigation might hope to achieve, it is necessary first to take account of an objection that might view it as a wasted effort. Explorations that seek to elucidate human practices in constructive terms, providing ideals that are candidates for universal acceptance, draw trenchant criticisms nowadays from post-modern standpoints. Such standpoints furnish new forms of scepticism that have, in recent times, become prevalent in the humanities and social sciences. Far from ignoring such standpoints, our investigation must negotiate its path through them.

2   Overcoming a post-modern debility

Being brought down to size

The rise of post-modern currents of thinking has been one of the more conspicuous tendencies in Western intellectual life in the last decades of the twentieth century and the opening decade of the twenty-first. It has produced an abundance of works which give an unprecedented prominence to newly sceptical forms of critique in the humanities and social sciences, and also in scholarly debate more widely. One of the consequences of this shift of mood is that it has relegated an earlier kind of thinking and writing; one that gave its major energies to visionary theories of change. This is not just a relegation in the form of a displacement by external forces. Rather, it arose mainly from something self-imposed, from a widespread reticence or an unwillingness among writers to put large-scale ideas for humanity's betterment into the public arena. This is the post-modern debility referred to in this chapter's title. But here I am running ahead of the argument that needs to be made, so let us begin at the beginning.

During the 1960s and early 1970s, there appeared a wide range of writings that gave visionary expression to education as a force for transformation. At the more well-known end of this range were works like *Deschooling Society* (1971) by Ivan Illich and *Pedagogy of the Oppressed* (1972) by Paulo Freire. Other less widely known, but nevertheless influential sources of educational ideas, included *Compulsory Mis-Education* (1962) by Paul Goodman, *Freedom to Learn* (1969) by Carl Rogers (both American), and the writings and work of Lawrence Stenhouse in the United Kingdom. Bodies such as UNESCO, OECD and the Council of Europe championed concepts such as 'lifelong learning', 'recurrent education' and 'permanent education'. The Faure Report, *Learning to Be*, was published by UNESCO in 1972 and became a landmark of new educational thinking. It envisaged a visionary restructuring of education, superseding older notions of occupational preparation and drawing confidently on ideals of self-realization and creative humanity. Leading political figures such as Olof Palme did much to advocate such a vision at an international level as well as in his native Sweden.[1]

Of course, there were many contrasts in substance as well as in style among the range of emergent educational visions. Illich's criticisms of formal schooling were frequently couched in provocative declarations, for instance: 'school makes alienation preparatory to life … by teaching the need to be taught.'[2] Freire's writings also had a provocative cast, but unlike Illich, whose criticisms arose from his own reflections on institutionalized learning, Freire's radical pedagogy was based on his successful experiences as an out-of-school educator with oppressed adults in Brazil and Chile. More generally, the emergent ideas of the lifelong learning movement tended to find practical application more in non-formal education than in mainstream schooling. Still, very many teachers were deeply influenced by what they acknowledged as new and worthy inspirations for their actions in schools. The envisaging of better futures by writers who devoted constructive energies to the articulating of such inspirations could expect a wide and sympathetic hearing among educators.

By contrast, there is a strong sense today that far-reaching moral–political visions, whether those of a Rousseau or Marx, of a Freire, Faure, or Palme, are no longer convincing. It is as if they have become *passé* in an age that is suspicious of utopias. This conclusion finds a potent, if terse, expression in Jean François Lyotard's seminal book, *The Postmodern Condition: A Report on Knowledge*. This was first published in French (Quebec) in 1979, as a report on the condition of knowledge in the world's more technologically advance societies. Lyotard describes the post-modern as a stance of 'incredulity' towards 'grand narratives' (*grands récits*).[3] By grand narratives, Lyotard means large-scale 'discourses of legitimation' or, more plainly, philosophical accounts that make an appeal to one or more foundational ideas as sources of justification and meaning. Marxism, for instance, would be a good example. Its account seeks to illuminate the exploitation of an underclass and the necessity of class struggle, and its appeal is to the grand ideal of emancipation through revolution. More generally, grand narratives would include anything that falls into one or more of the following categories:[4] (a) political and economic 'isms' of all kinds (e.g. nationalism, socialism, etc.); (b) any philosophy that combines a comprehensive explanatory position with an orientation for ethical commitment (e.g. classical metaphysics, idealism, Enlightenment rationalism); (c) finally, but not least, major religions such as Christianity, Islam, Judaism, Hinduism, etc.

Grand narratives would include the entire diversity of ideals that sought to engage human commitments and actions on a major scale from ancient times onwards. The 'incredulity' that Lyotard discerns as the trademark of the post-modern condition is a scepticism towards such ideals – a scepticism that he maintains has become a deeply rooted feature in the cultures of technologically advanced societies. This incredulity he views as 'a product of progress in the sciences', but he also suggests that such progress, in turn, presupposes this incredulity. On this account, the advancement of scientific and technological research requires a progressive falling away of both traditional and more modern beliefs in grand ideals for humanity and its prospects. On a first reading, one can see a certain force or plausibility in this argument, but there is also something curious about it. Its sweeping style overlooks any hint that scientific research might sometimes proceed, not from a loss of all enchantment, but from a different kind of enchantment, or perhaps a transformation of enchantment. We will return to this point later (Ch. 11, section on research).

The Postmodern Condition analyses the manner in which large-scale economic interests combine with the power-producing knowledge of advanced research. This combination, Lyotard argues, becomes the new driving force of government and public administration, and of higher economic activity in society more generally. One of the decisive changes that occurs in this event, according to Lyotard, is that 'learning is translated into quantities of information' and that 'anything that is not translatable in this way will be abandoned'. He concludes from this that '[t]he old principle that the acquisition of knowledge is indissociable from the training (*Bildung*) of minds, or even of individuals, is becoming obsolete, and will become ever more so.' On this reading of things, knowledge becomes significant as a commodity and the relationships between its suppliers and its users increasingly resemble the established relationships between producers and consumers. This kind of knowledge, 'an informational commodity indispensable to productive power', becomes, on Lyotard's view, 'the major stake in the worldwide competition for power'.[5]

The goals prized most highly by the protagonists of such an order are those of 'performativity' according to Lyotard – namely, the 'optimization of the relationship between input and output'.[6] Lyotard rarely refers to leadership in approving terms, and *The Postmodern Condition* is well supplied with critical remarks about 'managers', 'decision-makers', 'technocrats' and 'the system'. Guided by the criterion of performativity, Lyotard continues, the actions of this controlling class have 'dehumanized humanity', by consigning to the past any notions of competence as defined by criteria such as 'true/false' or 'just/unjust'.[7] This dehumanizing is done in order to 'rehumanize' humanity (or re-energize it) by reference to the criterion of 'performance-oriented skill'. To describe the various spheres of discourse and action where power is exercised (e.g. commercial organizations, public administrations, colleges, government politics, etc.), Lyotard uses the phrase 'language games', borrowing a term of art from Wittgenstein. This enables him to present in a summary way his critique of the 'arrogance' and 'terrorism' of the new powers-that-be of post-modern society.

> By terror I mean the efficiency gained by eliminating, or threatening to eliminate, a player from the language game one shares with him. He is silent or consents, not because he has been refuted, but because his ability to participate has been threatened (there are many ways to prevent someone from playing). The decision makers' arrogance, which in principle has no equivalent in the sciences, consists in the exercise of terror. It says: 'Adapt your aspirations to our ends – or else.[8]

There is an arresting incisiveness about Lyotard's key arguments. His analyses have keenly brought to light decisive trends that were less than conspicuous before his 'report' was published, but that have become prominent features of what is now acknowledged as a globalized economic order. Countless instances can be cited from the workings of this order to confirm both the conclusions and predictions in *The Postmodern Condition*. We have already mentioned a few of them in the previous chapter. The fact remains, however, that Lyotard's analyses have a sweeping character that presents the reader with a completed, but sometimes one-sided, picture. They rarely call attention to counter-instances that might question the status (the degree of influence), as distinct from the reality, of the features he highlights. His arguments tend to leave little scope for possibilities other than those forces he presents as dominant, even the exclusive ones. In short, his analyses produce perceptive generalizations that allow for no significant exceptions.

On a more critical investigation, Lyotard's account of things seems to reveal some of those 'grand narrative' features that, on his own account, can hardly be taken seriously today. Let us examine this more closely. First, *The Postmodern Condition* is not just a 'report'. It is a wide-ranging account of the recent for-tunes of human knowledge that seeks to explain things in a new light. This aiming for comprehensive explanatory power is something it shares with the efforts of many of Lyotard's predecessors – for example, Descartes, Kant or Hegel. Lyotard would hardly object to this comparison, but he would be likely to insist that where such previous philosophers sought to recommend an ethics universal in scope, he refrains from doing any such thing. In this, he identi-fies himself closely with the sceptical stance, or 'incredulity', that his analysis presents as a feature of advanced technological societies. In Lyotard's analysis, legitimation of grand narratives, or of values universal in scope, becomes all too often a denial of difference, or of heterogeneity. He see the demand for such legitimation as a form of imperialism that can become 'totalizing' (imposing an oppressive uniformity), or even totalitarian.[9] The violent history of the twentieth century, including two World Wars, tyrannical versions of Marxism in Eastern Europe and China, recurring bloodshed in various regions of the world in the name of grand political or religious ideals – these events and their lasting effects on memory illuminate a context in which the incredulity Lyotard describes becomes an intelligible stance. They reinforce, as it were, the disenchantment with traditional ideals that he earlier associated with scientific and technological progress. But Lyotard's suspicion of universalistic ethical theories arises also from his view of their assimilation into political and economic life in peacetime, especially in the exercise of institutionalized power. Referring, in particular, to critical theories that spring from leftist inspirations, he writes:

'Traditional' theory is always in danger of being incorporated into the programming of the social whole as a simple tool for the optimization of its performance; this is because its desire for a unitary and totalizing truth lends itself to the unitary and totalizing practice of the system's managers.[10]

This sceptical stance towards what might be called grand ideals of humanity, including those of more ancient and more modern ancestry, is a pronounced note in writings in a post-modern vein, other examples of which we will consider shortly. It cultivates a disinclination towards large-scale mobilizations, whether of labour movements, of pressure groups, or of public opinion more widely. Lyotard's reasoning here echoes the points about 'totalizing' in the passage just quoted. But it also adds a gloomy note that seems to spring from Lyotard's assessment of political action in the decade after the youth revolts of 1968 in France and elsewhere: 'In any case, there is no question here of proposing a "pure" alternative to the system; we all now know, as the 1970s come to a close, that an attempt at an alternative of that kind would end up resembling the system it was meant to replace.'[11]

Lyotard is, on the one hand, highly critical of what he sees as the coercive nature of political and working life in a globalized economic order. On the other hand, he resists any inclination to confront these goals directly – particularly a confrontation that draws on major inspirations for transformation. That is not to say that he discourages confrontation entirely. In fact, he recommends it strongly in the form of a multiplicity of smaller-scale 'games' that 'accept agonistics as a founding principle'.[12] This combativeness would also take 'paralogy' (the search for dissensus as distinct from consensus) as a guiding principle. Its actions would be focused on destabilizing anything with 'pretensions to totality', actively encouraging heterogeneity, and continually seeking to unsettle coercive exercises of institutional power.

The fundamental scepticism of Lyotard's standpoint rejects ideas that seek to be universal in scope, such as emancipation, equality or truth. He believes that these obscure, or deny, or smother difference – or at least that their manifestation in human history have repeatedly done so. More radically, Lyotard seems to hold that universalist aspirations *cannot but* have such unhappy consequences. I hope to show later in the chapter that this is a stance that is self-debilitating, even self-defeating, for education as a practice, especially when it is reinforced by other currents that run in a similar or parallel vein. Two such currents spring from the works of Jacques Derrida and Michel Foucault, and these call for attention now.

Deconstruction and care of self

If one is claiming an inherent integrity for the purposes of learning, it seems reasonable to associate this integrity with the search for truth. The defence conducted by Socrates at his trial (and made famous by Plato in his *Apology*) can be taken as a public appeal to recognize the importance of this kind of search. It can also be taken as an appeal to grant this search some protection from the expediencies of commerce and from the shifting priorities of power politics. But the radical scepticism we are investigating can confront such a stance with a sharp criticism: that the search for truth assumes that, in some ultimate sense, there is truth to be known. This criticism suggests that the search for truth is all too often really a search for comfort or reassurance; one that seeks for presence over absence, for meaning over meaninglessness, for security over venture. In his early writings, Derrida described such tendencies in philosophical enquiry as 'logocentrism'. It is difficult to find an English equivalent for the Greek word *logos*. English terms such as 'reason', 'account', 'uttered word', could each be used, depending on the context in which *logos* occurs in a Greek text. In all such contexts, however, it has the sense of a meaningful fullness – a conclusive articulation that disposes human thought and action to certain ends rather than others.

Derrida developed the 'deconstruction' famously associated with his name as an approach to tackle the domesticating tendencies of 'logocentric' thought. For instance, in his book, *Of Grammatology* (1967), Derrida explained that his philosophical approach was seeking to accomplish 'the deconstruction of all significations that have their source in that of the logos. Particularly the signification of truth.'[13] To many of his critics this looked like an unintelligible exercise, to others an irresponsible or chaotic one. But Derrida's stance was that too many of the disclosures of 'truth' by Western philosophy were really *closures* of questions that should remain radically open. Such closures, on Derrida's argument, tended to supply definitive accounts and foundational meanings that marginalized whatever was inherently different or 'other'; whatever the search for truth failed to assimilate, or subject to its assured grasp. The thrust of Derrida's deconstruction then was to upset the authoritative readings of major texts of Western learning, to defer definitive meanings where traditional readings sought to pin them down, and to release a play of different possibilities for new generations of readers. What was not clear, however, was what productive purpose might be served by this release of new possibilities. Deconstruction seemed to abandon the ethical concerns of serious argument and to indulge itself instead in reckless aesthetic plays and counterplays. Critics accused Derrida of nihilism and of playing fast and loose with the major concerns of philosophical enquiry. One critic alleged that his ideas were 'poison for young people'.[14]

The controversy provoked by Derrida's work reached a crisis in 1992, when a proposal by Cambridge University to award him an honorary doctorate was objected to by some dons. This forced the matter to be put to a vote (336 to 204 in favour of Derrida) and made 'the Cambridge affair' an international incident among philosophers, and in intellectual circles more widely. Almost a decade before this 'affair', however, Derrida had emphasized, in response to his critics, that deconstruction was anything but a form of nihilism, or paralysis of responsible action. He insisted, on the contrary, that it was an exercise of reason, envisaging 'a new mode of questioning', 'a new relation of language to tradition', 'a new way of taking responsibility'.[15] During his later career, Derrida was at pains to highlight the underlying responsibility of his undertakings. In his writings of the late 1980s and 1990s, for example, wherein the influence of Emmanuel Levinas' ethical philosophy on his work becomes more pronounced, Derrida repeatedly argues that the purposes of deconstruction were inspired all along by the search for a kind of 'undeconstructible' idea of justice. As distinct from more traditional 'foundational' ideas of justice, familiar to both philosophy and history, the 'undeconstructible' is one that always beckons from the future. For Derrida, it is one that cannot be institutionalized, that resists determinate encapsulation, and that cannot therefore be taken control of and deployed by powerful human interests. One of Derrida's later books, *Specters of Marx* (1993 French, 1994 English), stresses the inspirations that reside in a transformed kind of Marxist thinking for an idea of justice that 'remains irreducible to any deconstruction'.[16] Elaborating on this, he speaks of a 'messianic eschatology ... a certain experience of the emancipatory promise, an idea of justice – which we distinguish from law or right, or even human rights'.[17] Likewise, in his 1990 address 'Force of Law: The "Mystical Foundations of Authority"', Derrida speaks repeatedly of the 'deconstructability of law (*droit*)' and the 'undeconstructability of justice'.[18]

This important distinction between deconstruction, on the one hand, and what remains beyond deconstruction on the other, sheds light on the relationship between Derrida's earlier and later arguments. It reveals a coherent purpose underlying those new possibilities, which Derrida's earlier attacks on traditional forms of philosophy sought to open up. It now becomes clear that this would be an opening up of human minds and hearts; or more precisely an opening up *in* minds and hearts of spaces, where inspirations of first ethical importance might thrive. The very nature of such inspirations, however, would be such that they would resist institutionalization. Deconstruction as a discipline would highlight the need to undertake this resistance with renewed energy as it detected tensions between a worthy idea (of justice, of democracy), on the one hand, and the tendency of even the best ideas to become 'welded to an orthodoxy'[19] on the other.

From a critical point of view, it could be said that the earlier charges of irresponsibility against Derrida by his opponents might now be dropped in favour of a charge of abstract mysticism. Derrida might accept the 'abstract' part of the charge, but would also wish to stress that the abstract is what safeguards the most worthy springs of human thought and action from deformation. What Derrida calls 'the messianic' identifies a committed, yet a somewhat indeterminate stance towards religious faith, and towards action that might spring from such faith. If one asks then, what it is for the sake of which deconstruction is carried out, the ultimate answer seems to lie in the answering of an ethical, even a religious call; one that indicates a certain direction for thinking and action. But for all practical purposes, this direction remains indistinct.

Turning now to the works of Michel Foucault, the conception of learning as a search for truth comes in for some hard times, at least in his early and middle writings. In a 1977 interview titled '*Truth and Power*', Foucault insisted that 'truth isn't outside power'; that each society has its 'regime of truth', its 'political economy of truth'.[20] Similar themes suggesting that truth is encapsulated by power and its exercise are to the fore in other works by Foucault during the 1970s. For instance, in his 1971 essay, '*Nietzsche, Genealogy, History*', he criticizes traditional and conventional history for providing comforting illusions for those human desires that seek a reassuring sense of identity. 'We want historians' he declares, 'to confirm our belief that the present rests upon profound intentions and immutable necessities'.[21] Genealogy is the contrasting approach that Foucault, following Nietzsche, recommends because 'it opposes itself to the search of "origins" (*Ursprung*)'. It seeks instead to disclose the exercise of power and violence through a careful documentation of actual happenings – of 'invasions, struggles, plunderings, disguises, ploys'.[22]

On a similar theme in his *Discipline and Punish* (1975 French, 1977 English), Foucault argued that there is no knowledge that 'does not presuppose and constitute power relations'. He went on to insist:

> These 'power-knowledge relations' are to be analysed, therefore, not on the basis of a subject of knowledge who is forever free or not free in relation to the power system, but, on the contrary, the subject who knows, the objects to be known and the modalities of knowledge must be regarded as so many effects of these fundamental implications of power-knowledge and their historical transformations.[23]

These arguments suggest that anything that claims, on behalf of human learning, to be a search for truth – a search that might provide resources for emancipation from oppression – is an illusion. Many critics have faulted Foucault on this score[24] and have pointed out that something like a serious notion of truth-seeking must underlie Foucault's own entire project if that project is to be coherent. Charles Taylor, for instance, writes: 'The Foucaldian notion of power not only requires for its sense the correlative notions of truth and liberation, but even the standard link between them, which makes truth the condition of liberation.'[25] Foucault's later work seems to have taken the point of such criticisms, although not by acknowledging them explicitly.[26] But there is an important shift in Foucault's later position. For instance, in his 1984 essay, '*What is Enlightenment?*', he speaks of his work as trying 'to give new impetus, as far as possible, to the undefined work of freedom ... work carried out by ourselves upon ourselves as free beings'.[27] More explicitly, in an interview shortly before his death in 1984, Foucault distinguished his work (which he regarded as critique) sharply from polemics and insisted that everything of importance turned on this distinction: 'I insist on this difference as something essential: a whole morality is at stake, the morality that concerns the search for truth and the relation to the other.'[28] The significance of this shift becomes clear when we realize that 'a morality that concerns the search for truth' would be a foreign theme in Foucault's early writings – one more likely to be attacked than to be pursued.

Two of the main themes in Foucault's later works are 'care of the self' (*epimelia heautou*) and 'truth-telling' (*parrhesia*). In exploring these, he returns in a major way to classical Greek thinkers. Here he is not seeking to apply ancient ethics to a post-modern age. He is attempting, rather, to uncover a suggestive originality that later became lost to Western ethical thought and practice.

Foucault's explorations in his earlier and middle writings (e.g. *Madness and Civilisation*, *The Order of Things*, *Discipline and Punish*) had already associated that loss with the dominance of metaphysical and later scientific conceptions of truth in Western civilization.

In relation to the care of the self, Foucault is keen to show that this involves, first of all, a self-mastery. This is a critically informed self-knowledge, as distinct from a mastery by others. It is also distinct from a mastery of self that is not overtly coercive but that has nevertheless been *imposed* by others. This latter kind of mastery attracts particular criticism from Foucault. He describes it in many of his writings as a 'normalization' of the self accomplished through institutionalized practices (judicial, medical, educational) that promoted oppressive forms of acquiescence. Second, Foucault's late work emphasizes that a proper care of self also involves a care of others, and that it is distinct from any kind of self-preoccupation.[29]

Exploring 'a morality that concerns the search for truth' became the theme of what turned out to be Foucault's last course at the Collège de France – namely, the practice of truth-telling (*parrhesia*) in the ancient Greek and Roman worlds. The course had a two-fold emphasis: truth-telling as a political virtue (telling the truth to the politically powerful even at the cost of one's life), and truth-telling as a moral virtue (telling the truth to others even at the cost of one's reputation or self-image). Foucault gives the *Apology* of Socrates a particular importance in this connection. Socrates' account of his own life's work before a large and powerful jury is revealed as combining both kinds of *parrhesia*. Foucault calls attention, however, to the point that Socrates continually maintains – that his first interest is not in politics but in the care of one's soul. He credits Socrates with exemplifying, by practising philosophy as a way of life, a 'new form of parrhesia'. For Socrates, Foucault points out, truth-telling was not just a political virtue, but *the* major virtue in living 'the true life' (*la vraie vie*).[30]

To summarize, in the case of both Derrida and Foucault, significant shifts are evident between their earlier and later works. In both cases, the concentration on penetrating critique in earlier and middle works expands to include an ethical orientation towards the future in their later works. But neither author provides, in his later work, anything like a substantial account of what emancipatory forms of practice would look like: for instance, practices of education, of medicine, of law, of religion. This is as true of Foucault's late writings on the 'care of the self' as it is of Derrida's late writing on politics and on religion. Whereas Derrida's accounts of 'a justice yet to come' remain elusively abstract, Foucault offers very guarded remarks, such as the following:

> For example, with regard to the pedagogical relation – I mean the relation of teaching, that passage from the one who knows the most to the one who knows the least – it is not certain that self-management produces the best results; nothing proves, on the contrary, that that approach isn't a hindrance. … The farthest I would go is to say that perhaps one must not be for consensuality, but one must be against nonconsensuality.[31]

There are further cautionary observations of this kind in Foucault's later writings and interviews, including this summary description of his stance: 'So my position leads not to apathy, but to a hyper – and pessimistic activism.'[32] Foucault's pessimism about action here echoes that of Lyotard, and seems to be based on Foucault's continuing belief that action on any large scale would result in new forms of tyranny: 'programs for a new man that the worst political systems have repeated throughout the twentieth century.'[33]

In reply to the practical focus of the question 'Critique for the sake of what?', it can be said that the investigations of Lyotard, Derrida and Foucault are critically illuminating, yet indecisive. So where this question is concerned, they are important chiefly in a preparatory sense. They provide crucial insights, necessary for the circumspect exploration of pathways for defensible forms of practice. Yet their shared reticence to venture farther than ethical orientations that remain couched in the most abstract terms brings such exploration to an effective stop. The insights of Lyotard come at the price of constraining the efforts of practitioners – and, in a particular way, teachers – to the point of a critique-induced incapacity for constructive action. It is difficult to see how educational practice could be nourished on inspirations confined to the search for 'paralogy', or the destabilizing of emergent hegemonies, or even the proactive recognition of previously unacknowledged identities and differences (i.e. Lyotard's 'bearing witness to differends'). But the thinking of Derrida and Foucault hardly fare much better in this connection. Foucault's writings provide perceptive illuminations of the often-unacknowledged exercise of violence in practices of education, medicine, pastoral care and law enforcement in Western history. But there are no contrasting illuminations, or even suggestive intimations, of what non-repressive practices in these fields might look like. Where Derrida is concerned, the 'messianic' emphasis in his later work seeks to articulate a just and trusting foundation for relations to others. Yet it remains fundamentally indistinct what this would look like in practice. It even remains indistinct in principle.[34]

Beyond critique: the features and necessities of practice

The previous sections have explored some of the main characteristics of the post-modern debility mentioned at the start of the chapter. This is not a debilitation of all philosophical efforts, of course. Rather, it marks a major concentration of energies on critique and a similar withdrawal of energies from envisaging, even tentatively, some promising and defensible possibilities for practice. It neglects or declines the necessity to articulate some constructive shape of that for the sake of which critique is undertaken in the first place. Practices need to be sustained and enriched by the best reflective efforts of practitioners themselves. Clearly this involves criticism, including criticism of those internal features of a practice that hinder its development and criticism of external factors that distort or subdue the practice. Such criticism lacks full coherence, however, unless the arguments and insights it brings together also place before practitioners some inspirations for the development of the practice that are both potentially fruitful and worthy of the convictions of practitioners as such. This reference to practitioners *as such* suggests that whatever ideas or courses of action are put forward as candidates for defensibility are presented in a universal sense – i.e. for acceptance of all practitioners *as* practitioners. It is also important to note here that what is offered as a defensible *candidate* for universal acceptance differs sharply from anything like an *a priori* principle that claims universality from the start, whether on logical or other grounds. A candidate for universality remains alert to the fallibility of human argumentation and thus remains open to criticism, correction and, indeed, refutation. To present candidates for acceptance in a universal sense, moreover, is not to overlook that there might be exceptions in a particular set of circumstances. It is to say, however, that such exceptions would be regarded as departures from the norm, exceptions for which good reasons might be expected to be advanced.

To put forward constructive ideas as universal candidates for the commitments of practitioners might be viewed from a critical viewpoint, however, as an attempt to impose – however civilly – a restrictive uniformity on practitioners; to deny practitioners the diversity of approaches that a practice itself needs in order to flourish. To deal with this criticism properly calls first for some closer exploration of the notion of practice itself and, more particularly, of education as a practice. Some practices allow for, and even demand, a wide diversity of approaches among practitioners. Examples would include creative writing, musical composition, acting and a range of practices that are generally associated with the arts. Towards the other end of the spectrum are practices wherein such diversity among practitioners might endanger the very purposes of the practice itself. Examples here might include surgery, structural engineering, air traffic control, or more widely, practices wherein expertise has to be exercised in a very precise manner. Between both ends lie practices that, in some respects, require a vigilant precision, but that also allow for the exercise of a greater or lesser degree of inventive spontaneity. Examples here include practices such as nursing, teaching, and other practices in the so-called 'caring professions'.

But to get to the heart of the issues in question here, we need to be clearer first about what distinguishes a practice from other forms of action. Here we are assisted by some recent researches by Alasdair MacIntyre and others. MacIntyre's book, *After Virtue: A Study in Moral Theory* (1981, 1985), furnished some surprising and seminal ideas, and the book remains a central point of reference for debates in a number of disciplines across the humanities and social sciences. In Chapter 14 of *After Virtue*, MacIntyre gives the following description of what constitutes a practice.

> By a practice I am going to mean any coherent and complex form of socially established co-operative human activity through which goods internal to that form of activity are realized in the course of trying to achieve those

standards of excellence which are appropriate to, and partially definitive of, that form of activity, with the result that human powers to achieve excellence, and human conceptions of the ends and goods involved, are systematically extended.[35]

The many features of this description provide a range of criteria for distinguishing between practices and other human actions. MacIntyre supplies the following examples to illustrate the distinction. Throwing a football with skill is not a practice he says, but the game of football is. Sowing turnips is not a practice, but farming is. Bricklaying is not, but architecture is. Other examples of practices he includes are chess, painting, music, physics, chemistry, biology, history, and, more generally, 'arts, sciences, games, politics in the Aristotelian sense, the making and sustaining of family life'.[36]

If we focus briefly on each of the four main features of MacIntyre's description, and apply these to education as a practice, the necessity for overcoming the critique-induced debility explored earlier should be all the more compelling. The four features we will take in turn are: (a) a coherent and complex human activity that is socially established; (b) the goods, or benefits, that are *internal to* that activity, as distinct from those external benefits that the activity might also make possible; (c) the standards of excellence that are appropriate to the activity and that help to define its distinctiveness; and (d) the enriched conceptions of the benefits of the practice that are cultivated by the practice itself.

Beginning with the first of these features, education can clearly be seen to be an established social activity, and a complex one at that. Its successful conduct, moreover, clearly requires co-operation among colleagues. Here, however, questions about coherence can arise. Sometimes, for instance, successful co-operation is curtailed by conflicting conceptions among practitioners about what constitutes the coherence of the activity. This conflict over coherence might also be evident in misunderstandings between teachers and students or parents about the basic purposes of the work being done. It might also be evident in disagreements between teachers as a body and state educational authorities. For instance, government policy might view the point and coherence of teachers' work chiefly in the maximizing of test scores. Many teachers, for their part, might view examinations and tests as an encumbrance – a necessary evil that periodically interferes with the real work of teaching and learning.

In relation to the second feature, the internal goods or benefits of a practice are what distinguish it most clearly both from other practices and from activities that would not count as practices. In the case of education, internal goods or benefits would include the insights, understandings and proficiencies, the cultivated capabilities, dispositions and other personal accomplishments that are nurtured by practices of learning and teaching. The external goods or benefits would include the social status, money, occupations and so on, to which qualifications and other credentials of learning might open the door. It is important to remark here that frequent confusions of external with internal goods give rise to many of the more intractable acrimonies in education.[37]

In fact, the term 'goods', despite its positive connotations as a widely used term in philosophy, might contribute to this confusion in educational debate, not least because of the common association of 'goods' with 'commodities'. I will discard 'goods' in favour of 'benefits' from here on, as this latter term has a more recognizable range of connotations, including, for example, the material benefits of an insurance policy, the benefits of someone's acquaintance, and not least, the inherent benefits of learning.

The third feature concerns the standards of excellence that are appropriate to the particular practice, and that help to define its distinctiveness. To highlight this feature is to emphasize that such standards of excellence arise directly from a keen appreciation of the internal benefits of a practice, not the external benefits. For instance, where inherent benefits are concerned, perfecting one's game in football requires a participant's understanding of the finer points and more refined skills of the game. This involves trying to master the exemplary ball moves associated with the game's great players, and even discovering some moves of one's own that add to the sophistication and enjoyment of the game. The external benefits of excelling at football might include fame and wealth, but such goals are also achievable by other means and their pursuit through football does not necessarily enrich the game. Similarly, pursuing excellence in the study of, say, biology, includes coming to understand and appreciate how utterly different the world of living things is from what the untutored evidence of our senses might lead us to believe. It also includes cultivating the desire and the capability to advance one's understanding to ever further levels. By contrast, where students' achievements in biology (or any other subject for that matter) spring mainly from the prospect of external rewards and prizes, the case is quite different. The inherent benefits that inform excellence, properly understood, now become clouded, or even obscured, from both learners and teachers alike.

Activities that enrich the practice itself constitute the fourth feature. This issue directs attention to the constructive initiatives of practitioners. Where the conduct of a particular practice is healthy, this will be marked by initiatives that publicly affirm its benefits, and that call forth the best efforts of practitioners to refine and further such benefits. Everyday examples would include: initiatives by communities of anglers to restock rivers, to safeguard against water pollution, to develop and share knowledge on new kinds of artificial flies; initiatives by established local drama groups and music societies to build on existing achievements by taking on more challenging productions; initiatives by farming co-operatives to improve drainage and irrigation and to secure an optimal balance between high-yielding agriculture and ecological protection. More formal examples include the establishing of professional bodies and associations, such as engineers' institutes, accountancy associations, or professional councils for medicine, nursing and teaching. Where a practice is not in healthy order, however, such initiatives are frequently lacking, or renewal efforts in which practitioners previously took a pride might have fallen into neglect. Where education is concerned, healthy practice can be identified by cultures of constructive self-criticism among teachers. Examples include regular seminars to explore, review and exchange innovative pedagogical approaches, and active debate among teachers on the kinds of developments and resources that hold the best promise of advancing their practice. Conversely, the absence of characteristics such as these identifies a practice in a less than vibrant state, whether occasioned by a lack of morale among practitioners, or an intrusive degree of control by external powers, or some adverse combination of both.

These four features of MacIntyre's characterization of a practice highlight a fourfold necessity for any critique of practice to press beyond the analysis of shortcomings and malaises. Mindful of the question, 'Critique for the sake of what?', critique must venture into the challenging and ever-changing landscape of constructive possibility. But such venturing must proceed with a keen sense of its own fallibility. For a practice such as education, this fourfold necessity might initially be outlined as follows: first, the necessity to clarify what constitutes the coherence of education as a distinct practice; second, the necessity to distinguish the practice's inherent benefits from other kinds of benefits often associated with it; third, the related necessity of ascertaining the kinds of excellence that are more appropriate – and therefore more worthy – than others for this particular practice. The fourth necessity is a more discursive one: that of disclosing, in some detail, the kinds of action – particularly imaginative action – that might best enrich and sustain the practitioners, the beneficiaries and the practice itself. All of this involves exploring the practice from the inside, as it were. The first three of these tasks will be attempted in Chapter 3, the fourth in Chapter 4.

3 The integrity of educational practice

Learning for its own sake?

A provisional definition of the integrity of any practice might run along the following lines: The integrity of a practice is that which entitles practitioners to the freedom to pursue co-operatively the inherent benefits of the practice to high levels of excellence, with due accountability to the public but without undue interference from outside interests. Now to claim this kind of integrity, or integral-ness, for education as a human undertaking is to give it recognition as a practice of its own kind, or a *sui generis* practice. Put simply, this means: a practice dedicated to advancing forms of learning that are not harnessed in advance to one or other external party or institutionalized interest. As we have already seen, however, so prevalent are the latter conceptions of education that it may be difficult to envisage what education as a *sui generis* practice might look like. In the plentiful literature of educational research, not many have given attention to investigating this issue. The critical investigations of authors such as Wilfred Carr have probed the relationship between philosophy and education in ways that yield promising orientations for educational thought and action. These investigations enable the domain of educational practice to be viewed as one requiring the elucidation of different species of thinking than those supplied by academic philosophy or scholarly theory.[1] The enquiry underway in this book is largely such an elucidation.

Among those who have focused explicitly on education as a *sui generis* practice is the late John Wilson, whose arguments on the matter are characteristically crisp and candid. Wilson correctly points out that conceptions of education that equate it with what currently goes on in schools, or with the current priorities of a ministry of education, are all too often taken as unproblematic – not just by the public but also by teachers and even by educational research literature. This, he continues, allows a surfeit of ideologies, prejudices and preconceived ideas to flood the arena of educational thought and action. Wilson is particularly critical of those who regard education chiefly as a subordinate instrument for advancing their own preferred outlooks:

[T]he idea is that either the content of education or (worse) what is to count as education must in the last resort depend on one's ideology, ultimate values, or beliefs about what constitutes the good life. ... Very few have treated education in its own right, or seen it as much more than a means of implementing their preferred ideology.[2]

Hoping to improve the 'conceptual hygiene' of thought and debate about education, Wilson argues that education is not an 'essentially contested concept'. An 'essentially contested concept' is one about which there are fundamental disagreements as to its core meaning. In support of his argument, Wilson identifies key features of education that can be seen as universal – that is, inescapable features of an educational practice, as such:

(1) that it aims to promote learning above the level of nature, (2) that it is conducted intentionally, (3) that the learning is of a long-term or sustained character, and (4) that it is directed at, or for the benefit of people as such, taking all or most of the important aspects of a person into consideration.[3]

But this important clarification of formal features helps to heighten our awareness of features of another kind – ones that bring substantive questions to the foreground and raise the stakes in education. For example: Who should decide the direction(s) learning should follow in any particular instance? How can more worthy benefits be distinguished from less worthy ones? How can benefits be properly appraised? How long, at a minimum, should be spent studying X as distinct from Y? How can progression in specific forms of learning be best advanced in this or that set of circumstances? The integrity of education as a practice comes properly into view only when we recognize that informed answers to these substantive questions arise from inherent, as distinct from extrinsic, purposes. For instance, suppose the answer given to the first question about who decides the direction were to be 'The Church', or 'The Party'. It would now be clear that the integrity of education as a practice was being subordinated – that its inherent purposes were taking second place, at best, to those of extrinsic but well-established interests.

But, since education, like every other practice, is ever and always laden with a history, questions like these will already have been answered to a greater or lesser degree by custom and tradition. If a sufficient measure of conceptual clarity could do the work John Wilson hoped it would do, one might confidently expect to wipe out distortions occasioned by accumulated preconceptions and then begin afresh. Such hopes were famously voiced by Plato when he said of his envisaged class of guardians of the *polis*: 'They will take the city and the characters of men, as they might take a tablet, and first wipe it clean – no easy task.'[4] But influences from previous experience cannot be thus disposed of, easily or otherwise. Although a self-critical alertness can profitably contribute to the disciplining of preconceived ideas, an understanding cleansed of all effects of history and tradition remains the dream of a rationalist cast of mind. It lies elusively beyond the reach of merely human efforts. The next section of the chapter will seek to illustrate this with a classical example, to be followed by further illustrations later.

But even an intuitive grasp of the point is instructive on a few counts. In the first place, it suggests that where the understanding needed by practitioners is concerned, experience may be a more potent source of learning, both for good and ill, than expertise mastered from books and theory. But it also cautions that experience is a genuinely fruitful source only to the extent that it has gained a critically perceptive capacity in relation to its own encounters. Pressing both these points a bit further, informed answers to substantive educational questions are much more likely to be furnished by discerning and capable practitioners, than by politicians, or church authorities, or industrial leaders, or other corporate interests. That's not to say that educators should be sole arbiters in these matters. Rather, it is to emphasize a few fundamentals: first, that practitioners should be properly acknowledged as having a particular capability in such matters, and properly faulted if they don't; second, that they should be expected to share the fruits of such capability in appropriately different ways with learners, parents and the public more widely; and third, that they should be given the necessary freedom to engage wholeheartedly in the practice, but in ways that remain accountable to learners, parents and society for the trust and resources they receive.

These are points that could be made about any practice worthy of the name, especially in what are loosely called the caring professions, such as teaching, nursing, social work and medicine. They call attention, positively, to what is distinctive in a particular practice, or set of practices. More negatively, they serve to remind us of distortions that can follow if a particular practice falls under the control of extrinsic forces. And here it should be recalled that practices such as medicine, social work and nursing, no less than education, can be turned to ends that are quite at odds with their inherent purposes as practices. Stark examples come from totalitarian regimes of the twentieth century, such as the widespread abuse of medical practice to experiment on victims of the Nazi holocaust, or the certification of political dissidents as mentally ill in the Soviet Union. Less graphically, we are regularly reminded by reports in national and international media of recurring instances of abuse when practices operating with much autonomy fall prey, not to authoritarian politicians, but to institutionalized neglect or fraud. But whether from political manipulation or from institutionalized abuse, in all such cases the integrity of the practice is violated, and the human benefits which the practice aims to promote become disfigured to a greater or lesser degree.

Not surprisingly, perhaps, requirements for practices to be more transparently accountable have become prominent features of work environments in recent decades. A difficulty with most recent forms of accountability, however, is that they tend to place heavy emphasis on an exacting, yet aloof policing of the practice. They thus tend to make accountability itself a form of accountancy: an accounting of measurable outcomes. Actions that build up trust between practitioners and the potential beneficiaries of the practice in question fall quite outside the observant capacity of such accounting. This neglect serves to aggravate forms of paternalism that might already affect a practice in any inherited set of circumstances. In short, it provides another obstacle that the practice has to contend with in order to establish and affirm its own inherent purposes. The most important of these purposes cannot be validly appraised by methods springing from accountancy. For instance, the gratitude of convalescents to doctors and nurses who have done their real work well is often beyond measure, as is that of many former students to teachers whose labours gave good reasons for warm remembrance.

Applying some of these more general points to education, it might appear that the case for the integrity of education as a practice comes down to a plea for 'learning for its own sake'. To a degree, yes, but unfortunately this phrase tells us too little to make a convincing case. Despite the commonplace use of 'learning for its own sake' to affirm the traditional cause of liberal education, the phrase itself makes no clear positive sense. Unless some further elaboration is provided, it simply means 'learning for the sake of learning', or at a push, 'learning for the sake of inherent as distinct from extrinsic purposes'. This extra push itself is helpful. For we can now ask: *What would count* as such inherent purposes? The demand for cogent examples becomes more pressing the more we investigate the phrase.

Let us turn to an instance of practice therefore to see what further light this might provide. As a practising teacher, let us say, I might claim that I believe in 'learning for its own sake'. Asked by a friend to say what this means in practice – say, in my work as a teacher of mathematics – I might reply along the following lines: my main purposes in teaching mathematics are to enable my students to experience the satisfactions of mathematical problem-solving, to become proficient in mathematical reasoning and to develop active mathematical imagination. My friend agrees that these sound like worthy purposes and that they also look more like inherent benefits than external goals. He is sceptical, however, about my degree of success in achieving these inherent benefits in practice. A colleague maths teacher who has been listening to our conversation agrees to observe my work over a period, in a critically discerning but friendly way. She eventually concludes that my purposes are sincerely held but that my belief that I achieve them is justified only to a minor degree. She says she can sometimes see evidence of the purposes I avow, but she also concludes that they are more often overshadowed by other purposes. She recalls, for example, that I rely too heavily on readymade exercises from the textbook, also that I miss some promising opportunities by setting the pace and substance of learning by the more responsive students. She points out that there is sometimes a predictability about my approach that seems to owe more to test and examination routines than to my own avowed purposes. She then adds an insight that highlights her own understanding of the inherent purposes of learning. The heart of the matter must surely lie, she says, in the *experienced quality* of learning; in the inherent benefits that are yielded (if they are) for learners in genuine instances of educational practice. I agree immediately, and add that I thought such benefits, like the three initially mentioned to my friend above, would have been evident from my work. She replies sympathetically that an understandable tendency on my part to respond to examination and other external pressures sometimes obscures my own better purposes. She smiles, and acknowledges that her own work, despite her convictions, could similarly be described. This example raises a number of important issues to be taken up later (Chapter 9). For now, however, it is clear that learning for the sake of inherent benefits that need to be made explicit indicates something more substantial than 'learning for its own sake'. This is the case, principally because one now has to give overt attention to what these inherent benefits might be, and also to their justification. One must equally attend to how they are cultivated through the experienced quality of learning.

The integrity of educational practice: a classical example

Hopefully the explorations and illustrations up to this point have rendered the notion of the integrity of educational practice less strange than it might initially appear. It is necessary now, however, to investigate this notion more directly and to challenge the rationalist notions that would have it remain a stranger. Probably the best way to do this is through an example that discloses this integrity within the to-and-fro of practice itself. To highlight the point that the integrity of educational practice is a notion of classical ancestry in Western civilization, the example is taken from the educational work of Socrates in Athens, as described by Plato in one of his earlier works, Book 1 of *The Republic*. This ancient example can be supplemented by more contemporary ones later, but beginning with a Socratic example has advantages additional to the point about historical origins just mentioned. First, it illustrates the kind of integrity in question with an unmistakable clarity that makes it a seminal point of reference. Second, in doing this it also shows that the modern tendency to regard 'Socratic method' as some kind of set of skills, to be turned to this purpose or that, is badly misconceived. It should be stressed from the start that anything genuinely Socratic is much more about insights and convictions that inform practice than about method. A third point should be added here, however, about the all-male character of the Socratic educational practice. Despite the originality and boldness of Socrates' thinking, he seems to have accepted the prevailing idea that public life (viz. in the *polis*) was exclusively an arena for males, whereas the concerns of females were confined to the arena of domestic life (viz. in the *oikonomia*). But there is no reason to believe that the educational environments nourished by Socratic practices might not include females. Indeed, a Socratic rationale stripped of sexist features would suggest that such environments would be all the more fruitful for the inclusion of females.[5]

The action in *The Republic* Bk 1 takes place in the house of Polemarchus in Athens. Here, Socrates has gathered with a number of people of mixed age – mainly youths. Their informal conversation gradually takes shape as an enquiry about the nature of justice, or right action (*dikaiosune*). A few of those present venture different views that try to capture the heart of what justice means. For instance, the elderly Cephalus suggests that justice is telling the truth and returning what one has borrowed. This definition is supported by his son Polemarchus, who then adds that justice means helping your friends and harming your enemies. Contributions from younger participants include the view that most people practise justice for reasons of compulsion (from Glaucon), and that most people practice justice for the reputation that being seen to be just brings (from Adeimantus). Socrates, who has apparently given the issue much thought previously, leads a discussion that highlights merits and shortcomings in the various contributions made. The collective nature of the enquiry helps to identify and remedy confusions in the underlying assumptions of the different contributions – not just for the participants but also for today's readers. In this sense, the discussion gives a satisfactory sense of making progress. Yet the reader begins to suspect that while a better understanding of justice will be taken home at the end of the day by those present, a conclusive definition of justice, defensible to one and all, is likely to escape the participants, including Socrates.

This suspicion is strengthened after the objections raised by a forthright contribution from Thrasymachus are investigated and weighed up by Socrates. Thrasymachus has been following the course of the exploration with growing agitation, but has been prevented from interrupting by those sitting near him. A momentary pause in the discussion provides him, however, with a new opportunity. His is an outburst that dismisses the debate so far as a polite exchange of nonsense. He insists that Socrates' practice of using the points put to him to raise further questions is merely a device for deflecting and confounding others. He then confronts Socrates with a direct challenge:

> You know perfectly well that it's easier to ask questions than to answer them. Give us an answer yourself and tell us what you think justice is. And don't tell me that it's duty, or expediency, or advantage, or profit, or interest. I won't put up with nonsense of that sort; give me a clear and precise definition.[6]

In his reply, Socrates asks Thrasymachus not to be so hard on himself and the other contributors to the enquiry. If they have made mistakes, they haven't done so on purpose says Socrates, and points out that if they were searching for gold they would not have permitted mere politeness to get in the way of their search. He then adds:

> Justice (*dikaiosune*) is much more valuable than gold and you must not think that we will slacken our efforts to find it out of any idiotic deference to each other. It's the ability that we lack and clever fellows like you should be sorry for us rather than angry with us.[7]

Thrasymachus now accuses Socrates of feigning ignorance, and of using his famous irony to dodge giving a straight answer. Thrasymachus then proceeds to give his own confident definition of justice as 'that which is in the interest of the stronger party.'[8] He becomes entangled in contradictions, however, as he tries to defend this stance before the assembled group in his ensuing debate with Socrates.

The ironic note in Socrates' reply to Thrasymachus is unmistakable, but the point of Socratic irony is bypassed if one sees it merely as sarcasm, or a piece of rhetorical weaponry. The real irony is that Socrates – the person reputed to be the wisest in all of Greece – knows that he doesn't yet have a conclusive answer to the kind of question put by Thrasymachus. And if one leaves aside its impetuous manner, the demand made by Thrasymachus for a 'straight answer' seems quite a reasonable one: a human desire for something definite, precise and conclusive. But Socrates' response suggests that such an answer won't yield itself to the 'lack of ability' of his co-enquirers and himself. And the irony here hints at an insight that lies much deeper than sarcasm. Socrates' comment about a collective lack of ability is a recognition of the limitations in even the best of human understanding, particularly when up against central questions of ethics, morality and meaning. It distinguishes perceptively between ignorance on the one hand – including the self-assured conclusiveness of 'clever fellows' like Thrasymachus – and an *educated awareness* of one's ignorance, or limitations, on the other.

In the case of Socrates himself, this educated sense of one's ignorance comes from renewed enquiries, over very many years, held with the most distinguished poets, scholars and other leading lights of Athens. On his own account, he engaged in these enquiries to try to disprove the pronouncement, attributed to the Oracle of Delphi, that Socrates was the wisest of men. Socrates' own account of his public life is documented by Plato in the *Apology*, the defence conducted by Socrates to a jury of 501 Athenian citizens when he was placed on trial for impiety and corrupting the youth of Athens. Unlike most of the other early dialogues of Plato that show Socrates in action, but where he remains enigmatically quiet about his own aims and convictions, the *Apology* contains many explicit references to Socrates' stance as an educator. These references throw a crucial light on just such aims and convictions. For instance, at a key point in the trial, Socrates makes the following declaration:

> Real wisdom is the property of God, and this oracle is his way of telling us that human wisdom has little or no value. It seems to me that he is not referring literally to Socrates, but has merely taken my name as an example, as if he would say to us, 'the wisest of you is he who has realized, like Socrates, that in respect of wisdom he is really worthless.'[9]

At first sight, this might look like a counsel of despair for all educational effort. The thrust of Socrates' testimony to the court, however, or more significantly his testament to posterity, is a sobering but thought-provoking lesson. This lesson is that his own efforts have been unceasing in searching for the highest degree of wisdom that human efforts might achieve, but that this wisdom is still an insignificant thing compared to that real wisdom that lies beyond even the best of human efforts. Rather than a counsel of despair, this is a counsel of intellectual modesty. It is an exhortation to give a self-critical thrust, as well as wholehearted energies, to the deliberate pursuit of learning. The importance and merits of this kind of engagement are stressed to the jury by Socrates when he compares it to less worthy pursuits that have become common preoccupations, not least in the schools of the sophists:

> Are you not ashamed that you give your attention to acquiring as much money as possible, and similarly with reputation and honour, and give no attention to truth and understanding and the perfection of your soul (*psyche*)? [10]

A related insight is to be gleaned from the larger testament of Socrates in the *Apology*, and from a study of the structure of the other early dialogues of Plato that depict Socrates' educational work. This insight directs attention first and foremost to the experienced quality of learning environments. It underlines the conviction that learning is best undertaken as a collective kind of enquiry, dedicated to seeking the truth, whatever the topic or theme of the investigation. Learning is thus disclosed as a collective search in which those present are prepared to contribute their best ideas to date, and to learn from the critical appraisals of fellow learners. The teacher, who would have heard many if not all of the ventured contributions before, would have a particular responsibility to make explicit the most pertinent points of each contribution, and thus get a lively interplay of well-focused perspectives under way. The teacher would seek, moreover, to encourage all to advance their insights by a jointly undertaken review of what was most sustainable, and what was not, in the different contributions. This would require an atmosphere where it was safe for each participant to venture his or her perspectives (i.e. one of mutual respect rather than superficial politeness). It would also require the twin virtues of constructive self-criticism and constructive criticism of each other's efforts to be habitually practised. Promoting such an atmosphere would be the responsibility of each participant and also, in a special way, that of the teacher. The teacher would also have the responsibility, to be exercised to the best of his or her ability, of introducing new perspectives to provoke fresh energies by the students and thus advance the enquiry further towards truth. And for Socrates, such references to truth mean truth not in a final sense of the 'real wisdom' that escapes the best of human efforts. They signify rather those advances in insight that have survived the best efforts of collective criticism to date. More suggestively, they are also intimations of the provisional character of any genuinely fruitful human learning. Learning is thus significant chiefly as a pursuit of truth that is an unfinishing, and probably an unfinishable, pursuit.

The picture emerges here of a learning community that is essentially self-governing. This is not to say that it is a law unto itself. In fact, to be a significant feature of the educational life of a society, such learning communities need to be understood as communities of practitioners, where 'practitioner' refers not merely to teachers-as-learners, but also to students as active participants in learning. On a Socratic perspective, such communities would be maintained from public resources (unlike the private schools of the sophists), with a mutual acknowledgement of rights and responsibilities between the learning communities and the providers of resources. What this picture contrasts strongly with is any provision that removes the essentials of governance from the learning community itself and gives to 'the stronger party' the power to impose its own stamp on the conduct of learning. The 'stronger party' here can be seen not just as authoritarian rulers, but as any institutionalized power – political, religious, commercial or other – which is content to view education more as a strategic vehicle than a distinctive practice.

It might be objected that this Socratic-inspired picture of the integrity of educational practice could apply to universities, with their traditions of academic freedom, but not to schools and colleges. But the objection misses something crucial about the character of learning in such communities. It also ignores a considerable body of published evidence. Let us take the latter point first. The best examples of such learning communities in Western societies, at present, rarely enough come from universities. In these, energies now tend to be preoccupied by the requirements of funding regimes for research projects, thus often making academic freedom a hollow notion in practice. Rather, as some recent official reports from a number of countries suggest, the best examples are likely to be found in primary schools, and frequently in the infant and junior classes.[11] To realize this is to highlight the first point that the objection overlooks. This point is that learning can be a highly co-operative and highly searching kind of experience from early childhood onwards, if conceived and carried out in age-appropriate and imaginative ways. This realization, in turn, emphasizes the often overlooked importance of the *relationships that constitute* the experienced quality of learning – a theme that will be taken up in the next chapter.

But the arguments of recent pages run counter to some powerfully established ideas, both of longer and more recent ancestry. So some additional objections – two major ones – have to be addressed first. Careful consideration of these objections might not only identify their misplaced character. It might also open the way for a more robust presentation of the case that has been launched here for education as a practice in its own right (a *sui generis* practice).

Insights from antiquity: being beckoned to learn anew

The case for the integrity of education as a practice is unlikely to be warmly embraced by contemporary forms of scepticism, particularly the kinds considered in Chapter 2. Consider, for instance, the references above to the search for truth as an underlying orientation for educational practice. These sit ill with post-modern misgivings about the very notion of truth. This is one issue to be taken up below. But there is also a contrasting one. Much of the critical force of post-modern thinking itself is directed against the predominance of foundational stances in Western philosophy – stances that are even less favourably disposed than post-modern ones to education as a practice with a claim to its own integrity. In short, the case for education as a *sui generis* as distinct from a subordinate practice would be attacked by more traditional forms of philosophy for lacking objective and secure foundations. From the other side, it would draw criticisms from many post-modern currents of thinking for still holding on to a notion of truth, especially as a source of inspirations and convictions for the conduct of public action of any kind. But some brief elucidation of terms is called for here in order to review these contrasting objections.

In its full sense, a foundational stance maintains that philosophical thinking must seek to lay hold of objective truth, make this explicit and secure, and then draw upon it for the organization and conduct of human affairs. Even widely different currents of post-modern thinking discern versions of a foundational stance in traditional philosophy, especially in metaphysics and in rationalist epistemology. Both of these latter intellectual enterprises have their own philosophical contexts of scholarship. It is rarely pointed out, however, that both also underlie hugely influential patterns of control and study in the wider history of learning, and not just in Western civilizations. So the explanation of terms must also include both of these. Metaphysics can be understood as the long and manifold elaboration, especially from Plato's later works onwards, of an authoritative and conclusive account of all of reality. It seeks a definitive conceptual framework that presents the full picture, as it were. And rationalist epistemology can be understood as that search of more recent centuries, beginning most notably with Descartes (1596–1650), for stable and certain foundations for anything that is to count as knowledge.

Whether Plato can rightly be regarded as the author of the metaphysical conceptions of truth ('logocentric' or 'teleological') that Derrida and others have attacked in Western philosophy remains open to question. Nevertheless, the ancestry of such conceptions can largely be traced to the historic legacy of an all-embracing 'Platonism' that is associated with Plato's later works. Historically, moreover, such conceptions of truth regularly achieved an absolute status by becoming institutionalized doctrines of church or state. This is more an accomplishment of fourth century neo-Platonism than of Plato or his immediate successors. As we have seen in Chapter 1, the paternalistic cast of such conceptions and their strong emphasis on uniformity have been dominant forces in the history of Western education, at least until recent times. The 'incredulity toward grand narratives' that is a trademark of post-modern stances can thus be viewed as vigilance towards absolutist ideas that have, in the past, provided plausible warrant for institutionalized oppression or violence. That is not to say that such ideas were never other than oppressive. The absolutist philosophical systems that Karl Popper famously called the enemies of the open society – viz. those of Plato, Hegel, Marx – can still be regarded as sources that richly repay discerning efforts of study, even by post-modern philosophers. But that is another story.[12]

What cannot be denied, however, although the point is rarely acknowledged, is that the dominance of metaphysical outlooks in the history of Western learning eclipsed a more ancient conception of truth – a much more promising one for educational purposes. That eclipsed conception is the Socratic one that we have already begun to open up in the previous section. And such opening up remains a major educational research task that is yet to be accomplished. For all the respect paid to Socrates in more than two millennia of Western thought, his most distinctive *educational* insights never became an influential legacy, or an acknowledged educational tradition. Indeed, when critically viewed, the history of Western education can be seen, in large part, as a history of the effects of this eclipse. This is evident in a special way from the decisive part played in that history by metaphysical doctrines that came to infuse Christianity as an institutionalized religion. These ranged from more benign forms of paternalism to the most exacting forms of censorship and prohibition.

The revolts against metaphysical thinking that sprang from the efforts of Descartes, and later Kant, did not, however, win for the neglected legacy of Socratic educational thinking a fresh place in the sun. The revolutions in thought associated with the Enlightenment proved to be something of a false dawn where educational thought and action were concerned. The Enlightenment challenged the supremacy of metaphysics, chiefly by seeking to install a critical successor discipline in its place – namely, epistemology. This discipline became a hallmark of modernity in scholarly enquiry by elevating critical reason to a place of supreme importance. This regularly gave enquiry a rationalist cast that was blind to the preconceptions that remain in play in even the most critical forms of reason. In due course, critical reason became the focus as distinct from the arbiter of critique. As we have seen in the previous chapter, the pretensions of rationalist epistemology to universal knowledge, its quest for certainty and its preoccupation with unshakable foundations, have themselves been subject to sustained attack by post-modern critics.[13]

What remains curious, however, is that neither the critical educational writers of the Enlightenment (Kant, but roughly speaking Rousseau also), nor leading post-modern writers such as Lyotard, Derrida or Foucault, have called attention to the eclipse just mentioned. This is not to deny the radical force of much of Rousseau's *Émile* (1762), or the urbane thrust of Kant's essays on education (*Über Pädagogik*, 1803). Nor is it to diminish the incisiveness of the critiques furnished by writings in a post-modern vein. Yet all of these critical writings have bypassed a crucial point. That crucial point is that the life and work of the historical Socrates provide a unique gateway to pathways of educational thought and action that might have become a flourishing tradition in Western civilization. But to call attention to such a gateway would also be to appreciate the enormity of the eclipse that took place at an early stage in the history of Western education. All the more reason why the Socratic example, and especially its educational significance, calls for special attention now.

If, as Socrates' own renewed efforts show, even the best of human understanding is limited by the fact that humans are mortals rather than immortals, one consequence is inescapable: This consequence is that the most that such an understanding can achieve is a better *perspective* on truth – one that has stood up better to critical scrutiny than have contrasting perspectives. Equally important is the corollary: To claim to be in possession of truth in an absolute sense is, in effect, to claim to have arrived at some kind of super-human destination. It is to claim to have grounded a grasp of truth for good – to have overcome the kind of ever-renewed journeying Socrates engaged in with others throughout his adult life.

The chief practical import of the Socratic example is the view that human learning is probably most promisingly conceived of as a jointly undertaken search. This is a search that involves – in whatever field of study – an interplay with new perspectives and horizons, with forms of understanding that are sometimes disconcerting intruders on what one has already understood and made one's own. This search is warranted, indeed called for, by the kind of insight Socrates attributes to the oracle at Delphi (that human wisdom is 'worthless' compared to that of the divinities). It is also disciplined, however, by what the awareness of fallibility and limitation counsels to human aspirations. For these are aspirations that might otherwise become, sometimes all too quickly, unrestrained pretensions to mastery, to certainty, to absolute knowledge, or to the final truth.

On a Socratic account then, to understand the significance of human learning as a search for truth is *to be enjoined to practise that search ever anew with others*. It is to do so, moreover, less by applying theoretical expertise than by judiciously discerning and respecting the plurality of human perspective. But not only that. It is to begin to share the conviction that there is an emergent kind of universality in the faithful practice of this search for truth. This universality is not the same as consensus. It is manifest rather in a twofold recognition: first, that all human understanding is victim to the limitations of perspective, including in a particular way our own preconceptions and prejudices. Second, arising from this, is the recognition that the most promising stance for the cultivation of human learning lies in the readiness to try, *in particular practical instances*, to reason from another's viewpoint as well as from one's own. Such efforts will, of course, be attended by misunderstandings and failures, by pitfalls and acrimonies, just as they might also be attended by the detection of previous errors and the disclosure of fresh insights. As Socrates rightly saw, they are unfinishing and unfinishable efforts that have little to do with winning and losing, or having the last word. On the contrary, defensible educational efforts have everything to do with a joint renewal of attentive listening and with the readiness to take risks for learning. In fact, from an educational point of view (and the popular perception of Socrates as a rhetorical combatant obscures this), each of the early Socratic dialogues can be seen as just such a venture: to uncover unacknowledged preconceptions and to learn anew in the company of others.

The universality in question here arises then not from any doctrine or decree, nor from any form of *a priori* philosophy. It arises rather from what can be sustained, to the best of one's uncoerced belief, from the practice of active engagements with differences. Where educational practice is concerned, it includes engaging with differences in a number of quarters: differences that come to light in one's encounters with students, fellow teachers, parents and others; differences that disclose themselves in responding to inheritances of learning; differences that are uncovered in one's understanding of one's own beliefs and outlooks. The kind of universality then, is one that remains ever-provisional and open to revision. The forms of practice it indicates for teaching and learning are more suggestive than prescriptive, although not lacking in conviction on that account. They are practices that are inclusive in scope, and exploratory, self-critical and participatory in character.

It would take many pages to elucidate this suggestiveness, and to illustrate how it brings us to the heart of the matter that constitutes education as a practice in its own right. A few of its central attributes can, however, be indicated here, and explored more fully in subsequent chapters. First, an incisive awareness of the limitations and possibilities of human understanding itself is a necessity for any perspective that is described as an educational one. Of particular importance here is an alertness to the enabling and disabling effects of preconceptions in the experience of human understanding itself, not least the unacknowledged preconceptions that pervade the conduct of teaching and learning. Second, an educational perspective necessarily embodies informed, yet self-critical convictions about the kinds of actions through which defensible learning might best be advanced. Third, to call such convictions Socratic, as I am doing here, discloses a few related features. It highlights the point that 'Socratic method' remains mere technique without a particular kind of underlying conviction. It also distinguishes anything called an educational perspective from countless standpoints that view teachers and schools chiefly as part of the machinery for advancing established interests – political, commercial, religious or other. Finally, the practice of education as an ever-renewed and unfinishing search for truth restores to truth itself something of its inspirational force. It hardly needs emphasizing that such a force becomes disfigured to one or another kind of oppression once philosophy, or any other field of study, seeks to make truth absolute, and treat it as its own possession.

4 Disclosing educational practice from the inside

A surprising claim

To clear the way for exploring the suggestions identified at the end of the last chapter, it is first necessary to deal with a bold claim, which if justified, would curtail such exploration before it got underway. This is the claim by Alasdair MacIntyre that teaching is not a practice. In 2002, more than two decades after the publication of his most influential book *After Virtue*, MacIntyre took part in a dialogue on education with Joseph Dunne, subsequently published in 2004.[1] During the course of that dialogue, he declared that 'teaching itself is not a practice, but a set of skills and habits put to the service of a variety of practices.'[2] What is surprising about this claim is that the distinguishing features of a practice, perceptively described by MacIntyre in *After Virtue*, would seem to apply *par excellence* where the activity in question was the deliberate promotion of human learning through teaching. This is the heart of the point put to MacIntyre by Dunne, to question the claim that teaching was not a practice. MacIntyre's claim rests on his argument that 'the teacher should think of her or himself as a mathematician, a reader of poetry, an historian, or whatever, engaged in communicating craft and knowledge to an apprentice.'[3] At first sight, this characterization might appear plausible in the case of a teacher as subject specialist in a university, or perhaps a secondary school, although even in these instances it doesn't hold up under closer scrutiny, as I hope to illustrate a little later. But it is difficult to see, as Dunne suggests to MacIntyre, how it could apply at all to primary schools or to early childhood education. Equally important, as Dunne points out, 'good teachers not only instruct their students, but also create in their classrooms and in the school generally, the hallmarks of a community of inquiry and of virtue.'[4]

In response, MacIntyre says initially that it is not clear to him how far Dunne and himself disagree. He acknowledges that teachers are involved in a variety of practices and allows that teaching is an ingredient in every practice. He suggests that this might even amount to much the same thing as Dunne's claim that teaching is a practice. But then he demurs and adds two points that open again the gap that he had just seemed to narrow. First, he says: 'For it is part of my claim that teaching is never more than a means.' To this, he adds an equally controversial point: 'All teaching is for the sake of something else and so teaching does not have its own goods. The life of a teacher is not a specific kind of life. The life of a teacher of mathematics, whose goods are the good of mathematics, is one thing; a life of a teacher of music whose goods are the goods of music is another.'[5] There is something curiously unobservant about these two claims on the part of so incisive a thinker as MacIntyre. Exploring each of them in turn should enable us to get beyond what the two claims obscure, and to clarify a few crucial points in illustrating the distinctiveness of education as a practice.

Starting with the claim that teaching is never more than a means, there is no difficulty in accepting MacIntyre's point that teaching could be an ingredient of every practice. But the manner in which it becomes an ingredient reveals that teaching is *always* more than a means. Consider, for instance, the case of a newly qualified engineer whose first job starts with a 2-week period where she is assigned to one of her company's more experienced practitioners. On the face of it, the teaching done by the experienced practitioner during this fortnight could be regarded chiefly as a means of getting the newcomer successfully initiated into the way in which practitioners in this company conduct their work. But it is also more than that. Granted, insofar as the means are success-ful, the experienced practitioner will have got the newcomer to accomplish the objectives set for the end of the fortnight. But something else will also have happened. The newcomer will be influenced in one way or another by the experienced practitioner's knowledge, style of working and interpersonal qualities. She will be impressed or perhaps disappointed by the practitioner's level of knowledge, enthused or perhaps uninspired by the practitioner's style of accomplishing things, attracted or perhaps repelled by the practitioner's interpersonal qualities. And, of course, the same applies to the relationships of newly qualified teachers and their more experienced colleagues. It applies no less in all learning environments constituted by a group of students and a teacher. The means adopted inevitably become blended with the quality of the emergent relationships of teacher and learner. They merge with the events experienced by both teacher and learners, and with the other factors that go to make up a shared learning environment. Not surprisingly then, this environ-ment takes on its own particular flavour, and can do so in a period much shorter than the 2 weeks in our example. But to finish the example, when the fortnight is up, either or both parties might wish it could continue, or might breathe a sigh of relief, or might experience a mixture of emotions.

The claim that teaching is never more than a means draws too sharp a distinc-tion then between ends and means. If we examine now a few instances where such a sharp distinction is quite common, together with the consequences of this, the point at issue emerges more plainly. Drawing clear distinctions between means and ends is a regular feature of pursuing military strategy, of decision-making in commercial life, or of engaging in party politics. In each case here, the end can be viewed quite separately from the means, and the strategic importance of the end then serves as a justification for the means.

For instance, securing a town before the enemy forces do so may cost a lot of soldiers' lives and some civilian lives, but far less of each than if the enemy takes the town first. Moving a manufacturing facility from location X to location Y may mean a lot of job losses in the former, but the lower costs involved in location Y are likely to turn what would have been a loss in returns to shareholders into a gain. Running two of the Labour party's candidates in constituency Z is likely to increase the party's vote in this weak Labour constituency and thus secure a seat for the party through the transfer of second preference votes, even though it means that one or other of the candidates is destined for defeat.

It is difficult to envisage situations where reasoning of this kind could be justified in an occupation like teaching. That's not to say it doesn't take place. But, in fact, such reasoning is likely to undermine the end being sought. It may sometimes even do so in politics or in other fields of action, but it can hardly avoid doing so in education. Bertrand Russell provides a memorable, if grim, illustration of this in his comments on some of the letters of Thomas Arnold, renowned nineteenth-century educator and headmaster of Rugby School from 1828 to 1841. Russell writes: 'It is pathetic to see this naturally kindly gentleman lashing himself into a mood of sadism, in which he can flog little boys without compunction, and all under the impression that he is conforming to the religion of Love.'[6] Less dramatically, a similar point is made by John Dewey in his remarks on 'collateral learning', and on preparation as a 'treacherous' idea in education. On the former, Dewey points out that it is a great mistake to believe that a pupil's learning is confined to the specific material being taught, whether mathematics, spelling, history or whatever. More crucially, he says, 'collateral learning in the way of formation of enduring attitudes, of likes and dislikes ... often is much more important than the spelling lesson or lesson in geography or history that is learned. For these attitudes are fundamentally what count in the future.'[7] His point about preparation is the corollary of this. Preparation can indeed be a 'treacherous idea' if it means a teaching approach that sacrifices the learning potentialities of the present to a 'remote and suppositious future'. Getting the most out of each present moment of learning, Dewey points out, and doing so habitually, is the only preparation that profits in the long run in education. Contrary to MacIntyre's stance, these illustrations show that where teaching is concerned, there is always an inseparable connection, although often a subtle one, between means and ends. More succinctly, the ends must be embodied, or exemplified, in the means. Far from claiming that teaching is never more than a means, MacIntyre would be closer to the mark if he had argued that teaching is never *merely* a means, or better still, that there are few if any instances in teaching where the distinction between means and ends can hold up.

As for MacIntyre's second point, that teaching doesn't have its own goods and that all teaching 'is for the sake of something else', closer inspection shows that this can hardly be sustained either. Our investigation in the previous chapter of the ambiguities in 'learning for its own sake' made it clear that all learning is for the sake of some kind of benefits, whether intrinsic or external, and often some combination of both. The curious point in MacIntyre's claim that all learning is for something else is that the 'something else' is, in the first place, the intrinsic rather than the external benefits. When he says that the goods of a mathematics teacher are 'the goods of mathematics', he is referring primarily to an ever-higher quality of mathematical thinking and mathematical capability that teachers try to cultivate in learners.[8] This means, however, that all teaching worthy of the name, whether in mathematics, geography, art or whatever, shares a crucial feature in common, namely the cultivation of a high quality of learning. When MacIntyre says then that 'the life of a teacher of mathematics is one thing, … the life of a teacher of music is another', he is relegating or ignoring just this feature. He is also overlooking Dunne's point about primary teachers and early childhood teachers who teach a range of subjects. Bringing about a high quality of learning, and doing so in ways that nourish rather than take over the learner's individuality, are what give integrity to teaching as a practice. And this remains the case whether one is teaching a range of subjects in a primary school, one or two subjects in a secondary school, or a specialized aspect of one subject in a post-graduate seminar. What constitutes a high quality of learning, and what doesn't, needs more detailed exploration now, and this exploration can be started by focusing on the relationships that disclose educational practice from the inside.

Personal qualities and relationships

Forms of learning that don't bring teachers and students face-to-face have become increasingly common in recent decades. Traditional examples were the correspondence courses where all readings and assignments were processed through the post. The early work of the Open University in the UK, and similar bodies elsewhere, using television, radio and periodic tutorials, marked a second generation of such courses, and in time gave rise to the term 'distance education'. The development of internet and e-mail technologies led to a third generation, with virtual learning environments and other forms of online learning now playing a central part. What all forms of distance education have in common is the minor role played by the presence of a teacher among learners. That's not to say that the deliberate promotion of learning that takes place in distance education doesn't count as a practice. It is, in its own right, a complex practice, but different in key respects from teaching as a face-to-face practice in schools, colleges and other live environments of learning. Exploring these key differences will help to highlight what is most distinctive about teaching as a practice. It should also provide some promising ideas as to how the integrity of the practice, and the capabilities and dispositions of its practitioners, might best be advanced and sustained.

The most obvious difference between teaching and distance education is the daily, or almost daily, meeting of teachers and students in the former compared with the occasional or periodic meetings in the latter. A second difference is the importance of the teacher as a continual motivator of students' efforts in live environments of learning. This is not to say that tutors in distance education don't have a motivating role, but that role is not continual in the daily sense that a teacher's is. Distance education, moreover, presupposes a high degree of self-motivation on the part of students. Third, the planning necessary on the teacher's part for face-to-face learning environments is very different from that needed for distance education, including planning for different kinds of questioning, organizing and re-organizing group work, eliciting ideas from students, dealing with learning difficulties as they arise, and a host of other eventualities. Fourth, there are many interpersonal qualities that are crucial in the face-to-face encounter of teachers and students that don't arise, or at least not in the same immediate way, in the learning environments of distance education. These include: continual alertness and responsiveness; originality and resourcefulness in presenting lessons; imaginativeness in availing of students' contributions; keeping a number of different learning activities going at the same time; giving prompt feedback and providing well-judged criticisms and encouragement; dealing effectively with momentary or more serious distractions; having ample reserves of patience, firmness and foresight; and being fair and caring in dealing with learners.

The differences just drawn here could be extended to a longer list, but even this initial attempt serves to show something of the inherent complexity of teaching, and to indicate how it differs from other practices. At the same time, there is something flat in any characterization of teaching, no matter how exhaustive, that confines itself to an inventory of skills, competences or human qualities, almost as if they could be ticked off on a checklist. By contrast, what captures the distinctiveness of teaching is how these skills and human qualities *get embodied in the relationships* that give their experienced quality or flavour to instances of learning. It might be the case, for instance, that two teachers – let's call them Fiona and Peter – might rank almost identically on paper, or more precisely on a competence checklist, as regards their attributes. Nevertheless, as far as students are concerned, the experienced quality of learning with Fiona might be very different to that of learning with Peter: more imaginative, or more arresting, or more memorable, or whatever. Such differences are commonly explained by saying it's a matter of personality, or that it's impossible to put your finger on what's most distinctive in teaching, or that good teaching has a certain elusive style, or *je ne sais quoi*. And, so far as they go, such explanations are true. But they don't really advance understanding very far. Their very ubiquity detracts attention from the need to understand the experience of teaching and learning from the inside, as it were. They fail to explain what happens when skills get embodied in certain kinds of relationships and thus bring into being a particular kind of learning atmosphere, or ethos. It is important, in other words, to explore the cultural and interpersonal landscape over which the common usage of a phrase such as *je ne sais quois*, or 'it's down to personality', draws a veil.

Here, it may be helpful to venture a personal note. In my own early years as a teacher, it struck me that the heart of my work was a kind of wooing of the students – not so much of their affections, as of their best imaginative efforts. But it also became clear that these imaginative efforts were inextricably linked to the students' emotional responses and dispositions. These were practical insights that arose from experience, different from the theoretical disclosures of educational research (as it was then) and from the formal discourse of the teaching profession. While the language of teachers' staff meetings was often that of student abilities, student needs and student behaviour, I felt that factors such as these, and others as well, were intertwined in something more elusive, yet near at hand, that all of us as teachers confronted every day, but never named as such – in short, the students' sensibilities. Where environments of teaching and learning are concerned, sensibilities, or the capacity for emotional response, disclose themselves chiefly as dispositions. For instance, enthusiasms, aversions, inclinations, resistances, tolerances, prejudices, susceptibilities, credulities and so on.

Pushing deeper into this practical vein of thinking, the preconceptions lodged in so many students' responses suggested to me that teachers have to deal with students' *pre*dispositions perhaps more so than with their dispositions. I felt that educational research might have much to say about this. There were very few references to sensibilities, however, or to students' dispositions or predispositions, in the research literature on education. What could be found there was a mainly technical language, which, for all its precision in highlighting skills and competences, somehow beclouded the interhuman contexts of teaching and learning that research might properly have illuminated. Another realization that dawned on me from thinking in this practical vein was that the teacher's own predispositions, no less than those of the students, played a crucial role in cultivating or inhibiting fruitful environments of learning. Preoccupation with the teacher's competences, or the teacher's professional expertise more generally, tended to push this kind of awareness to the background, or even out of the picture.

I began to articulate the 'wooing' idea and to explore the importance of sensibility on the part of both students and teachers. It became clearer to me that if the teacher's efforts were to do justice both to the students and the subject matter being taught, the wooing in question might helpfully be thought of as an honourable kind of courtship – a courtship of sensibility that calls deeply on a teacher's originality and imaginativeness, but from which anything erotic must be ruled out from the start. Because of the emphasis that needs to be placed on this last point, I'm now more inclined to use the word 'heartwork' rather than 'courtship', although I'm particularly keen to retain the connotations of mutuality that are more evident in the term 'courtship'. In any case, it also became clearer to me that this kind of human interaction had an integrity of its own, unrelated to any extrinsic purposes that education is expected to advance, such as those of church, or state, or other bodies of interest. This integrity, I would argue, is associated with discovering and realizing each person's own potentialities for learning, but not just any kind of learning. The most concise description of such learning would be 'learning to become more fully human', although this suggestive term, as we will see in our later explorations, is laden as much with ambiguity as it is with possibility.[9] Working through an understanding of the courtship conception with teachers and student teachers over a number of years has led to a number of refinements.[10] Such refinements were also prompted by opportunities that enabled me to return to work as a secondary teacher at periodic intervals. These experiences have strengthened my conviction that the courtship conception is more promising, in the sense of being more fertile and inclusive, and is also more defensible, than are alternative conceptions of teaching. In the educational research of recent times, such alternative conceptions have increasingly placed emphasis on 'teacher effectiveness' and on schools as 'learning organizations'.

The courtship, or heartwork characterization, that I am keen to investigate calls for a shift away from a transmission-and-reception view of educational practice. In fact, this is a fourfold shift in the teacher's understanding, giving priority in each case to the experienced quality of a set of relationships. First, there are the teacher's relationships to the subject(s) being taught; second, the teacher's relationships to the students; third, the teacher's relationships to colleagues, to parents or guardians, and to the public more widely. Fourth, there is the teacher's relationship to him/herself or, in other words, the teacher's self-understanding, through which the other three sets of relationships are interpreted and accorded their particular significance.

But to put the matter this way is to run against much of the current of custom and practice in the conduct of educational affairs. Prevalent conceptions view teaching as a transmission of knowledge, of skills, of values, of a cultural heritage, and so on. Politicians and educational administrators frequently describe teaching in this way, as do many school leaders and teachers themselves. Sometimes even prominent philosophers, including Lyotard and MacIntyre, do so as well.[11] Such commonplace usage casts teachers mainly in the active role of instructors and students mainly in the role of receivers. One might protest that such a sharp division is rarely intentional in casual usage of the phrase 'transmission of knowledge, skills and values'. Even so, such usage still induces a habitual inattentiveness to the *joint* nature of teaching and learning; an inattentiveness that is sometimes evident among teachers themselves. In any case, the fact remains that any instance of teaching and learning is just such a joint experience, or set of joint experiences, shared from different perspectives by teachers and students. The responses called forth by a teacher's presentation to a group of students might be very varied, even in those instances where all the students appear to be quietly absorbed in a lesson. There is always an *interplay*, overt or tacit, direct or oblique, in educational practice. From the teacher's standpoint, this interplay seeks to bring about learning of some kind. From a student standpoint, the interplay might, for some, be close to what the teacher intends. But, for others, it might be influenced by something quite different, like trying to get under the teacher's skin, or sharing jokes with friends, or baiting the teacher with irrelevant questions or more ingenious distractions. The ever-emergent character of learning environments, even where predictable routine apparently rules, is invariably more complex and more subtle than any one-way descriptions such as 'transmission' can capture.

It is impossible to do full justice to this kind of interplay. But we can achieve a more inclusive picture by identifying some active features that give such interplays their character and distinguish them as instances of educational practice, properly so-called. We can begin to do this by illuminating, in turn, each of the four sets of relationships identified briefly above. This does not mean isolating each of the four from the others. Rather, it means focusing on the particulars of each set of relationships while remaining alert that the interweaving of all four constitutes the active context in which each set of relationships is embedded.

Four aspects of relationships of learning

Let us start then with the teacher's relationship to the subject, or subjects being taught. A subject that has secured a place on a curriculum – in school, college or other learning environment – can plausibly be seen as a body of facts, concepts, propositions, theories and procedures that has gained an acknowledged standing in a society. It gains such standing by having its cultural merits or social utility, or both, widely accepted as worthy of study by successive generations. This is not to deny, of course, that what gets placed on a curriculum might often be distorted versions, sometimes even intractable disfigurements, of the inheritances of learning from which a curriculum is drawn up. Be that as it may, subjects such as mathematics, music, languages, and what are normally included under terms such as 'the arts' and 'the sciences', enjoy widespread standing as being worthy of study. Subjects such as astrology and witchcraft do not. Other fields of study stand at an intermediate stage. A field such as Chinese medicine, for instance, has done much to strengthen its credentials in recent decades and is now accepted in some, although not all, Western institutions where medicine is studied.

Yet there is something amiss with the plausible description just presented. To understand subjects of study mainly as bodies of established knowledge may seem unproblematic from a layperson's perspective, but it is unsatisfactory from an educational one. This understanding fits too easily with a 'transmission' view of teaching: the teacher is deemed to have mastered a particular body of knowledge and then transmits this possession incrementally to students. Textbooks, prepared notes, CDs, DVDs, websites and other resources become seen as authoritative repositories of such knowledge. All too often then, on a transmission conception, the authority of teachers becomes associated with such secondary or reified materials, rather than with the originality of their own relationships to the subjects they teach. This originality lies, or at least a definitive source of it does, in a more vibrant understanding of subjects of study – one which associates each subject of study with a distinct voice, or recognizable range of voices. This more vibrant understanding has been around since antiquity, and it has doubtless been embodied in the actions of good teachers down through the centuries. But it has rarely, if ever, been a prevalent view, and has rarely been made an explicit theme by researchers or writers on education. Michael Oakeshott's essay *'The Voice of Poetry in the Conversation of Mankind'*,[12] stands as a telling exception in this respect, as it explores some perceptive insights that underlie the more vibrant understanding that we are now attempting to uncover.

Oakeshott challenges what he regards as a dominant tendency to reduce all discourses of inquiry to the pattern of argumentative discourse, and to give pride of place to the voice of science in this, with other voices being acknowledged 'merely in respect of their aptitude to imitate this voice.'[13] He is keen to uphold the plurality of voices, stressing that each has a distinctive character. In the course of his essay, Oakeshott identifies, in addition to the voice of science, the voices of 'practical activity', history, poetry, politics and philosophy, but also allows for others. Probing more deeply, he describes the different voices as 'various modes of imagining', each with its own idiom, each diverging not from some ideal 'non-idiomatic' voice, but diverging from each other. 'Each voice', Oakeshott writes, 'is the reflection of a human activity, begun without premonition of where it would lead, but acquiring for itself in the course of the engagement a specific character and manner of speaking of its own: and within each mode of utterance further modulation is discernible.'[14]

To understand a subject as a voice in this sense is quite different from understanding it as a body of knowledge, theories and procedures. It is not that the first denies the latter; rather, that it gives a particular significance to the relationship one has to a subject as a learner, and even more so as a teacher. A voice is something active, something that addresses us and calls forth a response. This response might be alert, careless, appreciative, critical, or other. It might involve a quickening of interest, an aversion, a perplexity, or a range of other cognitive-cum-affective stances, and in varying degrees of intensity. In short, a voice engages human sensibility in ways that something conceived as established body of knowledge does not. Where the sensibility in question is that of the teacher, everything depends not only on the character of the teacher's response, but on the *ongoing* character of that response.

To illustrate the point at issue, let us take as an example a fictional teacher who is nevertheless true to life. Paul, to give him a name, is a secondary teacher of history and mathematics who has a different relationship to each of these subjects. History he understands primarily as a body of accumulated information about the past, for transmission to his students – albeit a body that includes some conflicts of interpretation between historians. Paul is keen that his students will do well in their exams and he believes that they can best be helped in this by mastering the notes he has prepared for them: on colonialism, on the industrial revolution, on political leaders of the nineteenth century and on other reliable examination topics. Paul doesn't read recently published books on history as he sees this as academics' work rather than his. He watches some historical dramas and documentaries on television, but he doesn't make much use of this kind of material in his teaching. Mathematics, however, Paul sees as a fascinating world of exploration. Unlike his fellow maths teachers, he believes that this is a subject through which students can be brought to new imaginative neighbourhoods that will delight their minds and encourage them to a range of progressive achievements – for example, in problem-solving, in problem-identification and in logical thinking. He also believes that, if only students were introduced to it in the right way by their teachers, mathematics could be one of the most popular rather than one of the least popular subjects among the students. Paul finds himself getting irritated by teachers who can't or won't see mathematics this way. He takes a dim – but unvoiced – view of colleagues who allow the content, pace and method of their work to be dictated by the uninspiring mathematics textbooks that he feels are too much in evidence throughout the school.

A host of issues arise from these observations on Paul's contrasting relationships to his two main teaching subjects. Not all of these issues can be pursued here, but a few particular comments can be made at this point. First, and rather obviously, there is likely to be a higher quality of learning in Paul's mathematics lessons than in his history lessons, although the latter lessons are likely to meet formal measures of effectiveness in teaching. Second, contrasts like this are more usually made between one teacher and another, but when they are manifest in the practice of a single teacher they highlight the crucial importance of the teacher's relationship to the subject – a point that is overlooked by a widespread tendency, even among school leaders, to hold that all good teaching 'comes down to personality'. Third, this example shows that the relationship between the teacher and a particular teaching subject is more than a question of competence. That's to say, it is a recurrent interplay, just as much as interpersonal relations are. If the relationship is buoyant and balanced, it is one in which the teacher is continually attentive and responsive to new influences – a relationship that nurtures and relishes an ever richer fluency on the teacher's part. If it is neither buoyant nor balanced, something else displaces fluency – most often, a conformity to a regime of textbooks, notes and drill.

The second of the four relationships is the teacher's relationship to the students. So much has been written about this as a form of unequal power relations that it is difficult to establish a due recognition of the many other things that might also be going on in it. Presenting the relationship as a courtship, however, or as the heartwork of perceptive imagination, might prompt the necessary shift of thinking to facilitate this recognition. It's not that considerations of power are now dismissed; indeed, far from it. Rather, now, in thinking about relationships of teaching and learning, as well as engaging in them, we might become more critically conscious, and more conscientiously discerning, about the exercise of power and its consequences. For instance, power in relationships of teaching and learning could include coercion, earned authority, the use of defensible influence, or the unacknowledged exercise of violence, to mention just a few forms. It could, indeed, include some unlikely combinations of such forms. To appreciate this better, it is necessary to explore more closely both the nature and the defensibility of relationships of teachers and students.

In any exchanges involving cultural influences, no less than in the conduct of affairs of the heart, we can identify broad patterns, ranging from the predatory or possessive at one end of a continuum to the considerate and enabling at the other. In more practical terms, we can recognize, first, the kind of approach that declares its intentions with honesty, that pursues its purposes earnestly but refrains from forcing its suit – an approach that has the courage to face difficulties as they arise, that combines frankness with a keen sense of another's privacy and that seeks to evade the thrall of changeless routine. Such an approach discloses its special character through honestly encountering the disappointments as well as the delights, the frustrations as well as the surprises, of mutual discovery. In short, we recognize *a decisive sense of care* here in one person's basic attitude to another, or others. At the other end of the continuum, we recognize a contrasting – perhaps more common – kind of pattern, where considerations of a more calculating kind are to the fore. Here the arts of dissembling, manipulation and seduction are regularly nurtured and practised, and the characteristics of the first kind of interplay are at best secondary to the securing of the prize, or perhaps the imagined prize. Any purposeful human interaction could, of course, combine elements of both patterns, or move over and back between what we might call the more honourable and the more calculating ends of the continuum. Such fluctuations could occur often enough even in the approach of a particular individual. Relationships between teachers and students, like other relationships in which the quality of the influence exercised is critical, can be understood as occupying a fairly settled, or a more shifting place along such a continuum.

Turning now to the third set, this concerns the teacher's relationships to colleagues, to parents and guardians, and to the public more widely. Placing the focus first on relationships with colleagues, there is an inherited tendency in cultures of teaching that associates professional discretion with their classroom 'autonomy', but in a protectionist sense of 'autonomy'. This stance involves not venturing into discussions about how colleagues conduct their professional business in their own classrooms. It leads to what research studies, as well as inspectors' reports, have called the professional insulation and isolation of teachers from each other. This insulation and isolation lies in sharp contrast to the informality with which teachers regularly discuss friends and family, current affairs, sports, and not least, students' misbehaviour. Although it is declared as an affirmation of teachers' professional status, this kind of 'autonomy' stance is more accurately a form of defensiveness, associated with a discomforting awareness of subordinate standing. It often springs from an unhappy history. In any case, it precludes a consciousness of a more healthy orientation – one that sees the most encouraging affirmations of one's practice as coming precisely from colleagues. Autonomy claims that spring from defensiveness also lead too many teachers to shield the conduct of their professional lives from parents. This is despite the obvious fact that parents hear regular accounts of this life, often in biased form, from spontaneous comments by their children about their teachers. Finally, such a protectionist stance encourages a sense of victimhood. It tends to view the public at large as failing to understand the demands of teaching, or to regard the public as being generally unsympathetic to teachers.

A contrasting view of the teacher's understanding of this third set of relations envisages colleagues mainly as sources of constructive criticism and ideas, parents and guardians mainly as supportive partners, and the public mainly as a body whose trust is necessary, and is deservedly earned. To have naturally high expectations in these three domains is not to suggest that such expectations are thereby met. Rather, it is to highlight (to all concerned) the things that are worth struggling for, and to concentrate positive energies on the renewed articulation and pursuit of these. The absence of such expectations, however, is likely to lead, on the part of teachers, to a habitual inclination towards misapprehension, to a failure to see and seize opportunities, and to a demise in the kinds of productive energies that are particularly to be prized in educational practice.

The teacher's relationship to himself or herself is the fourth relationship for investigation. More simply, we can describe this as the teacher's self-understanding. This is where the other three relationships come together to orient in one way or another the teacher's thinking and actions. Important aspects of it have already been touched on in our consideration of the other three sets of relationships. For instance, recalling the case of the teacher Paul mentioned a few moments ago, it is clear that his relationship to mathematics has crucial implications for how he understands himself as a mathematics teacher. Because the same point holds true in the case of history, his understanding of himself as a history teacher is conspicuously different. The other sets of relationships are also affected by this. The kind of learning Paul feels himself answerable for to his students, and to their parents or guardians, is likely to be quite different in the case of mathematics and history. Looked at by an outsider, or by one of Paul's colleagues, the quality of learning among his maths students and his history students is also likely to be seen as very different. This difference is something Paul's students will have experienced directly, if any of them have him for both subjects. We have already noted that Paul feels a certain irritation towards colleagues who seem slow to see mathematics and its teaching with the kind of originality that he does. It might come as a shock to Paul's self-understanding as a teacher, however, if a few innovative history colleagues were to tell him that they experience a similar irritation towards himself when it comes to the teaching of history.

The previous paragraphs have sought to illuminate overlooked features of the kinds of relationships that are invariably in play in educational practice. They underline the point that teaching and learning constitute an active interplay of influence as distinct from a process of transmission and receiving. Conceiving of these relationships as a form of courtship, moreover, or conceiving of educational practice itself as a disciplined, imaginative heartwork, advances our understanding a bit further. It captures something of the venturesome character and the ethical responsibilities of practices that can properly be called educational. Let us try to illustrate this by considering an example of heartwork in practice.

Teaching and learning as heartwork in action: a first-person account

In this example, or more precisely this practical thought-experiment, it might be best to use the first-person singular, as it enables thinking to focus more centrally on the self-understanding of the teacher. Let the teacher, in this instance, be a primary school teacher.

As a primary school teacher of sixth class (12-year olds who will all hopefully be transfer-ring to secondary school next year), I teach a total of seven subjects. I feel well up to the different challenges of my work, although these make heavy demands on my energies. The feedback I get from inspectors' reports, from parents and from the school principal, tells me that my work in all areas of the curriculum is highly regarded. I admit however that I'm more attracted to some of the subjects than others. I have a lively interest in some of them and following up on this interest has made these subjects part of my personal culture, you could say. As for my students, I'm happy to note the progress quite a few of them have made as autonomous learners – some have become eager readers, a few are really excited about maths, some have warmed to science, most are keen on web-browsing and there are regularly well-informed contributions in class. Some of them come from homes that are really vibrant as learning environments, and this gives them distinct advantages when it comes to our work in the classroom. Others come from homes where learning is not the only thing neglected, and the consequences of this for the students' learning call for a range of different kinds of interventions daily in the classroom. Despite this diversity of background influences, I notice the students' reactions to the different subjects are still very much associated with the quality of my own presentations of these subjects in the classroom. And by their reactions, I mean both their enthusiasm for learning and their work effort as learners.

Although the curriculum for primary education is officially called 'child-centred' or 'learner-centred', I'm not altogether happy with this term. It's not that I prefer it to be 'teacher-centred', rather that the term 'learner-centred' tends to suggest that the students learn chiefly as individuals. This doesn't do sufficient justice to the social nature of the learning environments in which we work, including the diversity just mentioned. I know that the child-centred concept springs largely from Rousseau. It fits well in his case, as Émile was his teacher's only student. There are 28 students in my 6th class (and similar numbers in my colleagues' classes) and, although I know each of them pretty well as individuals, our learning is done as a group, or often in a number of smaller groups. I'm continually trying to turn to best advantage what I know of different students' backgrounds, and of their particular potentials and limitations.

I have become increasingly conscious of the fact that my work with these students, but also with other classes of previous years, involves a lot more than instruction. Despite my basic commitment to the 'child-centred' nature of the curriculum, my actual practices of teaching were a bit domineering, sometimes to a pronounced degree. What pulled me up short was a DVD recording of episodes of my own classroom work that I watched as part of a professional development course. (Video technology wasn't used in teacher education when I qualified as a teacher.) That recording made it clear to me that what I was watching, and what the students were experiencing, was an unfolding interplay with leading roles and minor parts, much as a drama on stage is. But this was an interplay in which I was clearly taking centre-stage for most of the time. Different members of the 'audience' were periodic participants – some much more so than others. I had previously thought about my work more as a process that usually ran to plan than as an unfolding interplay. But now, looking at myself from the perspective of an outsider, 'process' somehow missed the heart of the matter. Apart from my tendency to take most of the active parts myself, I could see that there was invariably something of a venturing in what I was attempting. I also discovered that the students, including some of the ones I had regarded as essentially passive, could in different ways be venturers themselves. They could surprise themselves, myself and fellow students if the climate was right, and if given the right opportunity and encouragement. I thus stumbled on the critical importance of seeking pertinent 'unscripted roles' for different students.

Although I found I had been overlooking frequent opportunities for productive contributions from the students, I also discovered from the video that I was revealing more of myself than I had thought. Rather than try to suppress this, I found it a more attractive prospect, and also less contrived, to try to turn it to advantage. Where previously I viewed my work primarily in terms of getting through the material I had prepared, now I began to see this preparation itself as something akin to a sketch for a learning drama. In fact, it would be nearer the mark to describe it as a sequence of broadly envisaged scenes. Each scene marks some change in activity and atmosphere, but also seeks to invite impromptu contributions that add greater vitality and warmth to the learning environment.

My understanding of the nature of my work – including the curriculum, the students, their parents, my colleagues, the principal and other professionals with whom I deal – has been continually refined, and will probably undergo further refinement in the future. So also has my understanding of the broader context of my work. Like most primary school teachers in my country, I work in a denominational school. Yet our salaries are paid entirely from public funds. I'm aware of the historical reasons for this arrangement. I don't see myself, however, as working mainly on behalf of the state, or the church, or indeed parents, although I'm aware that some among these might see things otherwise. My first commitment is rather to the students, and to their flourishing as co-operating and mutually attentive learners. I believe that my students' parents, by and large, appreciate this. If I were asked to describe what precisely I mean by this flourishing, I'm not sure that I could answer the question in precise terms. But I would be happy to answer it by giving an account of the heart of my practice, and that account would run roughly as follows.

I regard it as important for my students to see that each of the subjects we study has something rich and enduring to offer. For instance, if I'm teaching history, or English, or science, or religion, I'm keen to encourage the students individually, and as far as possible collectively, to discover something of the historian in themselves; or to discover something of linguistic aptitude and appreciation in themselves; or to discover something of the scientist in themselves; or to discover something of their own religious sensibilities. None of this is to deny that it sometimes takes a lot of pain, faith and forbearance, and an alert sense of detection, to unearth this 'something'. Nor is it to deny that the 'something' may initially look unremarkable when it is unearthed. This kind of discovery, however, and it happens in smaller or more significant ways in daily classroom life, marks in each case a learning achievement with longer-term consequences. It enables the student to understand something more of her own particular promise, of her own aptitudes and limitations. That's to say, it advances learning in the best sense of the word. It helps the student to become better oriented to the renewal of effort and commitment in the subject in question – even to take a step in the gradual appropriation of an identity that is uniquely her own. I'm aware that I've spoken here as if I were personal tutor to each of them, and within limits this is true. But discoveries of this kind are frequently also collective ones, or are made by individuals in the midst of collective undertakings.

The picture is quite different, however if, in teaching history, I seek to inculcate in the students any allegiance to a tendentious version of the past; if, in teaching science, I seek to privilege one perspective over others, say in energy use and environmental care; if, in teaching English (or any other language for that matter), I intimate that this language confers a badge of cultural or racial superiority; if, in teaching Religious Education, I treat matters of faith as if they were matters of fact. In short, I've put a foot wrong if, in any instance, my approach presumes some proprietorial claim on the minds and hearts of the students. I'm regularly struck by how powerfully influence works in unannounced ways in the to-and-fro of teaching and learning. In fact, I believe that the explicit disavowal of such proprietorial claims is a 'must' for professional discipline in teaching. Otherwise the interplay of influence between teachers and students can become rapidly disfigured, although often unnoticeably so.

It has come home to me more and more when I'm reviewing a day's work and preparing the next day's, that I'm something of an actor in my work in the classroom. That's not to say that I'm merely pretending, or that I'm not myself. In fact, I try hard to be myself, because I know I could all too quickly become 'role-cast' through habituation. I've learned that authenticity is important in the relations of teaching and learning. This means that I don't become a different person with my students compared to the person I am when I'm with my family or friends. Yet I do become different in some ways, because I'm on stage, and in a more real-life sense than in the theatre. My actions in the classroom are very much on view and are being continually appraised by 28 young critics; being judged, that is, for things like fairness or favouritism, alertness or absent-mindedness, consistency or unreliability, lucidity or obscurity, adventurousness or tediousness, humour or dourness, and so on. So I have to put a lot of thought in advance into how things might go; in effect, to do a mental rehearsal of the day's main episodes and encounters. But I have to be able to think rapidly on my feet as well when the unexpected happens, as it does many times daily. With every new topic or important idea I introduce, I have to make overtures to the students on behalf of that idea. I have to try to open up a fresh imaginative neighbourhood, as it were, and draw all of us into it. Occasionally, this backfires, or sometimes it falls flat on a first attempt. But when it works well, it's great, and it's here that some of the students' contributions are often real eye-openers.

I'm not saying that routine, or predictability, or boredom are strangers to the learning environments I try to build with my students. In fact, the students experience some of my more important expectations (rules if you like) in the form of routines that all of us must follow. Routines and predictability are good if they contribute to sustaining a richer climate for learning. As for habit, I don't worry about us becoming creatures of habit if initiative and innovation have themselves become habitual features of our work together. Boredom, however, is something that I know will invariably bring trouble and conflict. I continually try to forestall it, although not always successfully. I often think that if I had an abundance of good ideas for all the topics we have to learn, boredom could be kept to minimal proportions. In this connection, I'm stronger in some of my subjects than in others, and I can see that some colleagues are stronger in subjects in which I'm weaker. In fact, with some topics I get really stuck for ideas and I sometimes find myself wishing I could be a fly on the wall in the classes of those teachers who are strongest where I'm weakest – and I mean colleagues more widely than just in our own school. I need hardly say that I've picked up a lot of practical ideas from colleagues informally, and hopefully they have picked up a few from me. But we need to be at this kind of exercise more formally as well, through workshops or seminars at regular intervals in our ongoing professional development. To be the kind of teacher I'm keen to be, I need to be learning from new experiences on a continuing basis or, more accurately, from observant reflection on such experiences. I believe we all need to do so, right throughout our lives as teachers. This means that constructive self-criticism, including the mutual practice of such criticism, should be defining marks of practitioners who have chosen the promotion of good learning among others as their way of life.

The various dimensions of the heartwork theme – relations with students, with colleagues, with teaching subjects, with one's self – can be seen to interweave in the first-person account just offered. But there is a long-established contrasting picture – namely, a stereotype that sees teachers as needlessly bossy people: people who use a 'teachery' kind of voice that's higher and louder than natural speech and who spend much of their time giving orders and reprimands. There are still plenty of examples today to show that this stereotype is far from groundless, and few teachers can claim that there are no traces of it in their own practice. But as a stereotype, it presents a kind of barrack sergeant view of teachers: maintaining order and discipline among the ranks below themselves while conforming to the orders of a class of superiors. Everything about the account being presented in this book seeks to counter such a subordinate view of teaching. To be sure, the relationships that comprise the heartwork perspective being developed here are not neglectful of a necessity for firmness, even for resoluteness. But such necessity remains wrong-sighted unless it is informed by a perceptive understanding of learning environments themselves, and of the kind of imaginative capabilities that actually make such environments fertile. Bearing in mind the historical patterns reviewed earlier, this involves a major shift of emphasis from an order of compliance to an order of originality. And such a shift now brings imagination, particularly pedagogical imagination, to the centre of our enquiry.

5   Opening Delphi

Steiner's Delphic vision

The stereotype considered at the end of the previous chapter – the teacher as shrill disciplinarian and as compliant subordinate – is one that is discomfiting to teachers, however much their working lives might sometimes conform to it. Such a stereotype can have a practical value, however, as a reminder of what teachers have all too often become, and still become, and from which their deliverance will invariably involve continual challenge and struggle. The point at issue here – the necessity to give imagination a vital place in teaching and learning – needs to be put into sharper context. A lively way to do so is to review a characterization of teachers that is both coherent and forceful, but which is even less complimentary than the stereotype just mentioned. This is George Steiner's characterization in his much acclaimed and much criticized book *Lessons of the Masters*. Steiner depicts the mass of secondary school teachers as follows:

> In actual fact, as we know, the majority of those to whom we entrust our children in secondary education, to whom we look for guidance and example in the academy, are more or less amiable gravediggers. They labour to diminish their students to their own level of indifferent fatigue. They do not 'open Delphi' but close it.[1]

It is easy to envisage the outrage that such a severe judgement provokes among teachers. Injured self-respect protests at the sweeping nature of the 'as we know' in the declaration. Offended justice, likewise, points to the lack of any empirical evidence advanced by Steiner to warrant such a conclusion. The reference to indifferent fatigue inflames the injury, suggesting that teachers are, by and large, mired in mediocrity. Of course, the dramatic eloquence of the charge makes it stand out in memory. Yet, Steiner hasn't so much thrown a gauntlet at the feet of teachers as casually dropped one in passing while proceeding to the heart of the vision that he wants to share with his readers. Rage, on the part of teachers, however understandable, is a fruitless response. One could, more patiently, point out that what Steiner calls indifferent fatigue might more accurately be described as a demoralization that has become endemic among many teachers. But even this is to go on the defensive and choose from the start an inferior ground for engaging critically with Steiner's stance. Concentrating on his remarks-in-passing bypasses the constructive heart of what Steiner has to say. And that constructive heart is more thought-provoking than provocative. What calls for careful consideration is Steiner's argument in its fuller dimensions.

That argument is informed by a lofty conception of teaching, articulated with eloquence and passion, if not circumspection, in *Lessons of the Masters*. The book presents a dramatic contrast to the kind of studied reticence reviewed in Chapter 2 above. The pages of *Lessons of the Masters* are well supplied with illustrations of memorable teaching and learning. Steiner discloses teaching not merely as a distinctive practice, but as a rare art. There is an aristocratic uniqueness in the educational relationships that he elucidates. This gains an added charge from the erotic quality that Steiner invariably associates with these relationships. Exploring his characterizations at closer range will help to show why Steiner's estimation of the achievements of the majority of teachers is so low. But this is just the negative side of the picture. More positively, this exploration should help to illuminate important substantial features of the heartwork conception that we have already begun to examine. It should help to remove misunderstandings from this conception and elucidate it in ways that recommend themselves to teachers more widely in twenty-first century democratic societies.

'Authentic teaching is a vocation', writes Steiner. The genuine teacher is accordingly aware of the 'dignity', the 'magnitude' and even the 'mystery' of that vocation. It involves an 'unspoken Hippocratic oath'.[2] Steiner locates the wellsprings of this understanding in Ovid's depiction of Pythagoras as teacher in *Metamorphoses* XV. He illustrates his starting premise by quoting the following verse from Ovid's portrayal of Pythagoras, which Steiner himself regards as 'talismanic':

> His thought
> Reached far aloft, to the great gods in Heaven,
> And his imagination looked on visions
> Beyond his mortal sight. All things he studied
> With watchful eager mind, and he brought home
> What he had learned and sat among the people
> Teaching them what was worthy, and they listened
> In silence ...[3]

The teacher, in this account, dwells, at least periodically, in marvellous lands of the imagination, and is mindful of an obligation to keep faith with imagination's own most cherished sources of inspiration. Again quoting Ovid, Steiner writes that such an orientation on the teacher's part has affinities with oracular traditions: 'I will now follow the god to the open Delphi that I carry within myself.'[4] This reference reveals an initial glimpse of the context of his criticism of teachers who close rather than open Delphi for their students. He then quotes a further verse from *Metamorphoses* XV, which highlights the eminence of the teacher's calling:

> There is no greater wonder than to range
> The starry heights, to leave the earth's dull regions,
> To ride the clouds, to stand on Atlas' shoulders,
> And see far off, far down, the little figures
> Wandering here and there, devoid of reason,
> Anxious, in fear of death, and to advise them,
> And to make fate an open book.[5]

These quotations from Ovid reveal the elevated standing that Steiner gives to the first of the four relationships we considered a little earlier: the teacher's relationship to the subject matter he or she teaches. Steiner even uses the word 'exultation' to describe it.[6] Where the relationships between teachers and students are concerned, the initial picture that emerges from these verses seems to be that of the student as attentive listener, even awed listener. But the fuller picture Steiner presents is more complex, and his remarks on this relationship are particularly striking. The daring nature of these remarks, moreover, makes it difficult to give a presentation of his arguments without comment or interruption. I will try, however, to summarize his account of the main features of teacher–student relationships, and of good and bad instances of these, before attempting any analysis of that account itself.

Going promptly to the heart of the matter, Steiner writes: 'To teach seriously is to lay hands on what is most vital in a human being. It is to seek access to the quick and the innermost of a child's or an adult's integrity. A Master invades, he breaks open, he can lay waste in order to cleanse and rebuild.'[7] In this, Steiner points out, the stakes are high, and laden with dangers. Bad teaching succumbs to these dangers, he maintains. It is ruinous, as 'it reduces to gray inanity the subject being presented'. As well as destroying the subject, however, it progressively ruins the student's capacity for responding to what the subject might seek to say. 'It drips into the child's or the adult's sensibility that most corrosive of acids, boredom, the marsh gas of ennui.' Steiner claims that millions of students have had poetry, or mathematics, or logical thinking killed for them by dead teaching, 'by the perhaps subconsciously vengeful mediocrity of frustrated pedagogues'.[8] He then suggests that good teachers are more rare than virtuoso artists, and adds the remark about 'closing Delphi' that has already been quoted.

For Steiner, to respond to a summons to the vocation of teaching, is to accept the responsibilities involved in being a master. The word 'Master' clearly has a special significance for him, and he writes it invariably with a capital 'M'.[9] There is, however, nothing sexist intended here on Steiner's part. Female masters, although less often in evidence than their male counterparts, feature in his arguments and examples. In any case, to be an authentic teacher on Steiner's account is to be a master: to be both 'a bearer and a communicator of life-enhancing truths.'[10] This twofold responsibility puts the master at a distinct remove from those who charge a fee for their services. Steiner draws a contrast between Socrates, who remained an impoverished truth-seeker all his life, and the sophists, who charged fees and whose schools were acknowledged as advancing the aspirations of students to positions of power and influence in Athenian society. For Steiner, the taken-for-granted fact that teachers in today's colleges and academies, including himself, are paid, 'hides the problematic strangeness of their trade'.[11] For if the teacher is 'a being inspired by vision and vocation of no ordinary sort, how is it possible for him to present a bill?'[12] There is, Steiner suggests, something 'demeaning and risible' about the situation. However 'normal' the payment of teachers may have become, Steiner insists that authentic teachers cannot be in it for the money.

In addition to the exalted inspirations called for on the teacher's part, and the unmercenary character of the work of the teacher, a third feature that Steiner identifies is the 'orality' of teaching. Commenting favourably on Plato's remarks on the spoken, as distinct from the written word, Steiner suggests: 'Only the spoken word and face-to-face can elicit truth and, *a fortiori*, guarantee honest teaching.'[13] Socrates and Jesus, he points out, left no writings to posterity, yet they 'stand at the pivot of our civilization'.[14] Their radiance as teachers is unsurpassed and the example of their lives and of their deaths has imbued Western awareness with both 'an irremediable sadness and a fever of hope'.[15] Their particular genius as teachers, Steiner believes, is in the capacity 'to originate myths' (Socrates) and 'to devise parables' (Jesus). This capacity, he continues, is exceedingly rare. It 'incarnates' what is 'most decisive and inexplicable in Mastery, in the art of teaching'.[16] Steiner emphasizes that figures such as Socrates and Jesus share an originality and imaginative power that provide 'inexhaustible multiplicities and potentialities of interpretation'[17] – in the first instance among those present, but then, through seminal influence, on a much wider public and on succeeding generations.

Steiner devotes much attention to a fourth feature: what he sees as the erotic nature of the relationships of teaching and learning. Initially, he associates this with persuasion, saying: 'The pulse of teaching is persuasion. The teacher solicits attention, agreement, and, optimally, collaborative dissent.'[18] But he also insists on the presence of a sexual dimension. 'Eroticism, covert or declared, fantasized or enacted, is in-woven in teaching, in the phenomenology of mastery and discipleship.'[19] He briefly cites some examples. In 'the Platonic Academy, the Athenian gymnasium, the Papuan long house, British public schools and religious seminaries of every hue', Steiner maintains, 'homoeroticism not only flourished, but was regarded as educative.'[20] He also highlights some celebrated examples of heterosexual eroticism in teaching and learning, notably in the master–disciple relationships of Abelard and Heloise in twelfth-century France, and of Martin Heidegger and Hannah Arendt in twentieth-century Germany. And he concludes:

> The erotic sway available to the *magister*, the sexual temptations exhibited, consciously or not, by the pupil, polarise the pedagogic relation. I believe that there inheres in effective teaching, as in realized discipleship, an exercise of love, or that of hatred which is the dark of love.[21]

Pursuing the theme that '*eros* and teaching are inextricable', Steiner says that this can introduce some intractable complexities into educational relationships, including 'modulations of spiritual and sexual desire, of domination and submission', the 'interplay of jealousy and faith', and 'role reversals' between teacher and student.[22] The dangers ever in attendance here include 'sadism, both mental and physical' and the lurking presence of 'sexual favours on hopeful and calculated offer'.[23] Even where learning environments are less erotically charged, Steiner calls attention to an ever-recurring interplay 'of fidelity and betrayal, of *auctoritas* and rebellion, of mimesis and rivalry', in the relationships of teacher and student.[24]

There are additional features of the relationships of teachers and students that Steiner considers in *Lessons of the Masters*, although the above four – the richly imaginative, the unmercenary, the oral over the written, the erotic – are representative of his main lines of thinking. These illustrate for Steiner's readers something of each of the three scenarios of relationship he outlines in the book's Introduction: first, masters who have destroyed their disciples (both psychologically and physically); second, masters who have been subverted or ruined by their disciples, students or apprentices; and third, 'an eros of reciprocal trust and, indeed, love'.[25] In the book's Afterword, Steiner provides some retrospective views on the importance of teaching as a vocation and of the significance of his arguments as a whole, and I will conclude this summary presentation with two brief extracts from that Afterword. Steiner writes: 'There is no craft more privileged. To awaken in another human being powers, dreams beyond one's own; to induce in others a love for that which one loves; to make one's inward present their future: This is a threefold adventure like no other.' And then he adds: 'Even at a humble level – that of the schoolmaster – to teach, to teach well, is to be accomplice to transcendent possibility.' [26]

Masters and disciples, teachers and students

Turning now to review some of the more salient points in Steiner's account of the relationships of teaching and learning also provides an occasion to explore further the perspectives introduced in earlier chapters. Especially relevant here are the perspectives that understand teaching and learning as a form of courtship, or what I would now prefer to call 'heartwork'. Perhaps the first thing that needs to be stressed is that Steiner's conception of teaching and learning arise mainly from his experiences as a university teacher. In fact, many of his remarks suggest even a graduate-student context as distinct from an undergraduate one. Still, Steiner's main purpose is the wider one of considering the occupation of teaching as such. This is evident from his periodic use of 'child' as well as 'adult' when talking about students. It is also clear from his reference to the secondary school teachers whom he criticizes for their 'indifferent fatigue', and from his comment on the 'humble level' of the schoolmaster. To do justice to this wider purpose, however, one has to draw important distinctions between teacher and master that Steiner doesn't make, or that he passes over too lightly. Equally important is the distinction that has to be drawn between student and disciple. Steiner's reluctance to draw such distinctions is evident throughout the book, and the consequences of this provide the first point of investigation in reviewing his vision of teaching and learning.

The relationship of master and disciple is different in key respects to that of teacher and student. 'Master' can include a range of connotations. Starting from the more figurative end of this range, the term can designate certain human qualities that are linked more to personality and experience than to formal education or training – for instance, a master of irony, or of deceit, or of subtlety, and so on. It can also refer to a person who has an expertise that is the product of training and dedicated practice – as in a master potter, a master golfer, a master musician. It is a traditional term for a schoolteacher, often (although not exclusively) a male school principal. In a related sense to this, it can refer to the head of an institution, such as a university or hospital of long-standing reputation. It is the term that commonly marks a university degree between a bachelor's and a doctorate. It refers in a particular sense to a revered scholar, or a thinker whose wisdom most people lack. Here, we have touched only on a sample of the range of meanings – *The Concise Oxford Dictionary* gives no fewer than thirteen. For Steiner, however, it is clear that the last of the meanings just mentioned is particularly important, as revealed by the suggestive remembrance in his comment: 'Where men and women toil barefoot to seek out a Master, the life of the spirit is safeguarded.'[27]

That masters are sought out in this way reveals something of the acknowledged difference in standing between their students and themselves. This very seeking-out, whether by travelling long distances or resulting from an unexpected local discovery, cultivates a culture where deference and reverence, even awe of the master, find fertile ground. While taking nothing from the riches to be gained by students from 'sitting at the feet' of masters in this way, there are dangers for both; most notably perhaps, a dulling of critical discipline on the part of students and a lack of self-criticism on the part of the master. Many students quickly outgrow the limiting consequences of early adulation of a master, while still cherishing privileged educational experiences associated with that master. Even where they don't outgrow such attachments, they tend to pass on to other teachers or to other things in a few years. Masters, however, tend to be more long-term presences. The master who is ill-disposed to invite criticisms of his knowledge from students, or who fails to see such criticisms as sources of learning, is likely to make trouble for himself, or for others, and often for both. Among the many illustrations of this in the history of Western learning, two striking ones spring to mind. The first is the case of the Athenian politicians and poets whose 'high reputation for wisdom' frequently came to grief in public encounters with Socrates, but who took their revenge on Socrates in due course by legal contrivances. The second is the case of William of Champeaux and Anselm of Laon, in twelfth-century France. Their illustrious reputations, and that of their schools, came similarly to grief from a certain conceit associated with their public standing as masters; in particular, form their inability to deal with the searching questions of their assertive student Peter Abelard.[28] Steiner is clearly right to stress the ongoing necessity to dwell lovingly with the subjects one teaches. If this can be called a mastery, however, it is a mastery that is ever on-the-way, as distinct from any final destination at which one has confidently arrived. It is a modest, provisional kind of mastery that sees the necessity, with Socrates, of having an educated sense of its own ignorance.

Discipleship is scarcely less problematic in relation to learning than mastery is in relation to teaching. Discipleship identifies a disposition to learn that is different in central respects to that of the student. This difference is tellingly evident from Christian scriptures, particularly the New Testament, in which disciples and discipleship feature prominently. In Matthew 13:34, one reads: 'All these things Jesus spoke in parables to the multitudes and without parables he did not speak to them.' Two verses later, however, it becomes clear that when the multitudes had departed and he was alone with his disciples, Jesus gave literal explanations of the parables. In Mark 4:34, the contrast is contained in one verse: 'And without parables he did not speak to them [multitudes]; but apart, he explained all things to his disciples.' This distinction between more didactic teaching and parables mirrors a distinction between discipleship, on the one hand, and a range of more venturesome relationships of learning on the other. Parables are imaginative creations that invariably contain a moral, or other food for thought, but that make no proprietorial claim on the minds and hearts of listeners. They are particularly apt when exploring themes in ethics or religion with a plurality (i.e. a 'multitude') of learners. Here, the learner is free to take the point of the parable, or disagree with it, or just leave it. If, however, having thought about the challenges to one's beliefs and actions provoked by the parable, the learner wishes to become a disciple, the relationship changes somewhat. The learner now becomes a willing listener to the teachings of a master. Both the style of teaching and the style of learning have changed, as have the relationships between the teacher and the taught. The master–disciple relationship presupposes, on the part of the learner, a trusting faith in the truths taught by the master and a seeking after better understanding of these truths. It is understood by both parties, moreover, that the master's truths actually constitute an important kind of arrival, or destination. Properly viewed, these truths are articles of a shared faith, as distinct from something established beyond question. They are also distinct from a scientist's or a teacher's best hypothesis to date. These latter 'truths' invite critical comment and have to remain open to refutation, or to being superseded by a better, perhaps contrary, understanding.

This means that the relationships of teacher and student are, in principle, less hierarchical than those of master and disciple. Even in the junior classes of primary school, teachers seek quite properly to elicit critical discernment on the part of the children; to draw learners onto disciplined pathways of enquiry, both critical and receptive, on which the teacher has previously travelled. Crucially, however, these are pathways the teacher herself remains exploring, in her readings, reflections and exchanges with colleagues, as well as in her work with students.[29] The student is seen not as material to be moulded to the teacher's design, nor as a mind to be furnished with a preferred body of teachings and outlooks. Rather, the student is acknowledged as a new participant in the venture of learning, whose pathway will in many ways be similar to that of fellow students, but will also be hopefully marked by turns and achievements that are particular to the student's own range of promise.

Imaginativeness: aristocratic and pedagogical

Steiner's images drawn from Ovid – of thoughts reaching far aloft, of imagination looking on visions beyond mortal sight, of leaving the earth's dull regions – are striking ones. But they may also be daunting ones for teachers, by and large. His comments on good teachers being as rare as virtuoso artists would seem to underline this last point. The importance he attributes to the lofty imagination seems inseparably linked to a mentality that looks haughtily at the 'little figures far below', who 'wander here and there devoid of reason'. It is also akin to his dismissal of the bulk of secondary school teachers as 'amiable gravediggers', and to his less caustic remark about the 'humble level' of the schoolmaster. Steiner's conception of pedagogical imagination is avowedly aristocratic. He complains in the Afterword that 'any manifest turning towards an elite, towards that aristocracy of intellect self-evident to Max Weber, is close to being proscribed by the democratization of a mass-consumption system.'[30] His complaint here cannot just be dismissed, especially as he recognizes that democratization in education often springs from 'honesties, liberations, hopes of the first order.'[31] Yet there is a deep-seated fusion, indeed confusion, of the notion of excellence with that of aristocracy in Steiner's thinking, and this bedevils his whole outlook on education. It tends to confound the reader, even to repel the reader, at those very points where Steiner's insights are at their most suggestive. It is important then to address this confusion to see how his key insights stand if their aristocratic clothing is stripped away.

The notion of aristocracy has its origins in the Greek *aristos*, meaning 'the best', and *aristokratia*, meaning 'government by the best'. Throughout Western history, moreover, it is a notion laden with a keen consciousness of being the best in a socially exclusive sense; of being part of a class or group that ranks decisively above others in things that matter. Aristocracy is also historically associated with privileges of birth (even more so than of wealth), of preserving pedigree and lineage, and of keeping commoners outside. Not surprisingly then, the notion of aristocracy can provide a seductive and reassuring home for that of excellence. But this is an inappropriate home, one that any genuine notion of excellence should remain outside, and especially where educational matters are concerned. To excel in any field can, of course, mean surpassing the best achievements of others in that field. In a more specific sense that is particularly important for education, it can also mean surpassing one's own previous personal best. For a student to excel in this latter sense may not always mean being among the top percentiles, but it might indicate a heart-warming journey of progress – in mathematics, in technical drawing, in reading – from what may initially have looked like unpromising beginnings. In addition, when we consider the vast range of human possibilities – those in sport, in craftwork, in music, in art, in home-making, in scientific research, in diplomacy, and this list could fill pages – it is clear that excellence in one field might not at all be associated with excellence in another. Indeed, excellence in one or more fields could be accompanied by a lingering incapacity in others. For reasons such as these, associating excellence with the notion of aristocracy, and particularly an aristocracy of abstract intellect, gives rise to a prejudicial understanding of excellence itself.

The stripping of aristocratic associations from Steiner's demand for exalted imagination on the part of the teacher does not amount to throwing out the idea itself. Fertility in pedagogical imagination is to be unfailingly encouraged in the teacher's relationship to the subjects he or she teaches. Steiner is right to say that the 'gray inanity' of subjects poorly taught becomes the corrosive acid of boredom for students. But even if the teacher's relationship to the subject is healthily alive, even if it is a treasured and vibrant rapport, that is still only half of the picture. The students are likely to remain unacquainted with what might summon their best attentions unless the richness of the teacher's rapport with the subject becomes, in some degree, embodied in the learning environment shared by the students and the teacher. Just as a person who is alive in mind but dull or artless in conversation is likely to make a poor suitor, a teacher whose imagination is inwardly active but who is apparently uninteresting to everyone else, cuts a sad figure in school, college or university. There are, of course, many teachers for whom, for one reason or another, the torch is quenched, and who rely on a formula of textbooks, ready-made notes and past examination papers to see them through their work. Yet contrary to what Steiner may believe, where there are shortcomings of imagination on the part of teachers, these occur more often in the relationships between teachers and students than between teachers and the subjects they teach. Indeed, teachers frequently take comfort and shelter from the wounding rebuttals of students in the imaginative landscapes of their subjects.

In the case of most teachers, apart from those working with advanced research students, it is important for their originality to feature more in relationships of learning with students than in relationships of understanding with leading-edge research in their subjects. To be *pedagogically* at home in a subject is to place the main emphasis elsewhere than Steiner does. It is to be possessed of diverse human qualities that enable the genuine voice of the subject to speak: to make well-judged overtures to the minds and hearts of students, especially differently disposed students. The exercise of imagination here is at once more inclusively attuned to learners, and less emotionally intense, than in Steiner's account. Recall his observation that 'to teach seriously is to lay hands on what is most vital in a human being, ... to seek access to the quick and innermost of a child's or adult's integrity.' These descriptions are too forceful, too intrusive. They are like the movements of an impatient lover who presumes to have his (or her) way without impediment or protest. They ignore the discernments, the subtlety, the restraint, and not least the persevering foresight, called for in a courtship of sensibility, or as the title puts it, in imagination's heartwork.

This heartwork then, involves a perceptive and receptive communication with others more than an enraptured communion with the Muses. Most teachers know this all too well from their own practice. Teachers in special needs education and in further education are particularly aware of it. In most instances, however, teachers hold such knowledge – of wooing students' attentions and efforts – in intuitive and personal ways, rather than in ways that are explicitly articulated and documented. Comparatively little has been written on this theme in the research literature in education. It is all the more important then that we focus closely on it now.

Creating and sustaining a fruitful environment of learning is about as far away as one can get from the commonplace notion that 'anyone can teach'. Even accomplished teachers sometimes find, on inheriting new classes of students or moving to a different school, that they are pulled up short; that their best-prepared plans are swiftly sabotaged. The traditional reaction in such circumstances was to use corporal punishment to restore order, or to 'put the fear of God' into scoundrels whose agitations not only made their own trouble, but also stirred others to commotion. Today's remedies from the 'get tough' repertoire of responses include sarcasm and ridicule at the cruder end (sometimes by different teachers acting in concert), to punishments such as detentions, deprivation of entitlements, suspensions and expulsions at the more legalistic end. I am not decrying the use of these latter forms of punishment. Verbal and physical violence towards teachers remains on the rise internationally, and demands for redress frequently highlight urgent rather than restorative action. In the absence of parallel action along constructive lines, however, even the more scrupulous of negative punishments will damage relationships of learning. When relationships go sour, the energy and insight needed for building mutual trust are in short supply. But if reconciliation isn't worked on, the sourness tends to settle into a coldness in the longer term. Thus, the enduring sense of care for students emphasized a few pages ago can incrementally atrophy in a teacher. In such circumstances, even where test and examination results are kept up to satisfactory averages, greyness is likely to hold sway over vitality in the conduct of teaching and learning. A simple but irrevocable fact remains: Healthy relationships of learning are not something that can be made at will by the teacher. They are a joint achievement requiring, to be sure, diverse qualities of originality in the teacher, but requiring also a response-in-kind from students. Close attention to these responses, and to building productively on them, is one of the most neglected aspects of the study of teaching. Such responses can originate something as yet unthought of, and take learning on paths which neither teacher not students had previously envisaged.

This point about the diverse qualities of originality needed on the teacher's part might better be put by saying that originality itself, in different kinds of manifestations, must become embodied in the enactments of the teacher. The voice of the subject in question must present itself in an invitational way to a particular group of students. From a practical standpoint, the pressing question for the teacher becomes: What can I do with this topic so that it comes alive in the experience of these learners? Equally important is the corresponding nega-tive question: What do I need to avoid to prevent the students from getting an aversion to this subject or topic? All too often, nowadays, answers to questions such as these are seen to lie in making better resources, especially technological resources, available for teaching. At the more advanced end, such resources include electronic facilities such as interactive whiteboards, web-based learning and an abundance of software for computer-assisted learning. The ubiquity of such resources tends to advance a conception of teaching itself as a technologi-cal, as distinct from an inter-human undertaking. But if the advantages of such technology are to be realized in more than a minimal sense, their use must spring from the resourcefulness of teachers themselves, not from any bypassing of the teacher, or by substituting technology for indifferent teaching.

Investigating the reasons for this will help to illustrate, contrary to Steiner's view, the unaristocratic nature of pedagogical imagination, properly under-stood. In fact, this illustration can be better achieved by starting at the 'low-tech' rather than the 'high-tech' end of the spectrum, and by taking a familiar rather than a remote pedagogical difficulty.

Geometry and algebra rarely feature fondly in most people's recollections of their schooling. The lore of maths teachers themselves is well furnished with accounts of the difficulties encountered in teaching these subjects, to all but that minority of students perceived to take naturally to mathematics. Predictable routines have tended to feature prominently, moreover, in the inherited practices of maths teaching in secondary schools. These routines involve a long familiar picture: line-by-line explanations on the board by teachers, followed by drill-and-practice exercises by students. Maths teachers themselves, however, have convincingly shown how students from ranks other than those of the maths 'naturals' can be drawn into productive engagements with geometry and algebra, and drawn in a sustained way. This evidence is especially convincing where a rich pedagogical imagination uses quite simple resources and resolutely sets aside the common belief that most people are not good at maths.

Students in such cases typically work under a teacher's guidance with a well-designed stock of cardboard (or plastic) circles, semi-circles, triangles, parallelograms and so on. Through insightful orchestration by the teacher, most students can successfully work out for themselves – alone, in pairs, or in small groups – the sequence of logical steps in proving Euclidian theorems. Similarly, in algebra, the availability of 'algebra tiles' (different shapes and colours to represent X, Y, minus numbers and plus number) allows equations to be worked out visually on his or her table by each student, or pair of students. In both subjects, becoming at home in using these materials enables the students to learn in a more engaging and sure-footed way the conceptual steps in solving equations. It also enables the teacher to group students in such a way as to allow some teaching as well as learning to go on in each group, while freeing the teacher to give particular attention to groups or individuals. Gradually, the shapes in geometry and the tiles in algebra can be used less frequently, as the students become confident, and more conceptually proficient, in different kinds of mathematical thinking.[32] Everything depends, however, on the *resourcefulness* of the teacher in availing of such resources. The teacher's action combines her own venturesome mathematical thinking with an equally venturesome, but shared, pedagogical action. This kind of combination gives an unmistakable originality to teaching. By contrast, it defeats any worthwhile pedagogical purpose to expect the physical resources themselves to do the bulk of the work. In fact, resources like those just mentioned are likely to remain worthless unless their use is creatively planned from the start and sensitively monitored at all stages. The more imaginative the teacher, moreover, the more likely it is that she or he will involve the students wherever possible in making their own resources.

Moving up the scale from the basic end, the case is somewhat different with audio-visual resources – for example, DVDs containing contrasting productions of Shakespearian or contemporary drama, or featuring difficult experiments in chemistry, or illustrating geographical concepts such as erosion, plate tectonics, volcanic action and so on. These can clearly bring about much learning on their own. But they can also sideline the teacher, even to the extent that the teacher comes to be seen as the person who complies with the students' demands: the person who digs out and puts on the DVDs that the students want to see and lets them run for most (if not all) of the lesson. Likewise, the use of CDs in the teaching of modern languages can become almost a teach-yourself approach for the students if the teacher is content to take a back seat in the process. Needless to add, in the hands of an inventive teacher, such resources can promote learning experiences that are particularly rich and memorable.

At the more advanced end, electronic resources are widely thought to be of a kind that keeps everyone on their toes. Indeed, their successful use requires continual moment-to-moment interactions by the student, attentive monitoring of these interactions by the teacher, and even frequent interventions by the teacher. But here it is frequently possible for the teacher to waste much time – for instance, browsing through too many websites or being uneconomical in using a data projector with a class as a whole. Similarly, students can waste time by exploiting the shortcomings of a lazy or unalert teacher and seeking to browse where their own wishes lead them.

These examples help to highlight the crucial point. The most important imaginative challenge for the teacher is not that of staying in touch with what has recently been occurring at a subject's research frontiers. Neither is it that of ingeniously keeping disorder at bay. Rather, it is bringing forth an engaged response from students; a response to what the genuine voice of the subject says to them through the resourceful enactments of the teacher. Apart from the technological examples just considered, other sample enactments include: lively stories and anecdotes that help to clarify difficult points; role-plays and other dramatic devices that quicken suspense and expectation and thus enrich the emotional atmosphere of learning; dialogues and exploratory discussions that allow judicious scope to humour and sympathy; learning exercises that are carried out alone, in pairs, or in small groups, involving a disciplining of the learner's own inclinations and an attentive respect for the contributions of others. What is at issue here is the thoughtful creation of new imaginative neighbourhoods on a daily basis, or on successive occasions throughout a normal day. This is not to say that each creation is totally new. Successive creations will frequently have a family resemblance to each other and the learning environments in question will have recognizable routines and habits. Prominent among these, however, will be the habit of innovation itself.

Looked at in this unaristocratic way, the 'everydayness' of teaching can be seen less as a burden with monotony ever nearby, and more as the recurring possibility to transform everyday occurrences into something more meaningful and enduring. This is difficult to accomplish, however, if the teacher is attuned to something other than the inherent benefits of learning. Indeed, the thought itself will seem foreign if a teacher's self-understanding is essentially that of a functionary, or a subordinate, or if it suffers the kinds of distortion or diminishment we considered in the opening chapter. Keeping in mind what has been said about the teacher's relationships to the subject and to the students, inventive energies are called for in both. In relation to the first (the subject), the teacher needs the capacity to call on a fertile repertoire of ideas, stories and examples that reflects the imaginative richness of her or his relationship to the topic being taught. This is a repertoire, moreover, to be continually added to by the teacher. In relation to the second (the students), the teacher needs the capacity to see promise not only among those commonly described as the brightest and the best. More importantly, the teacher needs to be able to discern new beginnings in the everyday efforts of unremarkable students; to be attentive to what Heidegger has memorably called 'the undisclosed abundance of the unfamiliar and extraordinary'.[33] These pedagogical capacities are nurtured by a particular kind of love, and they will atrophy unless they are continually nourished. This is a love that is essentially different from erotic love. The next chapter will explore it in some detail, with some practical illustrations. Our path to this theme will take us through a critical review of the centrality that Steiner gives to *eros* in teaching and learning.

6 *Eros*, inclusion, and care in teaching and learning

At the heart of *eros*

One of the most distinctive things about teaching as a form of human action is that it involves a particular kind of love. This includes a love of what one teaches and a love of those whom one teaches, or more precisely, a creative combination of both. This much is uncontroversial. Neither is it controversial to say that achieving this kind of combination is, in each instance, an original accomplishment on the part of the teacher, requiring perceptive understanding and discerning judgement. To regard this accomplishment as an erotic one, however, or to give *eros*[1] a central place in educational practices, as Steiner does, is to confound things in two ways. First of all, it is to give priority to a kind of love that is burdened with problematic associations where teaching and learning are concerned. Second, it is to detract attention from a proper exploration of the kind of love that is particular to, indeed essential to, educational relationships. This latter is a practical kind of love, requiring forms of insight, circumspection, restraint and inclusiveness that are largely strangers to *eros*.

The two claims just made are bold ones, although they may sound plausible enough. It is only when we examine what they mean in practice, however, that we begin to understand their full significance. Explorations of practice reveal, in a way that an exclusive reliance on a formal kind of analysis cannot, the problematic associations of *eros* in education. Such explorations also show, more convincingly, the necessity for an illustrative account of the kind of love that supplies education with its proper moral energy. Even more so than in previous chapters then, recourse to examples will be necessary in arguing the case for the claims in the opening paragraph above. Let us begin with a closer look at the notion of *eros*.

In his book *Dewey and Eros* (1997), Jim Garrison undertakes a perceptive critique of Greek conceptions of *eros*. He reconstructs an understanding of *eros*, for educational purposes, along pragmatist lines inspired by John Dewey. At the start of his enquiry, Garrison poses a highly pertinent question and ventures a bold answer, which he then explores in detail in the remainder of the book.

What is this thing that every teacher intuitively understands lies in the middle of everyday practice yet is missing from almost all theory and research on teaching? It is loving, life-affirming, passionate 'desire', or erōs. Erōs is the most basic type of love. All practical reasoning is about obtaining values we desire. It is the kind of reasoning that practitioners use every day to obtain the results they value. It is the kindling that fires their other professional passions.[2]

Garrison explains that, for the Greeks, 'erōs is one of the daimōns,' and that daimōns played a key role in Greek religion as 'intermediaries between heaven and earth, taking prayers up and bringing down rewards and commands.'[3] The commands in question, however, might frequently have the form of inner compulsions that the human soul felt powerless to resist. Particularly important is the point that, for the Greeks, 'at birth a daimōn seizes each of us, determining our unique individual potential and mediating between us and our best possible destiny'.[4] Daimons can be active in an overpowering way whereby experience becomes charged with intense emotion: vengefulness, power lust, erotic desire, grief, and so on. To be thus seized is to lose one's normal composure, to experience an intoxicating thrall, or more prosaically, to fall captive to the urgency of one's passions. In Plato's writings, the sexual nature of *eros* is frequently stressed, mainly in the context of homoerotic attachments between older Athenian males (often Masters in Steiner's sense), and youths in the full bloom of male beauty. Steiner's depiction of the actions of the teacher as 'laying hold of the quick of another' is laden with Greek associations and carries strong evocations of *eros* as seizure. *Eros* can be distinguished from other forms of love not only by the passion and urgency of desire, but also by the character of the desire itself – a desire to posses its object and delight in it to the full.

Through the characters that appear in his later works, Plato repeatedly emphasizes a purging of the sexual tenor of *eros*. For Plato, this purging marks an ascent of the human soul from its captivity by physical desires to an emancipation from all things sensual and physical; an ascent, in other words, from the physical to the meta-physical. The ascent culminates, on Plato's account, in a wholehearted embrace of eternal ideas – of love, justice, beauty, truth. Such ideas, he maintains, are more radiant *and more real* than any of their sensual or earthly manifestations. Even the best of the latter are but a pale shadow of the former.[5] The ideas in their pure form transcend any earthly manifestations of them and, for this reason, they are referred to as the transcendent Ideas (or Forms) of Plato's metaphysics. Countless people who are not interested in the finer points of Plato's metaphysics are still familiar with some notion of Platonic love, as a kind of purified or disciplined love – a love from which erotic desire is absent.

Garrison is keen to retain the notion of *eros*, despite the fact that the passions of the educator he explores and affirms in his book are not sexual in character. He shares Dewey's rejection, however, of the other-worldly character of Plato's eternal, changeless, ideas. In his book *Art as Experience*, Dewey particularly criticizes Plato's attitude to things sensual and Plato's attempts to place beauty beyond the sensual. This criticism of Dewey's is approvingly quoted by Garrison:

> Sense seems to Plato to be a seduction that leads man away from the spiritual. It is tolerated only as a vehicle through which man may be brought to an intuition of immaterial and non-sensuous essence. I know of no way to criticize the theory save to say that it is a ghostly metaphysics.[6]

For all its 'ghostliness', however, there remains something intuitively convincing, indeed powerfully suggestive, about Plato's distinction between human manifestations of love (or justice or beauty) on the one hand, and the ideals from which they spring on the other – ideals which somehow elude human reach. Historical experience shows, for instance, that human embodiments of justice, of freedom, of love, of truth (i.e. integrity), rarely live up to the imagined or anticipated ideals. To put it in everyday terms, they fall short of the 'the real thing' (or, in Plato's terms, are poor images of the real thing). Yet historical experience also shows that, for all the disappointment of human hopes, for all the shortcomings of human achievements in these domains, such ideals retain a perennial appeal. Even in the darkest times, they beckon anew, from afar as it were. They summon human energies to actions that evoke worthiness, and in due course, historical remembrance. Here, it is worth noting that most of the disagreements to which Plato's metaphysics still give rise spring not from its suggestiveness, which remains remarkably fertile.[7] They spring rather from the pretensions of this metaphysics to being a superior and changeless knowledge – a knowledge that attributes fixed essences and identities and, on this basis, proposes a hierarchical political order. When this kind of knowledge is understood as a destination to be achieved by the philosopher rulers in whose hands Plato would place exclusive political power, it looks uninviting to a wholehearted democratic sensibility such as that of Dewey, or indeed Garrison.

Garrison acknowledges that Plato's ideas remain critically important for Dewey, as for himself. But they are now stripped of their metaphysical character. 'Plato's transcendent Ideas become ideals for Dewey', Garrison writes. They become recast as 'possibilities that are desired', or values which Dewey liked to describe as 'ends-in-view'.[8] Conscious of the fact that '*eros*' is a term that does not appear as an explicit theme in Dewey's philosophy, Garrison says that Dewey held an 'implicit philosophy of erōs': a 'consistent, although constrained, philosophy of love that laced together his educational thinking.' More emphatically, Garrison writes of Dewey that '[i]t is not possible to comprehend his philosophy of education without appreciating his hidden philosophy of love.'[9] Few who are familiar with Dewey's writings would want to dispute this latter claim. What remains in question, however, is the kind of love that becomes crucial for education. For Garrison it remains erōs, although not an *eros* painstakingly purified of sexual desire by the upward spiritual ascent recommended by Plato. Rather, in Garrison's recasting of *eros*, informed as it is by Dewey's democratic pragmatism, the sexual seems just not to feature any more. As distinct from being purified, it seems to have just disappeared. Desire is still strongly in evidence, but without reference to key daimonic aspects of Greek *eros*. Garrison regards the education of this human *eros* as 'the single most important aspect of all education.' He immediately asks 'Why?', and responds with a strong flavour of Dewey himself: 'Because we become what we love. That is how we grow.'[10]

What conclusions can be drawn from this? In summary, the notion of *eros* is intimately associated with Greek sensuality and religious beliefs, and also with Plato's reformation of these beliefs in his metaphysics. But it is difficult to retain a clear and coherent notion of *eros* if one lays aside both religious-mythological and metaphysical considerations in favour of the purely naturalistic account that Garrison is keen to present. In fact, the notion of love that underlies that account often seems to draw less on *eros* than on other Greek notions of love that contrast with *eros*, such as *agape* (a love that gives regardless of being returned) or *philia* (a love that prizes enduring bonds of friendship). This is evident, in particular, from the practical examples provided by Garrison. Making these other forms of love explicit in his account would probably mean that the role of *eros* would be minimized, if not ruled out. Or else perhaps, the notion of *eros* might be redefined in a way that dealt more explicitly with the classical Greek dimensions that Garrison is keen to exclude.

At any rate, it is clear that *eros*, as an educational inspiration, remains encumbered by some problematic features. Further exploration is called for of those forms of love that are singularly appropriate to teaching and learning, and equally, of those that are not. A striking illustration from classroom life should help to put the point at issue here into sharper focus.

The unerotic character of teaching

This example is taken from a work of literary fiction, *The Rainbow*, by D. H. Lawrence, set in England in the early twentieth century. Despite its remoteness from the educational contexts of the early twenty-first century, it speaks revealingly of attitudes and practices that are perennially associated with relationships of teaching and learning. In a chapter that is graphically true to life, titled 'The Man's World', the novel's chief character, Ursula Brangwen, now aged 17 years, anticipates what it will be like to begin work as an uncertified teacher in a rundown primary school near Nottingham. Ursula is a 'high-spirited, proud girl' with a lively imagination, a natural vitality and a love of nature that is sometimes 'poignant to the point of agony'. She has won an interview for a place at a training college in Kingston-on-Thames, but her father won't hear of her going so far away from home. Instead, he has secured for her a kind of apprenticeship position that will enable her to go on to college on a fees-paid basis after 2 years. Placing her disagreement with her parents behind her, Ursula is now determined to make the most of what her circumstances offer her.

She dreamed how she would make the little, ugly children love her. She would be so *personal*. Teachers were always so hard and impersonal. There was no vivid relationship. She would make everything personal and vivid, she would give herself, she would give, give, give all her great stores of wealth to her children, she would make them so happy, and they would prefer her to any teacher on the face of the earth.

At Christmas she would choose such fascinating Christmas cards for them, and she would give them such a happy party in one of the classrooms.

The headmaster, Mr. Harby, was a short, thick-set, rather common man, she thought. But she would hold before him the light of grace and refinement, he would have her in such high esteem before long. She would be the gleaming sun of the school, the children would blossom like little weeds, the teachers like tall, hard plants would burst into rare flower.[11]

Ursula's early experiences as a teacher are a series of rude awakenings that relentlessly work their way towards the downfall of her hopes. The Headmaster's obsessive dislike of her refined ways, the brusque unhelpfulness of Mr. Brunt next door, and not least the brutalized sensibilities of many of her 55 pupils, confront her with successive setbacks, confounding her dream and unsettling her resolve. She is repelled by the system of teaching at the school, which forces her to set aside the imaginative riches she hoped to share with the children, but also to set aside her own individuality in favour of an official and alien order. She is taken aback to see the other teachers 'drudging unwillingly at the graceless task of compelling many children into one disciplined, mechanical set, reducing the whole to an automatic state of obedience and attention, and then of commanding their acceptance of various pieces of knowledge.'[12] She is unnerved to find that producing these effects means not only a forceful imposition of will but also a recurring clash of wills between pupils and teachers and between teachers themselves. She discovers, to her horror, that the whole situation is underpinned by violence: regular physical violence in the punishment of students but also an ingrained psychological violence in relations between the teachers. But it is not until she herself is reduced to physical brutality – her unrestrained caning of a boy who has been insolently baiting her – that she begins to realize that something tragic has befallen her relations with her pupils. The following extracts illustrate something of that tragedy:

When she went into Ilkeston of a Saturday morning with Gudrun, she heard again the voices yelling after her: 'Brangwen, Brangwen.'

She pretended to take no notice, but she coloured with shame at being held up to derision in the public street. She, Ursula Brangwen of Cossethay, could not escape from the Standard Five teacher which she was. In vain she went out to buy ribbon for her hat. They called after her, the boys she tried to teach. ... And one evening, as she went from the edge of the town into the country, stones came flying at her. Then the passion of shame and anger surpassed her. She walked on unheeding, beside herself. Because of the darkness she could not see who were those that threw. But she did not want to know. Only in her soul a change took place. Never more, and never more would she give herself as individual to her class. Never would she, Ursula Brangwen, the girl she was, the person she was, come into contact with those boys. She would be Standard Five teacher, as far away personally from her class as if she had never set foot in St. Philip's school. She would just obliterate them all, and keep herself apart, take them as scholars only. ... Oh, why, why had she leagued herself to this evil system where she must brutalise herself to live? Why had she become a school-teacher, why, why?[13]

Apart from the personal tragedy for Ursula here, there is a further calamity – both for her pupils as would-be learners and for the school as a place of learning. This lies in the fact that a person with human qualities such as hers is a naturally promising candidate for teaching. But her naivety, so evident in the ardent character of her aspirations, is her most vulnerable point. It makes her look ridiculous in the eyes of both pupils and teachers who are already inured to the rituals of enmity, resistance and the wilful exercise of force. Of her, it could be said that she loved not wisely but too well, and that the consequences of her naivety in such a cynical environment undermined her very capacity to love fruitfully as a teacher might. In contrast to the corrosive attitudes of Ursula's colleagues, a discerning kind of help is called for here, whether in the person of a school principal, mentor teacher or teacher educator. Such discerning help understands that a naivety of the kind she showed is a natural, youthful accompaniment of potentials that lie deeper, especially potentials for pedagogical forms of love. Unlike the failures of understanding, of example and of supportiveness that hastened the collapses of Ursula's hopes, this more perceptive and supportive stance concentrates on eliciting and cultivating such potentials. At the same time, it seeks to coach and refine the naivety towards a more mature and circumspect judgement.

This is to suggest that educational leadership, and indeed any action whose ends-in-view are properly educational, is marked by an inclusive, proactive kind of love. This love is attuned more to intimations of educational need than to evocations of sensual desire. Its compassion is less demonstrative than productively resourceful. Clearly, this is a love quite different from *eros* – whether the elemental kind of *eros* in Steiner's descriptions or the more ascetic *eros* of Plato. It parallels in central respects the 'sympathetic intuitions', 'generous recognition' and 'sensitive responsiveness' on the part of teachers, which Garrison explores in detail, and of which he gives some compelling examples.[14] Against Plato, Garrison argues that *eros* is less about possession than about a loving bestowal. He writes:

Education requires self-transcendence and growth. That is the richer meaning of erōs. It is not enough that we desire to possess the good for ourselves unless we can also give it away. Good teachers know we may give the gift without loss of self.[15]

The rich insight in this passage is occluded somewhat by calling this kind of love *eros*, as distinct say, from *agape*. Even when shorn of sensual desire, there are features that are central to *eros* that make it a stranger to relationships in education. On this point, Martin Buber has made some incisive observations. In his essay simply titled 'Education', written in 1939, Buber carries out a searching investigation of two contrasting orientations for the teacher in educational relations – namely, 'will-to-power' and 'Eros'. He speaks of the necessity for an educator to exclude the 'fire of Eros' from the work of teaching and learning. 'Eros', Buber points out, 'is choice, choice made from an inclination.' This, he argues, 'is precisely what education is not. The man who is loving in Eros chooses the beloved, the modern educator finds his pupil there before him.'[16] This latter situation Buber correctly describes as the 'unerotic' situation of the teacher, and he goes on to explain why:

> He enters the school-room for the first time, he sees them crouching at the desks, indiscriminately flung together, the misshapen and the well proportioned, animal faces, empty faces, and noble faces in indiscriminate confusion ...; the glance of the educator accepts and receives them all.[17]

As well as the absence of choice, the other feature that distinguishes the educator's action here from one characterized by *eros*, is acceptance; acceptance, that is, as distinct from possession. *Eros*, of whatever kind, finds its fulfilment not just in a choosing that excludes others, but also in an equally exclusive possession of what is chosen. This highlights its inappropriateness for educational thought and action.[18]

All too often, of course, and all too humanly, the teacher does *not* 'accept them all'. Rather, the teacher tends to accept those who are easy to like, who are clean, who do their homework regularly, who have full and punctual attendance records, who co-operate with rather than resist the teacher's efforts. Tackling this all-too-human tendency means that the teacher must *learn* to accept all of the students, and must continually renew such learning for as long as teaching remains his or her way of life. This learning, moreover, is likely to come to grief, as it did with Ursula Brangwen, without clear-sighted, sympathetic support from tutors, mentors and colleagues. And even where supports of this kind are judiciously available, it is in the nature of such learning to be accompanied by recurring pains and setbacks. It is, in effect, a learning to love *as a teacher* that involves many role-reversals and shifts in self-understanding. This shift becomes a seismic one if one goes farther and takes Buber's 'I-Thou' thinking as one's guide, or if one follows the ethics of 'absolute responsibility in the face of the other' proposed by Emmanuel Levinas. This latter ethics is currently the focus of much research attention. Authors such as Sharon Todd and Paul Standish have explored in some detail how the ethical responsibility of a teacher stands in the light of the thought of Levinas. Todd emphasizes, in particular, the importance of 'being-for the Other' and explains: 'To encounter the unknowable mystery of the Other is to be for her.' She also highlights the Levinasian 'requirement for the self to depose its ego, its intentionality and its consciousness in the service of the Other.'[19] In a somewhat similar vein, Standish writes: 'Levinas is emphatic that the Other teaches me, and this teaching involves the sense of this unscalable height and mysterious depth, and of the Other as both 'holy' and humble.'[20] The dispositions nurtured by such thinking are loving in a deeply reverential sense. They involve a poetic, or mystic kind of passivity that listens deeply and lets the world – of people and of nature – *be*.

This reverential thinking stands in striking contrast not only to the outlooks of a Mr Harby or Mr Brunt, but also to the rough and tumble of environments of learning in most schools and colleges. It summons the self-understanding of teachers to a keen awareness of the sometimes awesome responsibility of their way of life. Yet it is largely silent on the collective dramas of teaching and learning; the active to-and-fro of life as experienced daily in classrooms, laboratories and seminar rooms. Neither does it speak to how a responsible teacher might deal with the demands of *multiple* others. For example, students might more than occasionally be impatient for the teacher's attention, or might mistreat each other, or might deceive the teacher, or might play truant for all practical purposes while remaining in a classroom.

In addition to being responsible, the teacher's kind of love must be *responsive* in a variety of active but perceptive ways. The teacher must, for instance, continually try to experience the teacher–student relationship from the other side: to experience not just a student's sense of non-acceptance by the teacher, but also the effects of jealousy, conceit, overt or covert bullying, barely suppressed ridicule, and other forms of exclusion by classmates. Learning of this kind challenges the teacher to find previously undiscovered resources of sympathetic understanding, or compassion, in herself, but also resources of anticipation, of imaginative planning, of both strategic and tactical action, and not least of consistency and firmness. Here the concerns of practical judgement are necessarily more central than are reverential forms of solicitude.

To emphasize human qualities like those just mentioned is to highlight the inclusive and unselfish (as distinct from selfless) nature of the kind of love that properly informs teaching, or the ethical stance of the teaching as an occupation. It is to suggest further that teaching has a range, or family, of practical virtues that are particularly appropriate to it. It is also to say that this family of virtues is different in important respects from the family that might be appropriate to other occupations, including other 'caring professions' such as nursing, medicine or development work. Exploring more closely this family of educational virtues, and how these receive their character from an educationally promising conception of love, now calls for attention.

Ethics and educational practice

To suggest that there is a family of virtues that is particularly promising and defensible for education as a practice is to take a different approach, indeed a different point of departure, from most of mainstream academic philosophy. Where such philosophy deals with matters of ethics, centre stage is occupied for the most part by different major theories of ethics. These include, to name but a few: an ethics of duty (or deontological ethics), springing primarily from Kantian inspirations; an ethics of justice, associated in recent times mainly with the work of John Rawls; a virtue ethics, associated chiefly with Aristotelian, or more precisely neo-Aristotelian approaches (for example, that of Alasdair MacIntyre); an ethics of care, associated often with feminist perspectives and with authors such as Nel Noddings. Major ethical theories usually articulate, in each case, a set of general principles that seek to be rationally compelling, and thus to dispose a person's overall ethical orientation. Ethical action would then be a question of applying in practice the theory to which one subscribes. Application would be guided by the principles of the theory in question, or more precisely by the imperatives of that theory for the particular fields of action in which ethical issues arise.

To illustrate this, let us use an example from Rawls' theory of justice. This seeks to provide a standpoint that can overcome all partisan positions and furnish impartial grounds for just action. The theory uses the device of a thought experiment involving the adoption of an 'original position' or 'an initial situation that is fair', in matters of justice. The thought experiment seeks to establish what principles of justice might come to the fore if one placed oneself behind a 'veil of ignorance', thus depriving oneself of any knowledge of the beliefs, gender, social standing, ethnic background, religion or abilities of others. Adopting the veil of ignorance thus means ridding oneself of all assumptions and preconceived ideas that might otherwise cloud one's thinking and prevent one from taking an original position. The original position would therefore be a purely dis-interested stance.[21] A teacher committed to a Rawlsian ethics of justice stance, when confronting issues of justice in a classroom, would systematically apply the principle of the 'original position' and the 'veil of ignorance' to ensure that the objective demands of justice were met in dealing with the issue.

Critics of such a Rawlsian stance might argue that, whatever its merits as a general theory, this approach cannot adequately serve the teacher in practice. Far from employing a veil of ignorance, the just teacher, critics point out, must continually bear in mind what the students have merited by their previous record of work, co-operation, disruption and so on. That is to say, while the general ethical orientation elucidated by the theory might be salutary in important respects, it fails to elucidate, even to identify, the range of virtues called for in particular practices, such as practices of teaching and learning. This restricts the theory's appropriateness in specific domains of action.

From the perspective of practice, a similar criticism can be made, in varying degrees, of other general ethical theories – indeed of any ethical theory that gives priority to one set of principles (whether of duty, justice, care or whatever) to the comparative neglect of others. For practice, be it in the field of social work, of customer service, of teaching and learning, or other, calls in each case for a range of virtues that may sometimes be in tension with each other, but a range that nevertheless holds a coherence informed by the purposes of that practice. It is this coherence, including its inherent productiveness and its overall defensibility, that makes it appropriate to speak of a 'family' of virtues for anything worthy of being called a practice.

Where education as a practice is concerned, Noddings' ethics of care goes farther than other theories of ethics do in providing such a coherence. This is probably because the theory has been developed from contexts of education and upbringing, or more precisely from Noddings' many years of experience of such contexts. At the same time, because it is in the first place a theory of care, it asks one virtue to do too much of the work. This work is distributed differently, however, if we make practice itself our starting point, as I have tried to do in the case of educational practice from the beginning of this book. The family of virtues that is most necessary, as well as most promising for a practice, thus emerges from exploring the practice itself. This exploration, moreover, is from the inside as well as the outside, from a practitioner's point of view as well as from an external view, of what the practice might most fruitfully and defensibly accomplish. An objection to this approach could charge that it is eclectic – that it picks and chooses from different ethical theories to suit its preferred conception of practice, while conveniently ignoring important discrepancies between these theories. In response, it must be pointed out that the demands of practice itself show that an ethical theory giving a predominant place to one or other virtue falls short of what is necessary. This is already evident from the example of the teacher who was ill-served by Rawls' theory of justice. In that example, the practical inadequacies of an ethics of justice would actually leave the teacher reaching for guidance from additional sources. Such sources could, of course, include an ethics of care, an ethics of duty, or a particular virtue ethics supplied by one or other moral or religious tradition. They could also include less explicit sources; for instance, unacknowledged prejudices from the practitioner's previous experience, or from an uncritical acquiescence in inherited attitudes and routines.

Mindful of points such as these, Noddings' ethics of care seeks 'to avoid a concentration on judgement or evaluation that accompanies an interpretation of caring as an individual virtue'.[22]

In her book, *The Challenge to Care in Schools*, she calls on her earlier work where caring was 'characterized by engrossment and motivational displacement.' By 'engrossment' she means not 'infatuation, enchantment, or obsession but a full receptivity': 'an open, nonselective receptivity to the cared-for'.[23] Noddings describes 'motivational displacement' as the kind of responsiveness that takes one out of one's own preoccupations to 'help the stranger in his need'. Here 'I receive what the other conveys, and I want to respond in a way that furthers the other's purpose or project.'[24] Noddings stresses that engrossment and motivational displacement 'do not tell us what to do; they merely characterize our consciousness when we care'. Rather than a prescription or recipe for specific actions, she goes on to argue, caring is a way of being in relation with others.[25] In the light of arguments made earlier in this chapter, there are two issues in this sketch of central points in Noddings' ethics of care that call for brief comment. The first is the non-selective character of her conception of care, which sets it clearly apart from *eros*. The second is her resistance to the temptation to think of caring as an individual virtue; a temptation that also accompanies an ethics of justice, an ethic of duty, or any ethics that gives an exclusive role to one attribute or quality.

Not surprisingly then, *The Challenge to Care in Schools* sets out a conception of caring that links it less to a single virtue than to more inclusive concerns of moral reasoning. More concretely, Noddings explains her purpose as being an exploration of 'moral education from the perspective of an ethic of caring' and this means that care is attended by, or revealed through, some complementary virtues, or what she calls 'components'. Noddings puts the matter as follows: 'Moral education from the perspective of an ethic of caring has four major components: modeling, dialogue, practice and confirmation.'[26] She identifies the first of these, 'modeling', as the vital necessity for commitments of care to be shown in deeds of caring. Rather than telling students to care, she writes, 'we show them how to care by creating caring relations with them.'[27] The second component, dialogue, is not just talk or conversation, Noddings insists. Neither is it a 'sweetly reasonable' way of telling pupils or students of decisions that have already been made. Rather it is a 'common search for understanding, empathy or appreciation. ... always a genuine quest for something undetermined at the beginning.'[28]

The third component, 'practice', sounds a bit odd as a virtue, particularly if we think of this term as used in phrases such as 'legal practice', 'medical practice' or, indeed, 'educational practice'. What Noddings has in mind, however, is a regularity of experience that 'shapes minds', or cultivates certain attitudes and capacities rather than others, and which thus has strong predisposing effects. Perhaps 'habituation' might be a better word for this, if it could be dissociated from any confusion with 'creatures of habit'. In any case, Noddings points out that women, more often than men, have traditionally 'been charged with the direct care of children, the ill and the aged. The capacities and dispositions that result from such experiences, she continues, are likely to be close to an ethics of care; more likely than those resulting from experiences that shape 'a "military mind," a "police mentality," "business thinking," and the like'.[29] In short, Noddings' third component stresses the importance of regular practice in caring. The fourth component, Noddings calls 'confirmation'. She distinguishes this from formulas, slogans and behavioural recipes of all sorts. Drawing on the work of Martin Buber, she describes confirmation as 'an act of affirming and encouraging the best in others'. It attributes to the other person 'the best possible motive consonant with reality'.[30] It involves attentive listening, sympathetic responsiveness, and not least, trust and continuity 'founded on a relation of some depth'. This continuity, Noddings adds, is not required in all relations of caring, but is essential in teaching.[31]

The four components described by Noddings, together with her many practical examples throughout the book, helpfully illuminate the kind of love that is called for in educational practice. They also provide a richer understanding of the ethical context of teaching and learning than could be furnished by the major schools of thought on ethics within academic philosophy, including ethics of justice, or ethics of duty, or indeed virtue ethics. Despite her sensitivity to the practical contexts of education, however, Noddings does not explore some essential factors in the relationships of teaching and learning that we reviewed in Chapters 3 and 4 above. These include the teacher's relationship to the subject(s) she teaches, and the question of how the quality of this influences the quality of relationships between teacher and students. There is an evident reason why she doesn't. She is critical of a liberal education based on inherited disciplines of study, arguing that the rationale for such a curriculum makes misguided assumptions about 'the content that all children need'.[32] This is a valid criticism, particularly of latter-day reformulations of liberal education such as the 'The Paideia Proposal' of Mortimer Adler (1982), which Noddings faults. This envisaged a reform of American schooling by proposing, in the name of equality, the same subject-based programme of studies for all schoolgoers.[33] Noddings' rejection of such thinking, coupled with her advocacy of an ethics of care, leads her 'beyond the disciplines' to an 'alternative vision', as she puts it. This alternative vision would make care itself the interdisciplinary core of schooling and would take account of different 'intelligences', drawing on the researches of Howard Gardner. In such a reformed curriculum, and especially at secondary school level, material from traditional subjects could feature, but chiefly as and when it became appropriate to students' aptitudes, capacities and 'basic affiliations'. The contents of the curriculum would thus be organized under themes of care: 'care for self, care for intimate others, care for strangers and distant others, care for nonhuman animals, care for plants and the living environment, care for objects and instruments, and care for ideas.'[34]

In the interests of practicality and compromise, Noddings allows that up to half of the secondary school curriculum might be allocated to subjects as traditionally organized, and the other half to her themes of care. She suggests, however, that after some years of successful experience with innovations, subject disciplines might give way entirely to a new basis for curricular organization, based on care. Such organization might provide for four equally prestigious programmes in secondary schools, each embedded in an ethic of care: linguistic/mathematical, technical, arts, interpersonal. Combinations of these, as well as hybrid versions, might also be encouraged, she adds.

Noddings' arguments provide insightful explorations and illuminating examples of the forms of love that are most appropriate and promising for practices of education. They are a refreshing contrast to Steiner's aristocratic sponsorship of *eros* in educational relations – also to the ingrained occupational cynicism described by Lawrence, less dramatic forms of which still remain an everyday reality in all too many schools. Her proposals for curriculum reform seek an institutional provision conducive to the cultivation of such love in ordinary environments of learning, thus making these more inclusive and healthy places. Yet the importance that Noddings gives to an ethics of care passes too lightly over the educational significance, indeed the pervasive presence, of the different subjects of study. Her apt criticisms of the less-than-inclusive role that subject disciplines have traditionally played in liberal education nevertheless overlook the point that such subjects constitute, not just repositories, but distinctive *engagements* of learning. Each has its own distinctive voice, so to speak, as the latter two sections of Chapter 4 sought to illustrate. These illustrations also emphasized that engaging fruitfully with such voices discloses a vital dimension of relationships of teaching and learning that is all too frequently bypassed.

In conclusion, all of this signifies a significant shift in the self-understanding of the teacher – from the teacher as master, or expert, to the teacher as fluent, responsive, welcoming learner. Undertaking this shift is itself a form of critically important learning for teachers. It is a different kind of learning than that involved in mastering theories of learning in educational psychology, although it may provide a more fertile ground for such learning. It involves a more self-critical undertaking: coming to understand in a new way the experience of human understanding itself, and how the inheritances that are called subject disciplines come to voice, or fail to do so, in this experience. Most importantly of all, perhaps, it involves a different understanding of what to care about in teaching, and of how that care might be experienced, exercised and renewed. This shift of focus from an exploration of educational practices to the underlying forms of understanding that are properly native to such practices also marks the transfer from Part I to Part II of our enquiry.

PART II

Educational forms of understanding and action

7 Understanding in human experience and in learning

Preconceptions in human understanding

Let us begin here by recalling the example of Paul, the fictional teacher introduced in Chapter 4, whose understanding of his two teaching subjects – mathematics and history – contrasts sharply. Where mathematics and its teaching are concerned, Paul is alive with fresh ideas, but he regards history essentially as a body of information – knowledge of events, causes and consequences – for transmission to his students. That transmission, moreover, is guided chiefly by Paul's familiarity with reliable examination topics, and with the structure of the examination question papers. He is similarly familiar with examination topics in maths, but somehow this remains a background issue rather than a dominant theme in his maths classes. Paul hasn't made explicit to himself the nature of his understanding of either subject. He readily declares that he finds maths a fascinating subject, and he admits, somewhat reluctantly, that history can be a bit unexciting. He would be offended if it were suggested to him that he had a prejudice against history and a prejudice in favour of maths. Paul insists that he has no preconceived ideas about either subject, but that he just has a natural attraction to maths that he doesn't have to history. But he also insists that he is no less competent in history than in maths and that his students' success in examinations bear out this point.

Few teachers will take kindly to a suggestion that they hold prejudices, either of a positive or a negative kind, either towards their teaching subjects or their students. The word 'prejudice' carries unwelcome connotations of irrationality, and a charge of prejudice is likely to provoke a self-protective reaction more than anything else. When the suggestion is put more mildly, however – for example, that teachers are often differently predisposed towards the different subjects they teach, it is likely that it will be readily granted. Similarly, suggestions that teachers are differently predisposed towards different students, towards different colleagues and towards different parents, are likely to be accepted, even as self-evidently true. Predispositions, however, include such things as presuppositions, prior assumptions, preconceptions and a range of other influences that are picked up from previous experiences. Some of these influences might be ones of which we might be less than critically aware. They might thus predispose our beliefs and attitudes from behind our backs, as it were.

The requirements of rationality would seem to indicate that such prior influences need to be identified and set aside if practitioners are to carry out their work in an even-handed way. We are reminded here of the kind of instruction judges give to juries on the necessity to set aside any preconceived ideas that they might be carrying from beyond their direct experiences in the courtroom. Although their decisions are usually of less moment than those of juries, teachers' work calls on them daily to make countless decisions involving judgements that are even-handed. And the more we know of such situations, the more a requirement to set aside all prior influences seems problematic. It is probably not humanly achievable. Even if it were, it would seem to require setting aside many insights gained from previous experience that would contribute to, rather than hinder, the making of wise judgements. One is reminded here of Dewey's rather forthright advice to educators in his late work *Experience and Education*: 'The mature person, to put it in moral terms, has no right to withhold from the young on given occasions whatever capacity for sympathetic understanding his own experience has given him.'[1] Teachers' deliberations might sometimes involve sitting at meetings to review cases of particular students. But, more often, their judgements and decisions are arrived at through acts of reasoning carried out alone, silently, and often in quick succession during the successive episodes of a normal lesson. It is instructive to focus on one such episode, in this case a turbulent one, to reveal just how much relations of teaching and learning owe to prior influences. The episode can be presented first from the teacher's side and then from the student's. The teacher's reasoning goes as follows:

> We are now in our fourth week of term and Billy Doyle has so far produced no homework, or just a few untidy lines. He shows no appreciation of the trouble I've taken to make French interesting. He made a farce of the oral exercises during group-work on Monday, pretending to be a cross-eyed cripple with a stammer. He shouldn't be doing French at all because he has neither interest nor aptitude, and he'll never reach a pass standard. But he's no better in other classes, from what I hear in the staffroom. He seems as determined to make trouble as his brother was two years ago. His antics are a continuing distraction to others. Now he's torn out a page of his copy and is making a paper plane with some scribbled writing on it – probably obscenities. I'll try to intercept that when he throws it. He deserves to be suspended. My complaint to his Year Head hasn't brought any action, so this time I'm going to the Deputy Principal.

As for Billy, his line of reasoning goes like this:

> This French is just stupid. I hate it. Nothing sounds like it's spelled. The whole language is for ponces if you ask me. The role-plays we do in groupwork are ridiculous and I'm not going to look like a ponce in front of

the others. When am I ever going to be in a French tourist office anyway? The French teacher is a waste of space. Nearly the worst in the school, but that wouldn't be hard. … Maybe if I got suspended I could get my weekend job on weekdays as well. I could give some of the money to Ma. She might change her mind about me having to stay till the exams if she saw a bit of extra money coming in each week. … Now Fiona over there looks like she could do with a juicy love letter from Darren. I'll send it air mail as soon as the teacher starts writing on the board.

Using colloquial language to describe this episode, we could say that the teacher is not really aware of where Billy is 'coming from', and that Billy is hampered by a similar lack. We could conclude that the teacher has good reason to be unsympathetic towards Billy. We might also enquire, however, to what extent the teacher, or any of the teacher's colleagues, is acquainted with Billy's circumstances, or if where he's 'coming from' makes sense in some kind of context that might yet give hopes for Billy's educational future. We could conclude, and fairly safely, that unless the mutual lack of understanding is earnestly and perceptively addressed, Billy's experience of learning French, and his life in the school, is likely to get worse rather than better. Or from the teacher's standpoint, unless there is some opportunity for Billy and his French teacher to tackle honestly and quietly the preconceived ideas each has of the other, things look bleak. The chances are dim of achieving some respite, or provisional deal, that would enable the learning environment in the French class to improve. The possibility of such a deal would require Billy and his teacher to listen to one another, away from the attention of others. They would probably have to start by adopting improvised 'rules of the game', including some assurances of confidentiality to Billy. These 'rules' might enable each to listen, without interjection, while the other told a story that would very likely disclose misapprehensions, prejudices and surprises. For instance, the teacher might be surprised to learn that Billy is correctly aware that negative comments are made about him in the teachers' staff room. The teacher might be further taken aback to learn that Billy is convinced that he is despised by his teachers, one and all; that Billy believes his mother and brother are similarly despised because his mother has no husband or steady partner. Billy might be surprised to learn that this teacher is far from being the 'ponce' he thought; that the teacher would happily give him a break; that the teacher might even stand up for him with the other teachers if Billy could agree to a few things in return, just for a few weeks till they could meet one-to-one again for another 15-minute talk.

Each would have to be prepared to see the other differently, at least to some degree, and at least for the time being. This would involve something like a provisional change of heart on the part of each. The teacher might acknowledge Billy's dislike of French, but try to convince him that it's definitely worth sticking it out till the exam. Perceiving also that Billy's aggression and lively imagination might be turned to some fruitful purpose, the teacher might guarantee him regular opportunities to work with fellow students designing 'unponcy' scenarios for the role-plays. These could include: being overcharged in a French fast-food outlet; being refused entrance to an upmarket disco in Paris; being interrogated by a French police officer on suspicion of a drugs offence and for failure to produce ID. The teacher might also now see the wisdom in involving Billy and other students in thinking up more imaginative scenarios than the teacher's own efforts produced. This, it should be noted in passing, constitutes a shift in the teacher's relationship to the subject, and also a potentially promising shift in the teacher's relationship to the students. In line with this shift, there could be a prize at the end of the month for the best scenario and the winner could be chosen by the students in a secret ballot. Designing new scenarios wouldn't let Billy off the hook for other work, however. Under his negotiated settlement with the teacher, he might be expected, like every member of a group of say, four students, to contribute at least a quarter of the French vocabulary for each of the scenarios. He would have to take his turn as group leader, ensuring that each member had pulled his or her weight in preparing the dialogue for the scenario.

Efforts to reach settlements of this kind are time-consuming and call for rich reserves of the kind of unerotic love explored in the previous chapter. They also call for perseverance and ingenuity, as they are likely to suffer setbacks and even reversals. What they are not are efforts to render students docile. Neither are they an application of behaviour management techniques that can be turned to this strategic purpose or that. They are wholehearted efforts, not just in the sense of being fully in earnest, but also in the sense of responding with humanity – with heart as well as mind. For all their vulnerability and fallibility, they represent some of the most promising measures in repairing damaged relationships of learning and in building healthy learning environments in contrived institutions such as schools. Where such efforts succeed in turning things around for the longer term, the provisional change of heart mentioned above becomes a more enduring one. The corrosive power of negative predispositions yields, in varying degrees, to more productive orientations in relationships of learning. Crucial to all of this work of heart and mind on the teacher's part is an incisive understanding of the concealed role of prejudice – the word has been continually hovering since the start of the chapter – in human understanding itself.

Prejudices as conditions of learning

'It is not so much our judgements as it is our prejudices that constitute our being.' This bold declaration by the German philosopher Hans Georg Gadamer (1900–2002) is presented in different ways in his various writings.[2] On a first reading, the declaration looks like an affront to reason; it seems to discard the very rationality that philosophy is supposed to elucidate. Gadamer acknowledges that the declaration is a provocative one, but his purpose, he explains, is to recover a positive sense of concept of prejudice that the English and

French Enlightenment drove out of linguistic usage. The concept of prejudice, Gadamer argues, originally did not have the negative meaning that is now usually associated with it. Pursuing his point further he states:

> Prejudices are not necessarily unjustified and erroneous, so that they inevitably distort the truth. In fact, the historicity of our existence entails that prejudices, in the literal sense of the word, constitute the initial directedness of our whole ability to experience. Prejudices are biases of our openness to the world.[3]

The reference here to 'the literal sense of the word' that Gadamer is keen to reclaim is critical. He describes that original sense of prejudice as: 'a judgement that is given before all the elements that determine a situation have been finally examined.'[4] He argues that such judgements have to be made all the time, as people are rarely, if ever, in situations where *all* elements that determine a situation are consciously available for final examination. Thus, he concludes, that 'all understanding inevitably involves some prejudices'.[5] But there is a more decisive sense than this, Gadamer argues, in which predisposing influences feature in human understanding. This more decisive argument, one that Gadamer developed from the researches of Heidegger (1889–1976), defines the heart of philosophical hermeneutics. In summary form, it might be presented in two steps as follows. First, human understanding is wrongly construed when cognition is separated from interpretation, as this provides the misleading belief that the cognitive functions of mind could act independently of interpretation. Second, in contrast to this customary error, Heidegger and Gadamer argue that every act of understanding is unavoidably interpretative from the start. In other words, interpretation is not an ingredient, deficient or otherwise, that is added later. It is active and influential from the beginning in every act of human understanding.

Again, no less than Gadamer's argument on prejudice above, this stance is initially surprising. It seems to deny the most rudimentary logic, particularly the distinction between established facts on the one hand and the more subjective domain of interpretations on the other. But Heidegger counters that it is just this distinction that has, for too long, bedevilled everyday thinking and philosophy alike. The originality of those sections of Heidegger's *Being and Time*, where he deals with understanding (Sections 31 and 32), lies in their incisive, if terse, demonstration that human understanding always involves the unavoidable bringing to bear of a prior context of influences.[6] This 'fore-structure', or predisposing background (*Vor-struktur*), works as a kind of built-in interpretative filter. It already gives prominence to some things, relegates others and grants significance of one kind or another to what is encountered in the experience of understanding. In understanding then, everything gets interpreted *as* something, or *as* significant in one way or another. To put it more formally, the 'fore-structure' of understanding is already constituted by the 'as-structure' of interpretation.[7] Successive experiences of understanding, moreover, modify those that have gone before and continually re-orient understanding itself towards the *future*, or more precisely, towards further experiences. Heidegger is mindful that in order to 'take hold of the possibility of the most primordial kind of knowing', the predisposing influences ('fore-structure') must be carefully watched during acts of understanding to detect possible biases and distortions. He cautions: 'our first, last, and constant task is never to allow our fore-having, fore-sight, and fore-conception to be presented to us by fancies and popular conceptions.'[8]

In *Truth and Method*, Gadamer devotes many pages to what he calls 'Heidegger's disclosure of the fore-structure of understanding.' He explores in thought-provoking and frequently challenging detail what Heidegger moves through tersely in his analysis of understanding and interpretation in *Being and Time*. Gadamer investigates the historical character of human experience: how this predisposes understanding and how it sets limits to the claims of reason. He is particularly concerned with examining the effects of history on acts of understanding. These effects clearly include those of the historical memory of a society, and of communities and groupings within a society. But they also include those of one's own personal history, or one's experiences to date. Becoming conscious of the effects of history, including history in the wider and more personal senses, teaches a number of salutary lessons, Gadamer maintains. One of the more important of these he describes as follows: 'In fact, history does not belong to us, but we belong to it. Long before we understand ourselves through the process of self-examination, we understand ourselves in a self-evident way in the family, society and state in which we live.'[9] This is not to suggest that critical practices of self-examination are worthless. Far from it. Rather, it is to suggest that in undertaking such practices, which Gadamer highly values, it is helpful to be aware that they are unlikely to yield what philosophy traditionally sought, and what became a guiding ideal of the Enlightenment – namely, a vantage point from which all distortions and biases might become fully transparent to critical enquiry.

When confronted with one's own experiences of understanding, with what one knows of the experiences of others, or with what educational practitioners encounter daily in trying to bring about fruitful learning, Gadamer's case is very difficult to dismiss. Still, the apparent priority he gives to interpretation over objective reason raises a concern in the reader's mind as to how his position is going to defend itself from the charge of relativism. For if interpretation is inescapably active in all understanding, what is to distinguish a better under-standing from an inferior one? Investigating this charge of relativism should help to clarify a few crucial points in Gadamer's argument and provide some further insights into the happening of human understanding – insights that might be particularly helpful for education.

To begin with, Gadamer holds that it is mistaken to place reason and interpretation in separate and competing categories, so the question of giving one priority over the other doesn't arise. Instead, he points out that reason, in a better or worse form, is an already embedded feature of all human acts of understanding. As reason-in-use, it involves pre-influenced interpretation from the start. Again, consulting a practical example should illustrate this better. For instance, I hear a sound outside and I find myself thinking immediately: 'that's a Volkswagen Beetle starting up'. My instant response to hearing the sound is an act of interpretative reasoning, informed by previous experience, which thrusts a conclusion on me before I have time to think about the matter more formally. And if I hear a sound I don't recognize, I find that I've already interpreted it *as unfamiliar*, as my previous experience comes silently but busily into play. To illustrate this instance with an example, I'm likely to find myself thinking: 'It's a cry of some kind; not a child crying, nor a cat wailing; it's too full-bodied than either of these. In fact it's too high-pitched for anything human. Maybe it's a siren, but yet it doesn't sound mechanical, and it's intermittent in any case. Maybe it's the cry of an animal in distress, but certainly not an animal I've heard before.' My failure to name the sound accurately does not mean that it remains un-interpreted. Rather, as this example of my reason-in-use shows, a number of candidates have passed through my interpretative filter before I finally regard the sound *as something I can't pin down*; something that remains significant *as* being perplexing, perhaps also *as* being disturbing.

Rationality itself is here shown to be interpretative. Such rationality characterizes not just the understanding that takes place in response to sound, but also responses involving the other senses and, crucially, responses to encounters with books, newspapers, films, and not least, encounters with others. It invariably involves the coming-into-play of previously significant influences, and, through this interplay, the taking-up or modification of attitudes to what is experienced. Sometimes this happens beyond one's conscious awareness, as for instance when one picks up, from infancy onwards, prejudices that might be lodged in the mother tongue or local dialect that one learns naturally in one's home and neighbourhood. These might be prejudices of a favourable or unfavourable kind. The fact that some of them might be called 'irrational' does not alter the fact that a predisposing rationality, of one kind or another, is active in their origins and development.

'Reason', Gadamer writes, 'exists for us [humans] only in concrete, historical terms; it is not its own master, but remains constantly dependent on the given circumstances in which it operates.'[10] While humans can imagine a reason that is all-capable, and free from all prejudice, the full realization of this ideal escapes the best efforts of humans themselves as historical and finite beings. The actual accomplishments of human rationality never attain the perfect ideal of reason. Reason, in the ideal sense, can be imagined as something omniscient, but this makes it more god-like than human. There is a strong echo in Gadamer's point here of the crucial distinction drawn by Socrates between the elusive, or divine character of 'real wisdom' and the limitations of 'human wisdom', or reason in human concrete terms. This distinction became largely lost to the major traditions of Western philosophy after Socrates' death. The distinction has already been reviewed in Chapter 3 above, but recalling it now directs attention again to the modest achievements of even the best of human rationality. This latter rationality, Socrates seems to be suggesting, is ever likely to be partial, and in both senses of the word: incomplete and burdened by bias. Of course, Socrates didn't make these points explicit. To have done so would be to anticipate by more than 2,000 years some central themes in the thought of Heidegger and Gadamer. Neither does Socrates say anything of the historicalness of human understanding, although his uncanny alertness (in the early dialogues of Plato) to how previous influences predispose our human efforts to understand points in this direction. Had Socrates' suggestive insights been taken up and developed by subsequent philosophy, as distinct from becoming overshadowed by the magisterial force of Plato's metaphysics, Western philosophy itself might subsequently have taken fewer wrong turnings. In particular, the claims of metaphysics to achieve an all-encompassing overview of reality might have been subject to greater restraint, as might the later pretensions of epistemology to unshakeable certainty. Institutionalizations of reason throughout the ages, not least in schools, might also have been more modest and more humane.

Partiality in learning

Although these arguments seem to capture something inescapable about the nature of human understanding, there remains an uneasy suspicion that relativism hasn't quite been laid to rest. Gadamer's arguments, for all their cogency, seem to make things a bit too provisional and slippery. Even if we are convinced that our own histories orient our capacity for human understanding with particular interpretative predispositions, can some yardstick be identified to distinguish better predispositions from inferior ones? More candidly, how is a valid understanding to be distinguished from an invalid one? What kinds of criteria can we call on here, or have criteria been thrown out in putting interpretation at the heart of understanding? These are practical and urgent questions, not least for those whose daily work involves the promotion of defensible forms of learning.

Perhaps the initial thing to say in addressing these questions is that being provisional, or non-certain, in one's attitude towards knowledge might more properly be seen as a merit than as a deficiency. At a minimum, it should help to keep in check any tendencies one might have towards dogmatism, or a know-it-all stance. But there are also more positive merits. First, there is a recognition here that preconceptions, both overt and unnoticed, are likely to remain active even in one's best efforts at disciplined understanding. This places as high a premium on qualities such as self-criticism as is customarily placed on a capacity to critique the arguments of others. Second, there is also a recognition here that the fruits of systematic efforts to advance human understanding (for instance, research efforts in various fields of learning) are properly seen as stages on a journey, as distinct from destinations reached for good. The journeys themselves continually discover new regions and are probably unfinishable. They also include the recognition of previous wrong turnings, and the taking of new turnings that might turn out in time to be mistaken ones. Being aware of this helps to promote the emblematic Socratic virtue, an educated sense of one's own ignorance. More generally, it nourishes a healthy sense of humankind's relative ignorance, in the face of the immensity of all that is not yet known, or at least not known to humankind. Third, accepting that partiality is inescapable – both in the sense of incompleteness and of bias of perspective – highlights the desirability of inviting constructive criticism of one's best efforts, to date, from others who are similarly engaged. It also calls attention to the desirability of cultivating environments of learning where such criticism is jointly practised by participants.

These three points – the importance of self-criticism, knowledge as a journey rather than destination, the inescapability of the partial – need to be elucidated more fully to deal with the issue of relativism. But it can be noted at this point that the provisional kind of pedagogical stance that they describe is itself a distinctive ethical orientation. When joined with the kind of ethics of care explored in the later parts of the last chapter, this orientation reveals itself as particularly appropriate to the deliberate promotion of practices of teaching and learning. This is something to be examined in the next chapter, but for now our concern is the elucidation of the three points just noted, in order to deal with the charge of relativism.

Taking self-criticism first, suppose it were possible not just to take to heart, but to accomplish to the full, Heidegger's advice 'never to allow our fore-having, fore-sight, and fore-conception to be presented to us by fancies and popular conceptions'. Such an accomplishment would enable us to distinguish successfully between satisfactory and deficient instances of human understanding. We would thus have at least one clear-cut criterion. A perfected sense of self-criticism would now be able to unearth all the assumptions at play in a particular instance of understanding and to reveal the ways in which some of these act as distortions or hindrances. This accomplishment would require, however, achieving an all-transparent vantage point over our own historical experiences. Gadamer's perceptive point that we belong more to the flow of history than it belongs to us, far from conceding anything to relativism, reminds us that such complete self-transparency is just not humanly possible. It's important to stress that it's not just limitations of memory that are the difficulty here. Even if we were somehow able to recall to consciousness everything we once knew but have forgotten, there would still remain a host of significant influences of which we have never been critically aware. Perfecting a discipline of self-criticism to the best of one's efforts can result in salutary progress in detecting such influences. But this very discipline alerts us also, sometimes by embarrassingly pulling us up short, to how elusive to inspection many of these predisposing influences are. It also provides reminders of how subtly interwoven they are into the settled tenor of our thoughts and actions. Self-criticism then cannot do a flawless job as a criterion to distinguish between a valid and an invalid understanding. What it can do is help in many practical ways to deepen our appreciation of the hidden constituents of human understanding itself, as this understanding unfolds in our own experience and that of others. This deeper appreciation reveals the folly of believing that a methodically disciplined use of reason can safeguard us from all error. It also carries its own intimations that the kind of clear-cut criteria that would distinguish conclusively between valid and invalid understanding just might not be available – that it might, in fact, be a mistake to look for it.

Turning now to the second point, this is the argument that the fruits of truth-seeking enquiries are to be conceived as stages on unfinishing journeys, as distinct from destinations securely reached. One serious problem with the latter view, supposing we were to accept it for the sake of argument, is that the outlook of authoritative conclusiveness it promotes becomes all too easily institutionalized. Where this happens, there is a tendency to be closed to alternative understandings, as the case of Galileo's prosecutors, reviewed earlier, tellingly shows. Galileo's interpretations were more fully explanatory, and more widely convincing, than those that had been accepted as certain truth for many centuries. Yet they were themselves but stages, historic landmarks if you prefer, on astronomy's pathways of discovery; pathways that still continue to come upon galaxies beyond those of which the solar system forms but a miniscule part. It could fairly be said that Galileo had an educated sense of his own ignorance, although he had perhaps a less sophisticated appreciation of the inherited certainty of the ecclesiastical authorities who denounced his work. Had the distinction between 'journey' and 'destination' been publicly acknowledged in the sixteenth and seventeenth centuries as even a provisional criterion to distinguish scholarly enquiry from 'the certainties of faith', times would have been less traumatic for Galileo. This is to say, in effect, that a provisional criterion might not be the deficient thing it seems at first sight. Being provisional, it remains open to revision, or indeed to refutation and replacement by something more demonstrably convincing. On this account, it could do a better job than the demand for 'certainty' of knowledge as a defensible criterion of learning.

The third point concerns the issue of partiality – both as lack of completeness and as the presence of bias in each person's own efforts to understand. Where the promotion of learning is concerned, this highlights both the need for, and the potential richness of, perspectives from others. Such perspectives are crucial in identifying questionable preconceptions that had escaped one's own self-critical efforts. They bring to light gaps and wrong turnings in one's own investigations. They can transform the landscape of enquiry by suggesting extensions or alternatives to one's own lines of reasoning, or by taking a spark from something already ventured and launching out in new directions. There is a to-and-fro movement here, as what is ventured by one calls forth something new from others, reciprocity being the corollary of an acknowledgement of partiality. And since everyone's history of experience is different, at least in some degree, recognizing the inherent partiality of understanding is, accordingly, a recognition of its individuality, and of the plurality that needs proper acknowledgement in environments of learning. Far from giving the upper hand to relativism, or to anarchic subjectivity, the recognition of partiality suggests that deficiency attaches not to non-certainty, or to acknowledged modesty in human aspirations to knowledge. Instead, deficiency can now be seen to attach to their precise opposites, which for many centuries gave unquestionable status to successive enforced orthodoxies and sought to circumscribe from the start what could be thought and taught.

An ethical stance that perceives the significance of self-criticism, that embraces knowledge as a journey rather than a destination, and that acknowledges the inescapability of the partial also discloses a particular approach to learning and teaching. When to this ethical stance one adds the orientations yielded by the arguments on relationship of learning and ethics of care in previous chapters, a picture emerges of a teacher as a particular kind of practitioner. For all its distinguished ancestry in the long-eclipsed understandings and practices of Socrates, this picture of the teacher seems a radical one, perhaps a disquieting one to many. It seems, for instance, to allow long-standing traditions of learning no higher standing in educational undertakings than the newly arrived claims of plurality or cosmopolitanism. It seems to make of the teacher some kind of pragmatic intermediary, as distinct from someone who clearly stands for a body of sanctioned beliefs that might be passed onto students. It seems, in fact, to destabilize the place of cultural tradition in educational experience. Perhaps the explorations of the next and following chapters will allay this disquiet for those committed educators who sense it. Perhaps not. But these explorations themselves are committed, first and foremost, to making clear that the inherent benefits of educational practice lie on the far side of such disquiet.

8   Cultural tradition and educational experience

Contrasting views of tradition

The view that passing on a cultural inheritance to new generations is among the central purposes of education is a widespread one, not least among teachers themselves when they are asked about the significance of their own occupation. In countries with democratic forms of government, this view usually does not give rise to major political crises, although there are recurrent controversies about issues such as faith schools, multiculturalism in schooling, and the wearing of religious emblems or clothing in public schools. Most residents of democratic countries would find it repugnant, however, that schools should be used to promote a fundamentalist culture – as, for instance, the educational programme of the Taliban sought to do in Afghanistan from 1996 to 2001. There are also fears in many Western countries that the kind of learning provided in madrassas, or Islamist schools, seeks to indoctrinate students into cultural traditions that are violently sectarian.[1] And, of course, many countries that are currently democratic have experienced serious conflicts in the past over education as a cultural force, or indeed as an ideological or an evangelizing force. For instance, South Africa, Spain, or the Quebec region of Canada. In general, however, disquiet over the cultural role of schooling rarely reaches crisis proportions unless schools are perceived to be promoting attitudes and actions that conflict with values that are widely accepted in the society in question.

Yet to view education as a vehicle for the transmission of cultural heritage, is largely at odds with what actually happens in schools. Such a view presents a two-fold illusion. First, it suggests that a cultural heritage is chiefly a ready-made, or approved repository: a body of established knowledge, theories, customs, beliefs, skills and so on. Second, it assumes that transmission is what education is mainly about, and that it is to be accomplished through those who have appropriated the substance of the repository and mastered certain techniques of transmission. Even where teaching is poor, however, there is always more than this happening. Students are never merely receivers of transmissions. They invariably experience some qualitative response towards what is addressed to them by teachers. This could be one of enthusiasm, boredom, suspense, frustration, warmth, resentment, or any number of further attitudinal stances. Similarly, teachers rarely (if ever) just transmit. Even where they confine themselves to reciting from a script, they disclose in their actions some traces of their own relationship, albeit an uninspiring one, to the subject or topic in question.

Where attention focuses primarily on the contents of a syllabus, as it frequently does with teachers who feel continually under pressure to 'get the course covered', there tends to be a corresponding neglect of the attitudinal dimension just referred to. This is the dimension Dewey called 'collateral learning' – reviewed in Chapter 3 above. However, collateral learning takes place among teachers just as much as among the students. Consider the case where the teacher's proficiency in his or her teaching subject(s) falls prey to the semi-automatic routines of textbook-led teaching. Here, the collateral dimension of the teacher's work, both in learning and in teaching, is likely to be marked by an unexciting kind of predictability. In such circumstances, teaching could still be effective, particularly as measured by the outcomes of traditional examinations. But the students' encounter with a vibrant tradition of learning remains stillborn, or at best is unlikely to have amounted to anything memorable or culturally enriching.

Where the teacher's proficiency resists an imprisoning kind of habituation, however, that proficiency itself can properly be seen as an active relationship to a tradition of learning. Recalling what we explored of this relationship in Chapters 3 and 4, we can now see it as a relationship that is every bit as alive as inter-human relationships are. That is to say, it is a relationship marked by frequent discoveries, frustrations, delights, distortions, renewals and lapses. It is a relationship, moreover, not with a body of neatly joined-together concepts and theories, but with a wide variety of interpretations, claims, counterclaims and inherent power-plays. Not least, it is a relationship with those ongoing creative achievements that constitute a discipline of learning. Such disciplines range from music to home economics, from biology to literature, from woodworking to geography, to mention but a small sample.

To speak of tradition in this way is to see it as quite different from something official, or readymade for transmission. More positively, it is to view tradition in one form or another as something that always constitutes a background to our understanding of anything. But for tradition to be educationally productive, it would need to constitute that background in a challenging and enabling way. This contrasts with widely held conceptions of tradition that predispose experiences of learning to an uncritical conformity on the one hand, or provoke a dismissive stance on the other. It is important to recall here that appeals to the authority of tradition played a major role in justifications that were historically offered by paternalistic and authoritarian regimes, in education as in religion and politics. On first sight, Gadamer's influential remarks on tradition in *Truth and Method* seem to reflect this emphasis. For some critics, this casts his entire philosophical approach in a conservative light and advances a paternalistic stance in affairs of learning. For example, when exploring the historical grounds of validity for morals, Gadamer refers to tradition in the following terms: 'in fact, we owe to romanticism this correction of the Enlightenment, that tradition has a justification that is outside the arguments of reason and in large measure determines our institutions and our attitudes.'[2] Remarks of this kind have provoked critics such as Terry Eagleton to confront Gadamer with the following demand:

> It might be as well to ask Gadamer whose and what 'tradition' he has in mind. For his theory holds only on the enormous assumption that there is indeed a single 'mainstream' tradition; that all 'valid' works participate in it; that history forms an unbroken continuum, free of decisive rupture, conflict, and contradiction; and that the prejudices which 'we' (who?) have inherited from the 'tradition' are to be cherished.[3]

Eagleton's criticism alleges further that the conception of history underlying Gadamer's arguments fails to see that history and tradition can be oppressive as well as liberating; that it is a 'grossly complacent' conception, viewing history almost as 'a club of the like-minded'.[4] This trenchant criticism also sums up the kind of suspicion provoked by appeals to tradition among educators who champion the cause of critical thinking and independence of mind. Tradition, to such sceptical minds, can scarcely be other than resistant to emergent voices that threaten the position of established powers. Calling on tradition as a source of justification for educational or other forms of established authority could not, on this sceptical stance, succeed in establishing a rationally acceptable claim. Rather, it would constitute an exercise of power, even an unacknowledged exercise of violence, albeit violence of a non-physical kind.

The point at issue here is a crucial one, with major import for how educational practices are to be understood and carried out. So it calls for careful scrutiny. In response to critics who charge him with conservatism, Gadamer insists that he was taking up neither a conservative nor a radical position in his investigations of prejudice and tradition in *Truth and Method*. He explains in the Foreword to the second edition of the book that he was trying to focus on what inescapably happens, 'beyond our wanting and doing', when human understanding takes place, or is attempted. Accordingly, he continues, he had to draw attention to the point that the influences that lie over us (*überliefern*) from the past are invariably less transparent, and also more active, than a naive faith in reason or in method might lead us to believe.[5] To answer Eagleton's question directly, the totality and ceaseless flow of such influences is just what Gadamer means by 'tradition'.[6] Acknowledging the effects of such influences does not nullify critical reflection. But it alerts such reflection to the point that there are constraints, including hidden ones, on what even its own best efforts might be able to achieve. In his writings subsequent to *Truth and Method*, and most notably following his fruitful debate with Jürgen Habermas, Gadamer frequently emphasizes that there are inherent tensions within what he continues to refer to as 'tradition'.[7]

This initial response on behalf of what Gadamer means by 'tradition' needs to be expanded, and this might be better done by broadening the context of investigation and including another major figure who has contributed to this theme. That is Alasdair MacIntyre, whose arguments have also explored tradition and its educational import. Criticisms that allege a conservative attachment to tradition can also be made of some of MacIntyre's main arguments. There are, moreover, some striking parallels, but also some decisive differences, in MacIntyre's and Gadamer's accounts. A summary of some pertinent arguments of MacIntyre's is called for before appraising afresh the significance of tradition for educational experience.

Tradition and rationality

MacIntyre's arguments on tradition appear with increasing emphasis in the three books: *After Virtue* (1981/1985), *Whose Justice? Which Rationality?* (1988), *Three Rival Versions of Moral Enquiry* (1990). In *After Virtue*, MacIntyre argues strongly against a modern liberal individualism that is confident in the impartiality of its own rational powers. He discerns in this liberalism an unwarranted self-assurance, linked to a concept of human reason that divorces it from the social and historical circumstances of its use. More significantly, in all three books, MacIntyre develops a major argument that highlights the social and historical context in which human practices are inescapably situated. This context, he insists, constitutes the background for one's self-understanding, for one's understanding of others and for one's emergent identity. In *After Virtue*, he writes:

> I inherit from the past of my family, my city, my tribe, my nation, a variety of debts, inheritances, rightful expectations and obligations. These constitute the given of my life, my moral starting point. This is in part what gives my life its own moral particularity.[8]

MacIntyre stresses that each person has to receive his or her moral identity in the first place through membership, informal or formal, of a range of communities and groups. These form the social and historical context of the person's experience. Each of these groups and communities, he continues, has its own particular traditions, through which certain attitudes and practices are cultivated and others are discouraged or neglected. And MacIntyre adds that these particular traditions never exist in isolation from larger social traditions. None of this is to imply, he says, that the developing self-understanding of any person is necessarily imprisoned by the effects of tradition. The moral limitations of the particular groups and communities are not insurmountable influences. Yet, he points out that, in taking a critical evaluative stance towards one's own upbringing or culture, 'particularity can never be left behind or obliterated'. The individual who presumes to be independent of all tradition, living purely by universal maxims of reason as proposed by Kant, lives an illusion, on MacIntyre's argument. In Chapters 4 and 5 of *After Virtue*, he argues suggestively that there are intractable difficulties in basing morality on a rationality that is devoid of cultural influences. And that is what Kant's universal rationality claimed to be. MacIntyre concludes that Kant's moral philosophy draws the substance of its 'rationally universal' maxims from unacknowledged Lutheran influences – influences that would have pervaded his Prussian upbringing. MacIntyre is convinced that 'Kant never doubted for a moment that the maxims he had learnt from his own virtuous parents were those which had to be vindicated by a rational test.' [9]

Although MacIntyre's investigations in *After Virtue* deal chiefly with issues of moral understanding and moral identity, what he says of these applies no less to the development of self-understanding and personal identity more fully. This is evident from the conclusions he draws at key stages of his argument, where his references include one's self-understanding as such, not merely one's moral understanding. Take for instance this following conclusion, which carries strong parallels to Gadamer's position: 'What I am therefore, is in key part what I inherit, a specific past that is present to some degree in my present. I find myself part of a history and that is generally to say, whether I like it or not, whether I recognize it or not, one of the bearers of a tradition.' [10]

MacIntyre is more promptly cautious than Gadamer in countering any suspicion that his references to tradition place his arguments in a conservative camp. He makes two important points to remove his case from such suspicion. In the first of these, he says that 'we are apt to be misled by the ideological uses to which the concept of tradition has been put by conservative political theorists.' He identifies as such theorists Edmund Burke and those who have followed him, in drawing sharp distinctions between tradition on the one hand and reason on the other. Against such theorists, MacIntyre points out that 'all reasoning takes place within the context of some traditional mode of thought'. Clearly, this recognizes that much reasoning can have a conformist or acquiescent character, or that it may be inconsistently alert to its own presuppositions. But it also reveals that it is only through fluent and critical acquaintance with what has 'hitherto been reasoned in a tradition' that limitations in the tradition can be properly identified, and possibly overcome. He rightly adds that this holds equally for modern physics and medieval logic. [11]

Second, MacIntyre challenges the tendency of critics to contrast the stability of tradition with the occurrence and recurrence of conflict, or to identify tradition with forces protective of an old order and conflict with attempts to overthrow that order. Against this, MacIntyre makes the more insightful argument that institutions – he instances universities, farms, hospitals – are bearers of traditions of practice, or practices, and that it is the coherence of these traditions of practice over time that led to the institutions. He also adds the following important point. Where, in any tradition, stability has come to replace active debate, the tradition is dying or dead. But where a tradition is 'in good order', it is always constituted, less by stability than by ongoing arguments about the pursuit of the goals that give the tradition in question its distinct purpose. Or as MacIntyre puts it: 'Traditions, when vital, embody continuities of conflict.'[12]

The resonances here with the arguments of Gadamer and Heidegger on the 'fore structure' of human understanding are notable. Indeed, the following conclusion, drawn by MacIntyre in *Whose Virtue? Which Rationality?*, might have been written by any of the three of them: '[I]t is an illusion to suppose that there is some neutral standing ground, some locus of rationality as such, which can afford rational resources sufficient for enquiry independent of all traditions.'[13] The conclusion shared between all three would be, first, that all understanding takes place within some tradition, or within a context where influences from different traditions mingle together. Second, a central educational consequence of this shared view would be the necessity not so much to pass on a tradition, as to enable learners to experience something of the tensions and conflicts that are lodged within traditions themselves, when traditions are properly conceived.

But as MacIntyre's investigations develop from *After Virtue* onwards, an important difference between his position and Gadamer's becomes clear. MacIntyre views tradition not so much as the totality of influences (*Überlieferung*, in Gadamer's language) that predispose the efforts of human understanding. What he has in mind, rather, is tradition as a specific grouping of such influences within a larger plurality of such groupings. To the fore in this account is the particularity of one or other tradition, each tradition having its own claims to coherence and to superiority over other traditions. Two features of tradition feature prominently in MacIntyre's investigations: a concern with moral issues and a concern with the pursuit of enquiry. As these investigations develop, the two features regularly combine in the frequently used phrase: 'a tradition of moral enquiry'. MacIntyre makes many references to the phrase 'a tradition that is in good order'. This should not be taken, as it might on a Gadamerian view, to refer to a wide diversity of predisposing influences where strenuous efforts have nevertheless been made to identify and critically examine embedded presuppositions. Rather, 'a tradition in good order', for MacIntyre, refers to a coherent set of beliefs, interpretations, arguments and practices that makes claims to truth. This means something more narrowly circumscribed; for instance, a Marxist tradition, a Kantian tradition, a Thomist tradition and so on. MacIntyre's use of the indefinite article, referring to 'a' tradition, contrasts with Gadamer's continuing references to tradition as something much more wide-ranging: 'all that is communicatively experienced'.[14]

Elucidating his more specific conception of tradition, MacIntyre argues first that 'to be outside all traditions is to be a stranger to enquiry'. This rebuttal of rationalist claims that would give reason a vantage point independent of human culture and history would be widely shared, not only by hermeneutic and pragmatist philosophers, but also by prominent analytic philosophers such as Donald Davidson and John McDowell. From his criticism of the 'outsider' position, however, MacIntyre concludes, a few paragraphs later: 'genuinely to adopt the standpoint of a tradition thereby commits one to its view of what is true and false and, in so committing one, prohibits one from adopting any rival standpoint.'[15] The contrast here with Gadamer's account of tradition is striking. To use a religious metaphor, one has a denominational emphasis whereas the other has a more ecumenical emphasis. This contrast has a decisive import for educational thought and action, in which tradition, in one or other understanding of it, plays a crucial part. MacIntyre has made explicit in his writings many of the practical consequences for education of his arguments on tradition. In Gadamer's works, such consequences remain to be brought out, as he makes only occasional references to education. Comparing both should illuminate some key points about the manner in which cultural tradition *unavoidably* features in educational experience. But it might also yield insights about how it might *best* feature in that experience – that is, most defensibly and most promisingly.

Cultural tradition as partisan

MacIntyre's arguments on education are chiefly to be found in four sources: his essay 'The Idea of an Educated Public' (1987); the final chapter of *Whose Justice? Which Rationality?* (1988); the final chapter of *Three Rival Versions of Moral Enquiry* (1990); and the dialogue with Joseph Dunne published in 2004 (reviewed in the opening pages of Chapter 3 of this book).[16] In 'The Idea of an Educated Public', MacIntyre writes that two overall and familiar purposes can be identified in modern education, namely to prepare young people for some social role and function, and to enable them to think for themselves (i.e. Kant's independence of mind). He argues, however, that these purposes are now contradictory, because the social roles and functions available in modern society are largely incompatible with the kind of independence of mind championed by Kant and the Enlightenment's legacy. Proficiency in thinking for oneself, on an Enlightenment-inspired view, would mean being able to produce arguments that are rationally defensible in universal terms. MacIntyre insists, however, that arguments can be made only from within one or other tradition, and can be justified only in terms of the coherence of that tradition. On this basis, MacIntyre argues that an educated public, properly so called, would require three conditions: (a) a large body of individuals, proficient in rational debate, who are actively committed to debating questions of common social concern in a non-specialist public forum; (b) a shared assent by such individuals to recognized standards of appeal for argument, but not standards supplied by 'local precedent and custom'; (c) a large degree of shared background beliefs and attitudes, these being formed chiefly by 'widespread reading of a common body of texts.'[17] MacIntyre maintains that such conditions were fulfilled in eighteenth-century Scotland, to enable an educated public to flourish there. This, in effect, was an intelligentsia whose frequent conflicts were productive, not least because they were contained by shared standards of appeal – largely those of an erudite, moderate Presbyterianism.[18] MacIntyre is correct in holding that Kantian standards – namely, requirements for a universality that was independent of culture and circumstance – could not have sustained such a public. Whether the only alternative standards for rationality are the partisan ones that MacIntyre embraces is another matter. This is a critical issue for educational thought and practice, and it will be taken up below. But, for now, we will continue with the elucidation of MacIntyre's conclusions on such thought and practice.

The difficulties for an educational aim such as enabling people to think for themselves become more pronounced, MacIntyre claims, in post-Enlightenment pluralist cultures. In these cultures, shared standards of the eighteenth-century Scottish kind are largely absent, and thinking itself has progressively become fragmented into a range of specialisms. MacIntyre's regret over this state of affairs is voiced at many points in his writings. It is particularly evident in his criticisms of the modern liberal universities. As these new academies grew during the nineteenth century, many of the older, confessional universities came under pressure to replace their denominational religious character with the non-sectarian ethos of the new liberal universities. Thus, the liberal university became the dominant model in Western countries. These modern institutions, MacIntyre points out, require no tests of religious belief of their members. In the appointment of their staff and the organization of their curricula, they carry on '*as if* there were indeed shared standards of rationality, accepted by all teachers and accessible to all students'. But apart from the natural sciences, where shared standards of appeal rule out such things as astrology and phrenology, such standards are illusory, MacIntyre claims. The humanities, in particular, have been deprived of the standards of specific moral traditions, against which the texts studied might be rationally assessed. And he concludes:

> What the student is in consequence generally confronted with, and this has little to do with the particular intentions of his or her particular teachers, is an apparent inconclusiveness in all argument outside the natural sciences, an inconclusiveness which seems to abandon him or her to his or her prerational preferences. So the student characteristically emerges from a liberal education with a set of skills, a set of preferences, and little else, someone whose education has been as much a process of deprivation as of enrichment.[19]

This kind of argument suggests that inheritances of learning in the modern liberal university are in disarray, or even in chaos. MacIntyre's critique contrasts sharply with the vision of founders such as Wilhelm von Humboldt in Prussia and Thomas Jefferson in the USA, who envisaged the liberal university as a place free from the imposed order of either ecclesiastical or political power. Jefferson's aspirations for the University of Virginia included, for instance, his often-quoted declaration: 'for here, we are not afraid to follow truth where it may lead, nor to tolerate error so long as reason is free to combat it.'[20] The boldness of the declaration is a good example of the Enlightenment faith in the sovereignty of reason, self-consciously assertive in the face of the more traditional sovereignty claimed by church or monarch. Humboldt's newly founded university in Berlin (1810), made a similar act of faith – a belief in the powers of a freely cultivated reason to yield the most promising of research insights. In so doing, moreover, Humboldt also believed that the university would best serve the interests of the state itself. Humboldt's designs, influential in many countries in the growth of universities in the nineteenth century, preceded those of Jefferson and were, if anything, more bold: 'The state must ... demand nothing from them [universities] simply for the satisfaction of its own needs. It should instead adhere to a deep conviction that if the universities attain their highest ends, they will also realize the state's ends too, and these on a far higher plane.'[21]

MacIntyre holds that all such aspirations for the sovereignty of reason were doomed to failure. He points out that in pre-liberal universities, the requirement for declarations of religious belief, binding on both staff and students, 'ensured a certain degree of uniformity of belief in the way in which the curriculum was organized, presented, and developed through enquiry'.[22] Tradition, in the sense of manifold inheritances of learning, was filtered, so to speak, to become a more definite and more binding tradition. This gave the learning environment of the university a particular denominational ethos – Catholic, Anglican, Lutheran, Presbyterian in Western countries; Islamic in the Arab world. Such an ethos was cultivated through the daily activities of teaching, learning and higher studies, but the university authorities also retained powers to enforce it. The abolition of requirements of religious belief – a hallmark of the liberal university – was a profound mistake, MacIntyre holds. The new university authorities replaced these with the erroneous assumption that appointments could be made on a 'conception of scholarly competence, independent of standpoint'.

Insofar as the teaching practices of liberal universities, or some version of them, are found also in secondary schools, MacIntyre's criticisms would also extend to these. Of course, a prompt rejoinder to this might be that secondary schools in today's world (including High School, *Gymnasium*, *Lycee*, etc.) are too preoccupied with the pragmatic business of tests and examinations to be concerned with these more philosophical issues. Although there is much truth in this, it is also the case that the humanities are now rarely taught in Western secondary schools – including denominational schools – from the standpoint of one moral tradition rather than another. To insist that such a form of teaching might yet be a practicable possibility is to overlook a crucial point. Most denominational schools today are located in societies in which democratic institutions are more than a few generations old. A widespread tolerance of religious freedom of belief and practice is a more or less inherited feature of such societies. But central to this tolerance is an equally widespread inclination to ignore religious authority wherever it is perceived to diminish liberties that are widely taken for granted in social and political life. It is worth bearing this point in mind when considering, as we will now, MacIntyre's practical suggestions – especially those that propose that curricula should be organized and taught from within particular traditions.

MacIntyre is against recommendations – recurring ones in North America – that the core of a humanities curriculum should be a reading of 'great books', or what is frequently called 'the best of what has been thought and taught'. His criticisms spring from different origins, however, than those alleging that a 'great books' curriculum invariably privileges the works of 'dead, white males'. These latter criticisms are concerned almost exclusively with issues of selection and exclusion from inheritances of learning. MacIntyre insists that issues of how texts are taught and studied are every bit as important as the selection of texts. He draws attention here to the quality of the learning environment in which texts are received and discussed, particularly the necessity to engage in constrained conflict with a text from the standpoint of one's own tradition. He stresses as an especially important skill '[k]nowing how to read antagonistically without defeating oneself as well as one's opponent by not learning from the encounter'.[23] To those who find such a stance too aggressive or combative, MacIntyre replies: 'there is no way of either selecting a list of books to be read or advancing a determinate account of how they are to be read, interpreted, and elucidated, which does not involve taking a partisan stand in the conflict of traditions.'[24] This means, in practice, MacIntyre concludes, that teachers have two important roles to play. The first of these is to advance enquiry from within one's own tradition, preserving, building on, and transforming agreements with those who share an allegiance to the tradition. This enables the progressive articulation of 'a framework within which the parts of the curriculum might once again become whole'. A more assertive part of this first role would be engaging in controversy with those who don't share one's tradition. This would be done both to reveal what is mistaken in their standpoints and to test the 'central theses' of one's own stance against the strongest objections that opponents might bring against them.[25] The second role would be less partisan. It would involve sustaining the opportunities for 'ordered conflicts', and also endeavouring 'to negotiate the modes of encounter between opponents, to ensure that rival voices were not illegitimately suppressed.'[26]

MacIntyre's arguments on the place of tradition in education thus make a strong case for denominational schools and universities. These would be places where internal disagreements that inevitably arise in the course of learning would be constrained by an acknowledged set of shared religious beliefs and convictions. Where a diversity of such institutions of learning existed in society, the different institutions would be upholders of rival claims to truth. Their students would learn, first of all, to value the teachings of their own tradition, in which they would become increasingly fluent. The convictions born of such valuing would orient their standpoint towards everything else they learned. The more successful students of such institutions would be active and capable representatives of their particular tradition, not least by having learnt 'to read antagonistically, without defeating themselves or their opponents'.

Cultural tradition and conversation in education

MacIntyre's arguments give a firm denominational colouring and a combative energy to cultural tradition. Both are in contrast to the more conversational, but also more elusive tenor of Gadamer's arguments. Because MacIntyre's investigations are characteristically into ethics, or more precisely into differing 'moral theories', it is not surprising that arguments for and against ethical standpoints feature prominently in his writings. In short, an emphasis on advocacy is much to the fore. Gadamer's investigations, by contrast, have less to do with the evaluation of competing ethical theories than with finding out 'what happens to us over and above our wanting and doing', when human understanding, including mis-understanding, takes place in human experience. The moral consequences of these 'empirically-oriented' (*wissenschaftliche*) investigations are not ignored by Gadamer, but they are, for the most part, left suggestively implicit. From Gadamer's writings, what emerges is a deepening understanding of human understanding itself – one from which one's ethical orientation might be gradually reconsidered as one begins to appreciate the eventual significance of what his investigations disclose. This is not to say that reading Gadamer would lead one to abandon one's existing beliefs. It is to say, rather, that one would probably hold them in a different kind of way – an *un*-certain way as distinct from both an uncertain or certain one.

Gadamer argues that a genuine encounter with tradition (i.e. cultural inheritances) involves what he calls a 'fusion of horizons' (*Horizontverschmelzung*): on the one hand, the horizon of understanding the individual brings with him or her to the encounter and, on the other, the horizon of meaning that addresses the individual in this encounter. For want of a less imprecise word, let us call this individual 'the learner'.[27] Again, at first sight, the 'fusion of horizons' looks like a conservative notion. Unlike the deconstructive strategy of writers such as Derrida, for instance, which makes the most of differences and their articulation, the 'fusion of horizons' seems to dissolve all significant differences into the continuity and ancestral authority of received tradition. This, however, is a serious misunderstanding and, for that reason, 'fusion' (*Verschmelzung*) is an unfortunate word to convey what is meant. In many respects, 'frisson' would be more accurate, if it is understood that the frisson occurs *through* the supposed fusion. What Gadamer has in mind is not a melting together in which all tensions are laid to rest, but an attentive to-and-fro between the learner and the different-ness of that which addresses him or her. It is an interplay in which tensions are uncovered and brought to the fore rather than glossed or passed over.[28] In this interplay, a particular embodiment of tradition – scientific, literary, religious, etc. – is brought to active articulation. It *says* something to the learner. But that articulation, including *its* presuppositions and the learner's own, can also be questioned and re-questioned by the learner. This can happen when a text gets a second reading, for instance, or when challenging ideas are discussed in a participatory learning environment. The learner can become in this event a more fluent, more engaged and more discerning participant.

As Gadamer puts it: 'Reflection on the hermeneutical experience transforms problems back into questions that arise, and that derive their sense from their motivation.'[29] As an event of learning, moreover, whether formal or informal, this engagement alerts learners to twin dangers: unquestioning discipleship on the one hand and, on the other, the kind of critique that remains uncritical of its own embeddedness in historical circumstance.

One of the most important themes in Gadamer's explorations is introduced in a short phrase that emerges at the end of the second part of *Truth and Method*. That phrase is: 'the conversation that we are' (*das Gespräch das wir sind*).[30] The significance of this notion can be roughly summarized as follows. Recognizing that our human efforts to understand are inescapably predisposed by previous experiences suggests something further about the relationship involved in understanding itself. That suggestion is that this is more a reciprocal relationship than a one-way relationship; whether one-way in the sense of transmission and passive reception, or of an assertive one-way mastery. Active in the relationship is a to-and-fro of anticipation and disclosure. Tradition in any of its engagements with human experience – for instance, in the form of a book being read, a film being watched, a teacher talking about the suffragette movement – *says* something to one's human understanding. Moreover, it unavoidably calls forth a response – however mild or intense – from the person addressed. What is at play here is a conversation, Gadamer rightly points out, even if no words are uttered aloud. So even if the response of the learner is an unvoiced dismissal – a silent 'that says nothing to me' – it is still a response, coloured by a host of predisposing influences. And where the response can be elicited further, as in a subsequent conversation about the book or film, or by a teacher in a more formal learning environment, some of the prior influences are brought to explicit awareness. In becoming conscious of these, further questions are likely to be prompted on the part of the learner; questions that are put in turn *to* tradition: to a teacher as an immediate face of tradition, or to what the author has written, or to the issues addressed to one in a film. What is true here of tradition as literary and artistic works is also true of tradition in the form of mathematical or scientific accomplishments, and indeed of everything that addresses human understanding through newly encountered influences of all sorts.

In Chapter 3 we drew on Michael Oakeshott's lively depiction of subjects of study as voices, each voice having acquired 'a specific character and manner of speaking of its own'. Within each voice, moreover, Oakeshott points out that 'further modulation is discernible'[31]. Such modulation can break new ground through the enquiries and debates that help to develop each subject at the frontiers of research, and can add to its riches as an inheritance of learning. More significantly for our purposes here, this modulation can also occur through normal educational practices, when these bring the voice of one or other subject into an environment of learning in a conversational way. The energies released in such genuine events of conversation are strikingly described by Oakeshott's remark about thoughts of different species taking wing and provoking each other to fresh exertions.[32] Becoming proficient in a range of voices in such conversation, Oakeshott emphasizes, lies at the heart of any endeavour worthy of the name education: 'Education, properly speaking, is an initiation into the skill and partnership of this conversation in which we learn to recognize the voices, to distinguish the proper occasion of utterance, and in which we acquire the intellectual and moral habits appropriate to conversation.'[33] Needless to say, this is not what chiefly goes on in most schools and colleges. But this admission itself calls attention to how successive forms of custodianship of teaching and learning have promoted widespread attitudes and practices that are strangers to such conversation and its possibilities.

To regard cultural tradition as a kind of conversational partner, and to regard education mainly as a dialogue with tradition, is to place a central emphasis on actions of exchange as distinct from actions of transmission and reception. Gadamer realizes that it may seem odd to regard cultural inheritances, very many of which are preserved in written texts, as conversational presences. In this connection, he writes: 'It is true that a text does not speak to us in the same way as does another person. We, who are attempting to understand, must make it speak.'[34] This, he says, is not an arbitrary business of forcing the text to one's will. Rather, it is made possible only by the kind of familiarity and fluency that close and attentive reading, accompanied by critical self-reflection, makes possible. 'The anticipation of an answer presumes that the person asking is part of the tradition, and regards himself as addressed by it.'[35] Coming to regard oneself in this way is not an overnight achievement. It is the product of unforced advances in familiarity and fluency; of finding that one or more aspects of cultural tradition are quite naturally taking up more of one's inter-ests and efforts. Such aspects of tradition, we need to remember, could range from Spanish history and literature to woodworking, from biology to art, from religion to music. This is a form of self-education (*sich-erziehen*) that, at its best, becomes part of the settled tenor of one's ways. It may take place outside of formal education, but it can also be initiated and guided, or alternatively frustrated or undermined, by formal education. For many, it gets under way in only a few circumscribed areas of their lives.

The conversational stance in relation to tradition that Gadamer describes contrasts in some key respects with what MacIntyre calls 'knowing how to read antagonistically' in defence of one's own standpoint. It is more a contrast of emphasis than a fundamental disagreement about the nature of tradition and of humankind's relationship to tradition. Yet the contrast is a decisive one whereby practices of learning and of the cultivation of learning are concerned. In both the conversational and the combative approaches, there is an active interest in new voices; voices, that is to say, other than those with which one has become familiar, or which one has come to cherish. A major purpose in MacIntyre's scheme of things is 'to enter into controversy', to 'test and retest' one's own views against 'strongest possible objections', to 'exhibit what is mistaken' in rival standpoints in the light of one's own understanding. In the case of Gadamer, the approach is more exploratory than combative. That is not to say that controversy is thereby avoided. In fact, it is to uncover conflict and its underlying dimensions to the best of one's ability, but yet to experience conflict differently than as a protagonist. It is to dwell among issues more with anticipations of discovery and illumination than with thoughts of defence and attack. It is to be open ever anew to surprise, sometimes shock, at what can be disclosed about the world when experienced attentively. Among various disciplines of study, or voices of tradition to speak with Gadamer and Oakeshott, such disclosures are abundant. They include instances of inspiring greatness and calculating deceit, of noble compassion and breathtaking cruelty, of which humankind's efforts have shown themselves to be capable.

When considered as educational orientations, both approaches 'make texts speak' in ways that quicken the responses of learners and teachers alike. Both look promising if one wishes to bring tradition to active life and to infuse educational experience with a rich, imaginative quality. This quality, in both cases, is something incomparably richer than what is dreamt of in the 'quality assurance' approaches that have pervaded Western educational systems in recent decades with an elaborate machinery of performative evaluation. Yet despite the many shared attributes of MacIntyre's and Gadamer's approaches, the quality in question is different in each case, because a partisan approach makes texts speak differently, or to different purposes, than does a conversational one. Over the course of a extended period of study, a partisan orientation would have quite different consequences for learning, and for one's beliefs and outlooks, than would a conversational one. Recalling some of the arguments made against custodial conceptions of education in the early chapters, I want to suggest here that a conception of tradition such as MacIntyre's can hardly avoid becoming a form of custodianship. Notwithstanding its assured boldness, it is a weaker candidate for defensibility on educational grounds than is its conversational cousin. This becomes clearer when both are explored in the context of educational practice itself, and this exploration will be our chief concern in the next chapter.

9   Giving voice to the text

Texts as active presences

Can conformist tendencies be eliminated from the cultivation of learning? Kant provides an intrepid answer in his seminal essay 'An Answer to the Question: What is Enlightenment?', which was first published in 1784. He states: 'Enlightenment is man's emergence from his self-incurred immaturity.' Such immaturity he describes as 'the inability to use one's own understanding without the guidance of another.'[1] There is an energy-building attractiveness about Kant's answer. It manifests the spirit of challenge and the bright hopefulness of the Enlightenment itself; the anticipation that centuries of servile compliance with authoritarian tutelage might finally yield to the blossoming of the rational autonomy of each person.[2] We have already seen, however, that disposing of prejudice is a more intractable affair than Kant and the inheritors of the Enlightenment legacy supposed. The insight that 'we belong to history before it belongs to us' is unknown to Kant's thinking. Had he encountered the force and pursued the consequences of this insight, he could scarcely have claimed so much as he did for the powers of human reason. We are now more conscious of the limitations arising from human finitude and from the embeddedness of human experience within history. We have to acknowledge that even the detection, not to speak of the critical appraisal, of all of the previous influences at work in human understanding presents insurmountable difficulties. Such influences, as previously noted, include prejudices, both in the sense of prejudices against and prejudices for something. They also include preconceptions, presuppositions and prior assumptions of diverse sorts. All of these constitute the predisposed context from which a person's efforts to understand necessarily arise.

Far from forcing us to a relativist position, the more compelling conclusion to be drawn is that predisposing influences are simply the conditions that enable us to understand anything new. This, as philosophical researches increasingly acknowledge, is just an inescapable truth about the human condition.[3] But this enabling could also work negatively, and thus be a *dis*abling; as for example where one is unaware of some of one's preconceptions, or where one has an obdurate attachment to one's own outlooks. By contrast, where one is committed to practising a discipline of self-criticism, one's prior influences and their assumed preferences are likely to come to light more openly in one's encounters with others. Such a discipline is probably the best means of identifying invidious forms of bias and of keeping them in check in one's relations with others. It is the kind of discipline that can be recommended to educators, not least because it is conducive to promoting environments of learning that have an invitational or participatory character.

For all its merits, however, in alerting teachers to the possibilities of conformism and overlooked bias in their relations with students, this self-critical discipline hasn't touched so far on another source of bias, namely texts. Texts are a major feature of students' experiences in schools and colleges. In virtually all subjects, moreover, they furnish ready-made theories and opinions, and countless items of knowledge and information. Texts are already replete with their own inbuilt biases, but they cannot apply to themselves the kind of self-critical discipline that conscientious teachers might practise. The same is true of video recordings, websites and other such already-published materials. The frequently overlooked perils of textual bias are compounded wherever the text rather than the teacher is in the driving seat; where teaching, as the popular phrase puts it, is 'textbook-driven'. Students, in consequence, frequently believe their main task to be the taking-in and memorizing of key parts of the texts – although not usually verbatim memorization – for reproduction in examinations and tests.

Such a situation is arguably more invidious – i.e. more prejudicial in an injurious sense – than the 'apparent inconclusiveness of all argument outside of the natural sciences', which MacIntyre criticizes as the lot of students in liberal universities. It is also probably much more common, particularly in light of the renewed importance given to examinations and tests in international educational reforms since the 1980s. Committing a text to memory for extrinsic purposes, whether for an examination, a quiz, or other purpose, is, on the face of it, a form of non-encounter with the text. The text, in this instance, apparently has nothing to say to the reader. It may provide items of information for the extrinsic purposes that are highest in the reader's mind, but it seems that nothing much else of significance is happening. This, however, would be a wrong conclusion to draw. Recalling here Dewey's comments on collateral learning, and those of Heidegger and Gadamer on preconceptions that are acquired inconspicuously, it is very unlikely that the text that is read for extrinsic purposes communicates no more than pieces of information for short term, or even longer term, utility. Enduring attitudes of one kind or another are also invariably picked up, and, as Dewey rightly points out, these are what really matter for one's education in the longer term. As examples of this, one can still hear adults today talk of their dislike of Latin, or more particularly, their abiding dislike of Cicero or Virgil, despite the fact that it may have been a high grade in Latin that enabled them a generation or more ago, to matriculate and progress to university. In only a few instances are Virgil or Cicero remembered for their literary merits by yesterday's teenage students for whom they were required reading in school. Where they are, the memory is probably of something cherished as it brought to life again, as in Steiner's evocations of Ovid in Chapter 5 above. Where they are not, however, what is brought to life is more likely to be a memory of endless recitation, tedium and of punishments for failure to learn.

The bringing-to-life of texts, and of the different voices of tradition that seek to speak through them, is what is at issue if one seeks to 'make the text speak'. It presents an additional challenge to the teacher to that of keeping a vigilant eye on the biases active in his or her own experience. Making the text speak is not only a question of trying to bring about an engagement of heart and mind between the students and what the text seeks to say. It also means being vigilant about the play of prejudices that is also brought to life in this event; prejudices that lay previously dormant behind inscriptions on a page. In the teaching of history, for example, it is not an overly difficult task to evoke for students the turbulent world of the European Reformation, even if prescribed text-books present a pre-digested account in terms of 'the main causes', 'the main events' and 'the main consequences'. Where the acrimonies that actually constitute such causes and events are brought to life, however, as distinct from just memorized for recall, the stakes are also raised. The students are more likely now to treat the issues as live ones – possibly to identify with one or other side; perhaps to conclude that Popes Julius II and Leo X were villains and that Luther was admirable in all respects, or *vice versa*. Questions like the following illustrate some ways in which the stakes are raised in this instance by making the history text speak: What is the teacher to do here in the face of urgent questions about whose side was in the right? Should the teacher provide an account roughly in accordance with his or her own conclusions in the mat-ter? If so, are these conclusions coloured more by personal allegiances than by historical evidence on the teacher's part? Or should the teacher deliberately pursue a middle course? Or take a definite stance of neutrality? Couldn't such sensitive issues be thankfully evaded by putting the text and its handling of the matter firmly in the driving seat, and by concentrating attentions on the kinds of questions that typically come up in examinations?

The sciences provide no less intriguing examples. In the teaching of biology, for instance, the text's presentation of an apparently inert body of ideas can be transformed in the hands of an imaginative, resourceful teacher. This happens when the teacher's efforts succeed in bringing students to experience, as insid-ers, the fecundity of the theory of evolution, or the fascinating possibilities of biotechnology; when the students come to discover, even in rudimentary ways, something of the scientist in themselves. As students begin to understand biol-ogy from *within*, however, the stakes are similarly raised. A host of questions are now likely to arise, as issues that are presented matter-of-fact in the text-book are encountered in class or laboratory as live ones. For instance: Doesn't an evolution theory rule out other explanations of the development of living things, especially religious explanations? What gives humans the right to experiment on other species? If economic development invariably leads to the destruction of natural habitats, why is this allowed to continue? An abundance of further examples can be found in these and other subjects – in geography, economics, physics, modern languages, design technology; even in apparently neutral subjects like mathematics.[4] They are unlikely to be uncovered, however, unless, in each case, 'the text speaks'; unless it succeeds in saying something significant to the sensibilities of a particular group of learners.

It is already apparent that the 'text' here is to be understood not merely as written material that is studied, but as the product of human strivings and accomplishments in various fields; in other words, live experiences and achievements that have been preserved in written or other form. Making the text speak means not only bringing to life one or more voices, but also bringing *to light* a particular context from within which these voices speak. It is this twofold enactment that gives an event of teaching and learning its particular significance. It does so by enabling the learner to experience the world differently, or to experience a world different from the familiar one of everyday experience. The learner, in other words, enters a new imaginative neighbourhood and gradually becomes more familiar with some features of that neighbourhood. In further explorations, additional features of the neighbourhood are noticed. The learner becomes progressively acquainted with the more influential voices in this region, or field, but also with its recurring tensions and disputes. And becoming more at home in the field, the student may also perceive that certain voices are currently out of fashion, or are marginalized, or even silenced.

It would be unfair to expect that a student would achieve this kind of discerning fluency in engaging with texts as active presences, unless of course he or she has chosen a particular field for special study. The teacher, however, needs this kind of critical discernment in his or her relationships with the subject or subjects being taught. It is not something that can be mastered overnight. But decisive first steps towards it can be taken in the early stages of teacher education, where this is adequately conceived and carried out. But the foundational stages of teacher education can also take decisive steps in contrary directions; for instance, as a proprietorship, or custodianship, of minds and hearts, whether in potent or milder forms. These initial steps have the most far-reaching consequences for how texts actually speak through a teacher's actions during the course of his or her career; that is to say, consequences for what comes to be experienced by teachers and learners alike when texts come to life, or fail to do so, in classrooms and other environments of learning.

Pedagogical challenges in voicing the text

We need to probe a bit further then the contrasting positions of MacIntyre and Gadamer on understanding and tradition, and especially on texts as a key part of tradition. Summarizing the essentials of their positions so far, the matter can be put like this. Gadamer's explorations disclose that what one brings to an event of understanding is invariably coloured by a cluster of prior assumptions, and that these inter*play* with new influences from tradition, in its experienced diversity (*Überlieferung*).[5] By becoming self-critically alert, the learner can progressively improve in detecting these prior assumptions, especially as they are brought to light in encounters with others. Many of these assumptions might, in any case, be presuppositions that enable a more open encounter with tradition than prejudices that disfigure or disable it. When practised as a discipline, this alertness promotes in the learner an appreciation that his or her most fruitful efforts will probably always be partial, both in the sense of being incomplete and being biased. Among the main educational consequences of this for a learner would be: first, to cherish those beliefs, outlooks and convictions that are the fruits of one's learning to date, and that have so far withstood one's own critical scrutiny and that of others; second, to see learning itself as the recurring opportunity to experience new discoveries and to lessen the burden of partiality. In short, the opportunity to understand more, to understand better and to be ever disposed to learn anew.

MacIntyre's position parallels this insofar as he acknowledges that understanding is always coloured by predisposing influences. Gadamer includes, in tradition (*Überlieferung*), the full diversity of what addresses human experience in new events of understanding. MacIntyre also acknowledges this diversity but he perceives it differently. For him, tradition is seen more as a range of rival traditions, each with its internal coherence, its recognized virtues and its claims to truth. MacIntyre gives a prominence to contest between traditions that Gadamer doesn't, although Gadamer is no less attentive to the conflicts that arise from plurality in human understanding and interpretation. MacIntyre points out, moreover, that even where a tradition is 'in good order', it embodies 'continuities of conflict', but that this conflict is now contained within limits by the shared beliefs of those who are committed to that particular tradition. The most significant difference between Gadamer and MacIntyre, however, touched on just lightly in the last chapter, concerns the nature and quality of one's experienced relationship to tradition. MacIntyre insists that 'genuinely to adopt the standpoint of a tradition thereby commits one to its view of what is true and false and, in so committing one, prohibits one from adopting any rival standpoint'.[6] This highlights the more combative character of MacIntyre's stance, as distinct from the more 'conversational' emphasis in Gadamer's.

Bringing these comparisons to bear on the experience of reading texts, the first point to note is that no reading of a text can be neutral. This much, at least, can be agreed. All readings involve interpretation, and interpretation is coloured in each case by the preconceptions and other influences that the reader carries in her mind and heart, and that are actively called into play as the reading proceeds. Suppose we also agree, just for the sake of argument for the present, that a national curriculum council for schools, or a university faculty of humanities, has done its best to be even-handed in selecting a 'great books' curriculum.[7] Their declared aim is to provide a curriculum that represents 'the best of what has been thought and taught' – in this case, in Western civilization through the ages. MacIntyre maintains that such a curriculum, notwithstanding the good intentions of its designers, will abandon the students to their 'prerational preferences', unless the texts in question are read – i.e. interpreted and taught – from within the standpoint of a particular tradition. His case is that, unless teachers intervene in concerted ways to guide the interpretations of the students along tradition-approved pathways, these interpretations will be confused. They will be guided – not by a tradition-free universal reason but by something much more unruly: the student's own preconceptions and prejudices, many of which might lie beyond their critical awareness. And he adds that selection of books, not just the teaching, must be done from the standpoint of a particular tradition.

When set out in this detail, MacIntyre's case can be seen to be a substantial one. Unfortunately, he doesn't illustrate the case with practical examples. If he did, its merits would become even more evident, but so also would its short-comings. To explore the case more fully then, we might consider a few such examples here. A text like a modern play might provide a familiar instance, but a better one might be a play from a pagan period – one that might fea-ture alike on a curriculum approved by a national body or a denominational college. Sophocles' famous play *Antigone* fits this purpose well.[8] To get the illustration under way, let us join the story just as King Creon has rejected all arguments that Antigone's life should be spared. He has condemned her to death for disobeying his order that the traitor Polynices must be refused the rites of burial. His decree is that she must be left out in the open for vultures to devour. Antigone has brought about her own downfall by insisting on car-rying out what she saw as her sacred duty. She repeatedly attempted to give her brother a proper burial, but was discovered and arrested on one of her later attempts. Some time after Antigone is led away, Tiresias, an old blind priest to whom Creon is much indebted, enters. Tiresias reminds Creon of the mon-strous character of the decree that Polynices should be refused burial rights. Creon angrily rejects the counsel of Tiresias, to the dismay, indeed horror, of the chorus and the others on stage. Tiresias himself is badly shaken by Creon's continued refusal. Amid rapidly rising tension, he gathers his thoughts and he speaks again – this time, his 'yet unspoken mind', calling attention to the ter-rible consequences that portend. He points out that the city of Thebes has been scandalized by Creon's act, but has also been inspired by Antigone's piety and bravery. More ominously, he reveals that his own religious offerings have just that morning been rejected and this means that the Gods will take a terrible revenge on the city if Creon's order is not revoked. Tiresias' second speech has the desired effect. But it is too late – for Antigone, for her intended husband Haemon (Creon's only remaining son) and for Creon's wife Eurydice.

What kinds of interpretations might an 'unguided' reading of the play yield among its first-time readers. They might include the following, and many more: (a) regarding the play as a whole: a tragic battle to the last between two determined wills; a far-fetched story but a gory one; a warning that you don't mess with things sacred; (b) regarding king Creon: an obstinate despot who was puffed up with his own power and importance; a leader caught badly in a 'no-win' situation; an inexperienced monarch who tried too hard to prove himself before his subjects; (c) regarding Antigone: a stirring example of a woman 'speaking the truth to power'; a person who put family loyalties before politics and paid the ultimate price for doing so; a brave but stupid woman to do what she did, because when you're dead you're dead and the kind of burial you get is irrelevant; (d) regarding Tiresias: a kind of witch-doctor character who could see nothing that was there but everything that wasn't; a sage whose physical blindness might have made him more perceptive in other ways; the guy with the religious bag of tricks who could really call the shots, but who could have saved a few lives if he showed up earlier.

This sample of interpretations reveals something of the diversity of preconceptions that modern readers might bring to their reading of the play. Some of these interpretations show little appreciation of the context of the play; some fare little better when it comes to the attributes of the characters or the significance of the plot. For educational purposes, subsequent readings of the play, or preferably viewing it performed, might promote a deepening engagement of the learners with the characters, the issues and the context of the play. In other words, the learners might come to appreciate how the language of the play carries, in a vibrant way, the honoured traditions of a fourth century BC city in Greece. But, for MacIntyre, these subsequent readings would be guided by a teacher whose own commitment to a particular moral tradition would privilege certain interpretations and eschew others. The importance of this point can be underlined by considering more closely the peculiar kind of language of a text from another time – including its idioms, its common assumptions, its evocations, its force or gentleness, and so on. That language, even when translated into one's own vernacular, retains its strangeness and its emotional intensity (and here we are leaving aside the question of what might be lost in the translation). It is the 'language-in-use' of a bygone time and place. It speaks from elsewhere and it summons the reader to that different neighbourhood.

MacIntyre draws an insightful distinction here between language and language-in-use. A language-in-use defines a particular community of speakers at a particular place and time: 'Latin-as-written-and-spoken-in-the-Rome-of-Cicero … Irish-as-written-and-spoken-in-sixteenth-century-Ulster.' This he contrasts with modern internationalized languages – including English, Spanish, German and Japanese – that have become 'potentially available to anyone and everyone, whatever their membership in any and no community'.[9] He argues perceptively that to learn a community's language-in-use is to learn at the same time 'the paradigmatic uses of key expressions', 'the model exemplifications of the virtues' and 'the legitimating genealogies' of the community.[10] It is to be initiated into the traditions of that community.

In the case of the play *Antigone*, making the text genuinely speak does not mean making the readers proficient insiders in the language-in-use of ancient Thebes. It means, rather, enabling the learners to dwell, if only for a while, and if only vicariously, in the arresting presence of this 'language-in-use'. To say 'vicariously' here does not mean to dwell 'light-heartedly', or 'flippantly', but rather as wholeheartedly as possible, while knowing that one's experience returns, hopefully all the richer, to one's own time and place. Such dwelling-awhile in the world opened up by the text cultivates the kind of productive tension that Gadamer's ill-fitted phrase – 'fusion of horizon' (*Horizontzvershmelzung*) – seeks to capture. As suggested earlier, it is more a frisson than a fusion; an ongoing to-and-fro between one's own assumptions and those of a previously unencountered world of belief and action. This active interplay provides fresh inspirations for a challenging and deepening of one's self-understanding. It also gives pause to tendencies towards a self-assured superiority, or certainty, in one's beliefs and outlooks. It is the reverse, if anything, of the assimilation of one horizon to another that the phrase 'fusion of horizon' might suggest. In fact, this kind of assimilation is more likely to occur just where the import of MacIntyre's fine insights on language-in-use is occluded by one of his most controversial points: where an authoritative reading of the text is provided for students from the standpoint of one particular tradition.

Other prominent examples from 'great books' curricula include the language-in-use of Shakespearean plays. The tragedies periodically refer, with fearful seriousness, to past terrors and those yet to come. For instance, from *Hamlet*: 'In the most high and palmy state of Rome, A little ere the mightiest Julius fell, The graves stood tenantless, and the sheeted Dead did squeak and jibber in the Roman streets.'[11] Or to take Plato's most famous dialogue, the *Republic*, its language-in-use is that of Athenian citizens who at one point propose the most far-reaching censorship of poets and artists, in order to purge the state from the laxities from which it suffered. If modern readers of such texts understand what is said in the language, but fail to hear or understand the language-in-use, then their reading of the text will have largely been a failed encounter. The references to ominous happenings in *Hamlet*, or *Macbeth*, or *King Lear*, will seem like pieces of superstition, although perhaps quaint ones. Similarly, the musings of Plato's characters about censorship will likely seem significant chiefly as affronts to democratic principles.

Efforts to make the text speak therefore involve close attentiveness to the dangers that go with considering the play being studied (or any other such text) in isolation from its historical context. More positively, such attentiveness highlights, in each case, the singular ethos of such contexts, including their defining cultural, political and religious features. In the case of Sophocles' *Antigone*, becoming more conversant with the play's language-in-use gradually brings home to the readers the salient features of life as experienced in a *polis* such as ancient Thebes. It discloses the peculiar significance given to things such as burial rites and their proper performance, to one's patriotic duty to one's *polis*, to religious observances and sacrifices to the Gods, to loyalty to family members and their memory, to obedience to the rulers, to the reprehensibility of traitorous acts, to resolute courage in the face of mortal danger, and so on.

However, sensitivity to a text's language-in-use does not mean that priority must be given to one particular tradition's readings of the text. On the other hand, neither does it imply that a text can be read from the standpoint of some supposed universal rationality. MacIntyre claims, however, that the kind of reading typically given to books in institutions of modern learning is a 'distortion by translation out of context'. The appeal to truth underlying the original author's endeavours, and the historical experience out of which the text has been written, 'disappear from view' in such readings, or at most are referred to as 'an exploratory appendage'. Thus the text itself is 'rendered contextless'.[12] He believes this to be an unfortunate but necessary consequence of an ethos of modern liberalism in institutions of learning. On this point, he is characteristically frank:

> There is thus a deep incompatibility between the standpoint of any rational tradition of enquiry and the dominant modes of teaching, discussion and debate, both academic and nonacademic. … Where the standpoint of a tradition involves an acknowledgement that fundamental debate is between competing and conflicting understandings of rationality, the standpoint of the forums of modern liberal culture presuppose the fiction of shared, even if unformulable, universal standards of rationality.[13]

Universal standards of rationality in such institutions work out in practice, MacIntyre believes, to be predominantly those of 'modern liberal culture' and 'modern liberal, individualist society'. Modern liberalism, MacIntyre argues, is heir to an Enlightenment legacy and, despite its trademark stance of opposition to tradition, has itself become transformed into a tradition. This tradition is prevalent in pluralist democracies, MacIntyre continues, not least in their institutions of learning. In its unacknowledged failure to find universal standards of rationality, it persists in behaving as if such standards existed, thus involving its adherents in interminable argument. Furthermore, it is a tradition which, 'for the most part precludes the voices of tradition outside liberalism from being heard'.[14] Even if they are heard, they are likely to be regarded as being irrational, or mythological, or not to be taken seriously.

The few examples we have explored from a 'great books' curriculum – or from a humanities curriculum more generally – bring out the substance and subtlety of a central aspect of MacIntyre's argument. First, with regard to substance, the examples help to show clearly that where an educational relation to tradition is concerned, the question of how texts are read and taught is at least as important as the question of what texts are selected for study. Second, with regard to subtlety, MacIntyre's investigations of the significance of language-in-use, and of the historicality of writing and reading themselves, show *why* the 'how' question is so important. As already suggested, however, the other key aspect of his argument, that teachers must adopt a combative stance in upholding a tradition to which they themselves adhere, is more problematic. MacIntyre links this controversial aspect closely to his keen insights on the predisposed nature of human understanding. It is important then to show that this link is unnecessary, and, from the standpoint of educational practice, that it is a mistaken one; that it takes from the fertility of MacIntyre's arguments as a resource for educational thought and practice.

Educational practice and its claim to universal defensibility

What would it mean to teach a play by Sophocles or by Shakespeare from within the standpoint of a particular tradition? At a minimum, it would mean that pride of place would be given to certain preconceptions rather than to others in the interpretations taking place in the readings of the play that a teacher shares with students. These privileged preconceptions might be very different in the cases of readings undertaken from within, say, a tradition of Marxism, Freudianism, feminism, post-modernism, liberalism or Christianity. More particularly, what does this say about the teacher's own reading of the play, prior to any sharing of interpretations with the students? What would be the features of this reading, and how would they influence the readings undertaken with the students? Also, how would these features influence the teacher's own relationship to the play? The teacher's reading of the play *for teaching purposes* would probably be something undertaken alone,[15] and would probably be accomplished in one, or a few sittings, in order to anticipate and clarify some important pedagogical questions. The teacher might already have studied the play as an undergraduate and might have seen it a number of times on stage or screen. But the teacher's new reading of the play for teaching purposes would be governed by different considerations from those of an undergraduate's reading, or at least by additional considerations. Reading the play for teaching purposes is attended by new responsibilities, as pedagogical considerations come much to the fore. Everything the teacher reads is now accompanied by questions such as: How will I handle this scene with the students? (e.g. Hamlet's rejection of Ophelia – the 'Get thee to a nunnery' episode from Act 3, Sc.i). Should I give my own interpretation first? Should I elicit students' interpretations first? Should I press the more reluctant students for their interpretations? Should I give my own interpretations at all? Should I highlight a few contrasting interpretations as plausible candidates?

If the teacher views his or her relationship to tradition as MacIntyre does, thus subscribing to the standpoint that teachers must speak 'as protagonists of one or other contending party', then decisions favourable to that party will have to be taken during the teacher's own reading of the play for teaching purposes. These decisions will subsequently steer the teacher's actions with the students in certain directions rather than others. In particular, whatever latitude the teacher might decide to allow in the voicing of contrasting interpretations by the students, the teacher will be conscious of an obligation in the final analysis to give his or her own authoritative interpretation; one that is consistent with the tradition to which the teacher is committed – Marxist, feminist, Christian, or other, as the case may be. And what goes for the teaching of a Sophoclean or Shakespearean drama here also goes for the teaching of any other question or topic – in the sciences, arts, technical subjects – wherever the students' emergent understandings in the form of value commitments are called into play. Regardless of the subject being taught then, all environments of learning that involve a teacher and a group of students are also environments of moral enquiry, to a greater or lesser degree.[16] The students' attitudes and beliefs may be engaged directly by issues in the topic being explored, or in a collateral way, to use Dewey's term, by the teacher's handling of the topic and of the students' responses to the topic. The frequent neglect by teachers of the collateral dimension is something that Dewey has rightly highlighted.[17] It can now be seen as a neglect with consequences that might be unwittingly aggravated by the strength of a teacher's loyalty to a particular tradition.

If being a protagonist on behalf of a particular tradition is granted pride-of-place in education, as it is in MacIntyre's scheme, then it becomes clear why he insists on the point that 'teaching is never more than a means'. Teaching is cast here as subordinate set of actions, owing its first loyalties to one or other contending tradition. On this account, teaching lacks an integrity that is associated with a practice in its own right. This is also consistent with two of MacIntyre's related claims that we reviewed in Chapter 3: that teaching is *not* a practice and that teaching does *not* have its own goods.

In short, MacIntyre's explorations of the significance of tradition for education yield incisive insights, but these are wedded to a conception of tradition itself, which is partisan at its roots. To say that the consequences of this are necessarily divisive – in the sense of cultivating mutual animosities between different social, religious and ethnic groups – is to draw too strong a conclusion. For instance, many denominational schools and colleges are not notably divisive in the sense just mentioned.[18] And it is unlikely that MacIntyre wishes to stimulate anything beyond 'an arena of conflict in which the most fundamental type of moral and theological conflict was accorded recognition'.[19] Yet the evidence of denominational conflicts in the history of education is a turbulent, and intermittently violent, one. This vexed history, and the re-emergence in recent years of 'faith schools' as an issue of public concern in some Western countries, augur ill for a stance on education as partisan as MacIntyre's. Be that as it may, things look scarcely more encouraging for MacIntyre's stance from a specifically educational standpoint, as distinct from a religious or political one. Educational practitioners will look in vain among MacIntyre's arguments for pedagogical insights that might be candidates in any universal sense for their occupational commitments; insights that would sustain teaching and educational leadership as a coherent, conversational art, notwithstanding the religious or political beliefs of practitioners themselves.

This last point highlights the necessity to clarify what constitutes *an educational standpoint as such*, as distinct, say, from a 'Marxist educational standpoint', or a 'feminist educational standpoint', or a 'post-modernist educational standpoint', and so on. By contrast with the common view that makes an educational standpoint itself dependent on one's religious, political or socio-economic beliefs, I would like to put explicitly now the case that has been much in rehearsal in previous chapters: There *is* such a thing as an educational standpoint in its own right. Not only does this have an integrity of its own, but also *a nonpartisan tradition of its own*. If this argument can be sustained and made more prominent, perhaps it can fare better in supplying what MacIntyre's partisan arguments, and those of anything which goes by the name of an 'ism' cannot supply – namely, ideas, insights, fertile suggestions, that can be candidates in a universal sense for the reflections and actions of teachers. The tenor of this book as a whole rests on the premise that there is such a standpoint, or family of standpoints, and that there is a recognizable tradition in which such standpoints are naturally at home. This tradition, which has distinct origins in the educational practices and convictions of Socrates of Athens, has of course been largely sidelined, even to the point of eclipse, in the long history of Western education. It has not been extinguished, however. In fact, it is likely that its inspirations flickered even during the most oppressive regimes, or in the darkest days of sectarian and other conflicts. In such circumstances, there were still some teachers whose work with learners, in childhood or at more advanced levels, proceeded on convictions that were Socratic in one or more important respects.[20] That is to say that the relationship of such teachers, both to students and to inheritances of learning, were marked by a renewed questioning engagement. Working often in isolation, and more than likely unobtrusively, it would be difficult for such teachers to recognize their work as belonging to anything as substantial as a distinct educational tradition. The writings of authors such as Rousseau belong clearly to this kind of tradition. But in varying degrees, so also do those of Pestalozzi, Froebel, Montessori and Dewey. This is so in view of the centrality they give to learning as a new beginning, and more particularly to the experienced quality of learning itself. For all their pedagogical richness, however, these writings do not make the integrity of teaching and learning an explicit theme, or give to educational thought and practice the distinctiveness of a tradition in its own right.

To focus anew on such a tradition here is not to engage in any nostalgia, or to claim that ideas from Greek antiquity can be applied to twenty-first century circumstances. Rather, it is to call attention to a range of attitudes and practices that have a claim of long ancestry to being educational before being anything else. It is to call attention, moreover, to the kinds of convictions that underlie these attitudes and practices. It is to show that such attitudes and practices, together with their underlying convictions, can be instanced in an inspirational, if not quite flawless, way in the work of Socrates with his students. It is to argue further that such attitudes and practices are not tied to a single time and place, but can flourish in different historical and social circumstances. It is to reveal that they can receive further illumination and new definition through the kinds of relationship to tradition (*Überlieferung*) that explorations such as Gadamer's uncover.

Bearing these points in mind, and recalling in particular the conversational cast of Gadamer's standpoint, we might now look again at MacIntyre's conclusion – which marries a relationship to tradition to the necessity for a partisan standpoint. MacIntyre's conclusion was: that to adopt the standpoint of a tradition 'commits one to its view of what is true and false' and that this commitment 'prohibits one from adopting any rival standpoint'.[21] From the standpoint of a non-partisan educational tradition, MacIntyre's argument might now be put as follows. Genuinely to adopt the standpoint of a tradition commits one to its view of what is true, in the sense of being worthy of one's deepest convictions. In being thus committed, one would not abandon these convictions lightly. Not surprisingly then, one would be likely to be predisposed against traditions with a contrasting view of what is true. But because of one's awareness of the incompleteness and bias that invariably mark even the best efforts of understanding, one would also be alert to the necessity to keep such predispositions in check. In practice, this would mean the necessity to place them at risk in encounters with others, and in all that one encounters in inheritances of learning. Finally, if one were an educator, one would first of all be conscious of the continuing necessity to renew one's conversations with such inheritances. Second, one would be also conscious of the desirability of exchanging the fruits of such conversations, in age-appropriate ways, with different groups of learners.

To speak like this is to identify the convictions that lie at the heart of a tradition that is educational in its own right. It is also to stress that such convictions yield practices of teaching and learning that make a claim to universal defensibility, but do so as candidates that recognize their own provisional or fallible standing. This has strong parallels to what Seyla Benhabib has called 'historically self-conscious universalism' and 'interactive universalism';[22] but only if the 'universalism' in question is understood as a beckoning kind of universality, as distinct from an 'ism' of any kind. The imperatives of a tradition that is educational before it is anything else are conversational more than combative ones. 'Conversational', it should be recalled, refers to the fluencies and moral energies required for a double engagement – first with a *range* of voices of tradition; second, with learners who are differently disposed and differently ready to attend to such voices. Such fluencies and moral energies define the relationships of learning that have been and remain our major concern in these chapters. The building and sustaining of such relationships as one's occupational way of life requires certain capabilities and dispositions rather than others. In particular, it calls for a fresh investigation of the question of teacher education.

10 Neither born nor made

The education of teachers

Disagreements about teacher education

There is a fairly widely held view that says 'teachers are born, not made'. Against that there is a more exclusive view that teaching is essentially a matter of an assured fluency on the teacher's part in the subject being taught. This latter view, which overlooks pedagogical considerations, has been quite common until recent times in universities and academic secondary schools. At its most precious, it regards good teaching as that which occurs when students assemble to overhear a dedicated scholar communing with his or her muse. They catch something of the Olympian drama as it were, although essentially as spectators. Now for all its self-preoccupation, this viewpoint emphasizes an often-overlooked aspect of teaching that we explored in Chapter 3 – namely, the active character of the teacher's relationship to the voices of the subject being taught. But it quite neglects the point that these voices seek to engage students through the quality of the teacher's own enactments and the teacher's pedagogical accomplishments more generally. This exclusive view waned, but didn't disappear, as universal post-primary education became the norm, and later as students from an unprecedented diversity of backgrounds began to fill institutions of higher education.

'Born teachers' are seen as those who can take such diversity in their stride – who are ever-resourceful and innovative in their handling of learning relationships, even the trickiest. The qualities that make a 'born teacher' are characteristically taken to be attributes that one possesses as a form of giftedness, as when it is said that someone is a 'born artist' or a 'born athlete'. To be a 'born teacher' is thus to be favoured in some way by nature. Unfortunately, such attributes are not bountifully enough distributed among populations to enable 'born teachers' to be found for all the teaching that needs to be done. It has long been recognized that efforts have to be made to nurture these attributes, and to bring them to high levels of accomplishment, through teacher education programmes. Yet the second half of the declaration cited at the start – 'teachers are born, *not made*' – raises a question as to whether such efforts can really be successful; or even if they are, whether they can achieve anything more than second best.

In this connection, it is sobering to recall that the history of teacher education in most anglophone countries is a frequently vexed one, beset by recurring
controversies. It ranges from the 'model schools' of the nineteenth century to
the reform efforts of recent time springing from 'competencies' approaches.
A critical survey of that history reveals a number of prevalent themes, among
which the following three remain central: (1) contrasting conceptions of how
pedagogy should properly be understood, and what it should accomplish;
(2) controversies over how teacher education should be designed and carried
out in practice; (3) battles over who should control teacher education and how
that control should be exercised. A thorough review of such themes would run
to a large volume, with many instructive instances of ideological acrimony,
institutional power struggles, moderate advances and missed opportunities.
A summary review is all that is feasible for our present purposes, drawing from
time to time on an ever-expanding bibliography.

Let us begin the review with the first of the three themes: contrasting conceptions of how pedagogy should properly be understood, and what it should
accomplish. In the model school era of the nineteenth century, teacher education, or more precisely, teacher training, was perceived as being necessary only
for primary teachers. It was based closely on the idea of apprenticeship. Where
the formation of the trainee teachers' attitudes was concerned, this included a
strong habituation into a culture of deference, acquiescence and emulation. As
for teaching practices, learning by rote was predominant, with a major reliance
on repetitive drill. Pupils were to be taught as a single group in large classes,
although some of the more able pupils might be called on to act as 'moni-
tors', or assistants, who might take sub-groups of pupils for specific tasks and
periods as instructed by the teacher. Questioning was to be used essentially as
a form of testing, or keeping pupils on their toes, rather than as a strategy for
provoking further thinking and learning. Idleness and playfulness were to be
shunned in the classroom. Discipline was to be strict, with recourse to corporal
punishment for any serious infringements. What the work of teaching could
accomplish would be assessed chiefly by tests and examinations based closely
on prescribed syllabuses and textbooks.

Conceptions of teaching in marked contrast to this had been introduced in
European educational thinking by Rousseau in the late eighteenth century.
These were developed by Kant, Pestalozzi, Herbart, Froebel and others into
the nineteenth century. Despite their many differences, these latter currents
of thought had, at their heart, an investigative approach to learning and its
promotion. They shared an opposition to paternalistic conceptions of teaching,
which tended to lose sight of the experienced quality of learning. Although
ideas from such authors were making some headway in parts of Continental
Europe, they were largely strangers to teacher education in English-speaking
countries. Many of them were given a fresh and original articulation in
America in Dewey's writings from the 1890s to the 1930s and became associated with the progressive education movement there. These ideas attained an
international prominence in educational debates, not least because of Dewey's

standing as one of the world's leading philosophers. The controversy fuelled by conflicting conceptions of pedagogy became more intense during the twentieth century, and especially between advocates of traditional and progressive education. Towards the end of his active life (1938), Dewey summed up the main dividing lines between the contesting parties as follows:

> To imposition from above is opposed expression and cultivation of individuality; to external discipline is opposed free activity; to learning from texts and teachers, learning through experience; to acquisition of isolated skills and techniques by drill is opposed acquisition of them as a means of attaining ends which make direct vital appeal; to preparation for a more or less remote future is opposed making the most of opportunities of present life; to static aims and materials is opposed acquaintance with a changing world.[1]

In his late works, Dewey stressed the necessity to think 'in terms of education itself rather than in terms of some 'ism about education, even such an 'ism as "progressivism"'[2] In an era when 'learner-centred' education is being increasingly embraced as a strategy to promote 'lifelong learning' in the 'knowledge society', much of the dust is finally settling on arguments about Dewey's pedagogy. For instance, his emphasis in the quotation above on a range of approaches that were once considered dangerously radical, would find much favour with current official demands that education should promote entrepreneurship and commercial innovation. In the field of teacher education, such demands have featured in an inconsistent way: on the one hand, an official discourse that acclaims individual initiative and enterprise, and on the other, official policy measures that promote compliant submission.

This brings us to the second theme: controversies over how teacher education should be designed and carried out in practice. The historical background for this theme, until comparatively recently, is essentially the same as that for the first theme: how pedagogy should properly be understood. Teacher training colleges gradually moved away from apprenticeship models of teacher education and, during the mid-twentieth century, sought to upgrade their programmes of initial teacher education to degree level or post-graduate diploma level. By the 1970s, this goal had largely been achieved. Linking these programmes to university studies increased the importance of theory in their composition, particularly the growth of 'foundation courses' in educational psychology, sociology of education, philosophy of education and history of education. But the new emphasis on theoretical studies gave rise to much disquiet by the mid 1980s. Some of this sprang from student teachers, who complained about a lack of relevance of 'theory' to their daily experiences in the classroom. Disquiet of a more ominous kind arose among politicians and educational administrators. These concerns were mainly of two kinds. First was the concern that a preoccupation with critique – Marxist, feminist, 'progressive' and other – was cultivating radical attitudes among student teachers that were inhospitable to the inherited traditions and work practices of schools. Second was the related concern that this very preoccupation with theory drew time and energy away from those basic skills of teaching that training programmes should promote to an acceptable degree of proficiency among student teachers.

Following the major Education Reform Act of 1988 in England, Wales and Northern Ireland, and despite recurring expressions of protest and dismay, successive waves of change in teacher education were enforced during the Conservative administrations of Thatcher and Major. Changes of a similar coercive nature were enforced to a greater or lesser degree in most anglophone countries, Ireland being a notable exception.[3] Among the main ingredients of these changes were: (a) a requirement to align the design of teacher education programmes to a range of specified competences (sometimes more than 90 competences); (b) a shift in the main location of many teacher education programmes from campus to school through new 'partnership' requirements; (c) the introduction of a hierarchical inspection system for teacher education programmes; (d) the reorganization of a university's or a college's funding for teacher education so as to tie the level of funding to the institution's performance on the new requirements. The more far-reaching consequences of these changes will be pursued in the next section of the chapter. What needs to be stressed here is that the reforms occasioned a major emphasis on practices of conformity in institutions of teacher education – an emphasis that was in conflict with that on innovation and entrepreneurship in the new official priorities for higher education as a whole.

As for the third theme, battles over the control of teacher education, the historical origins of these battles lie in conflicts between church and state. In many countries during the nineteenth century, France and Ireland being conspicuous examples, recurring acrimonies occurred between political and ecclesiastical powers over the control of training institutions. In France, the Napoleonic state made it clear, much to the chagrin of the Catholic church, that teacher education would answer to the state's priorities. Thus began a prolonged period of church–state tensions in education, examples of which still persist in a country that is among the most secular in Europe. In Ireland, Catholic authorities were unhappy from the start with teacher education establishments that were not under religious control. Through a persistent campaign from the 1850s, the denominational churches won successive concessions from the British administration until, by the mid-1880s, most teacher education for primary teachers was under denominational control.[4] Thus it remained for a century or more. But the sharp decline of church authority in recent decades in Ireland has meant that the once-strong denominational ethos of church-controlled teacher education colleges has effectively become a thing of the past.

In recent decades, the control of teacher education internationally has been gained by governments who became strongly wedded to a 'competences' approach. Versions of this approach have been prominent in the educational reforms of the last few decades. As we shall see, these have shown an attachment to doctrinaire policies that rivals, or in matters of enforcement often exceeds, the certainty and zeal of their nineteenth-century ecclesiastical predecessors.

Competences and the making of teachers

Early versions of 'competences' approaches were based on the assumption that teachers could not only be made, but that they could be made to a specified design, and an elaborate design at that. These approaches located their conceptual home in a behaviourist outlook. For behaviourism, anything that is significant in human action can be classified as one or other item of observable behaviour; observable, moreover, by operationally defined categories that employ pre-specified criteria. This latter requirement would seek to ensure maximum uniformity in the assessment of a piece of behaviour by more than one assessor. From its early pioneers such as Pavlov and Thorndike onwards, one of the central tenets of behaviourism is that behaviour that is rewarded becomes reinforced, whereas behaviour that is denied reward tends to disappear. On this kind of account, leadership and management become significant chiefly as sets of techniques that use rewards and disincentives to bring about changes in specific items of behaviour.

Variants of a 'competences' approach to teacher education had been around for many years, especially in parts of North America. But the enthusiastic embrace of the approach in the early 1990s as a policy measure by the then Department for Education for England and Wales marked an unprecedented departure. Dissatisfaction with teacher education programmes in the United Kingdom, and more particularly with their alleged left-leaning emphasis, was forcefully expressed in the publications of influential think-tanks such as the Hillgate Group and the Centre for Policy Studies.[5] These groups' wholehearted preference for free-market approaches to social policy, together with their aversion to anything that hinted of left-wing critique, found receptive ears within the Thatcher administration. In addition, a certain complacency among institutions of teacher education – that the future would remain much as the past had been – caught them off-guard and allowed a shift of historic proportions to take place with remarkable speed. By the end of the century, the landscape of teacher education had been transformed, not only in England and Wales but also in Northern Ireland, much of the United States, New Zealand, Australia, Canada and also some Continental European countries. Common to many of these reforms was the sustained enforcement of a 'competences' approach.

The case of Northern Ireland at the turn of the century provides a good illustration of such enforcement. As a part of the United Kingdom, it reflects the thrust of the key reforms in England and Wales; but as a later version, after the turmoil that arose from the first wave of enforcement on the other side of the Irish Sea had settled somewhat. In 1998, the Northern Ireland Department of Education issued a publication called *Northern Ireland Teacher Education Partnership Handbook.*[6] The *Handbook* listed a total of 92 competences, to which all programmes of teacher education would have to be aligned. The competences were grouped under five headings: (1) 'Understanding the Curriculum and Professional Knowledge'; (2) 'Subject Knowledge and Subject Application'; (3) 'Teaching Strategies and Techniques and Classroom Management';

(4) 'Assessment and Recording of Pupils' Progress'; (5) 'Foundation for Further Professional Development.' [7]

When closely examined, few of the 92 competences in the *Handbook* provide anything like the operational definitions one would expect. In fact, many of them are exemplars of ambiguity. For instance, under Section 1, 'Understanding of the Curriculum and Professional Knowledge' (25 competences), competence 1.3 reads: 'Demonstrates understanding of social, psychological and cultural influences in children's attainment.' Competence 1.8 reads: 'Demonstrates knowledge of the principles involved in fostering good discipline.' In relation to the first of these, problems persist even if one were to amend the text to read 'demonstrates a *rudimentary* understanding of the social, psychological and cultural influences etc.' Understanding this competence in a uniform way would still be very difficult. The same is true of 'the principles involved in fostering good discipline' mentioned in competence 1.8. Some might hold that such 'principles' are essentially connected with a system of punishments and rewards. Others might insist that any discipline worthy of the name arises from an unforced commitment by students to engage in the work in question. Ambiguities like this are evident in most of the 92 competences listed. Far from providing clearly defined examples of things that need to be mastered, the wide scope for interpretation here increases the power of enforcers and the anxieties of those on the receiving end of enforcement.

The main effects of such a policy are to force those involved in teacher education, both tutors and student teachers, to comply. However, compliance of this kind is characteristically laced with dismay and resentment. New policy regimes sweep aside the practical judgement that is properly native to educational practice. It becomes clear that long-held professional purposes, whatever their merits or shortcomings, now count for little.[8] But resentment itself is both interrupted and intensified by the practical necessity to adapt quickly to the newly required procedures and performances – procedures and performances that will be subject to detailed scrutiny when the inspectors call.[9] This kind of experience is a contemporary instance of the conquest and colonization referred to in Chapter 1 above. The professional demoralization to which it leads has been examined in much detail in the research literature dealing with the 1990s reforms in teacher education.[10]

Yet despite the determination with which reform programmes were implemented, the hopes of governments to recast teachers as compliant agents of official policy fell far short of original expectations.[11] To be sure, the academic autonomy enjoyed by teacher education institutions (especially in the UK) after their widespread reorganization as university level institutions during the 1970s has all but disappeared. The standardization wrought by the enforcement of competences approaches has seen to that. But the crucial fact remains that successive political attempts to reform teacher education, and education systems more generally, have done much more harm than good.[12] Their net effects include making teaching less attractive to those with an imaginative cast of mind, and a large-scale shift among the international research community, away from exploring the kinds of learning most promising for student teachers. Research energies here, as in other fields, are attracted to topics that are likely to draw resources from funding agencies – especially topics that give prominence to measurable outcomes or that fit comfortably with narrower conceptions of 'evidence-based research'.

Meanwhile, in policy-making quarters internationally, one can trace some new directions. 'Competences' have been quietly shedding their connections with a behaviourist rationale. They are becoming associated instead with something quite different: with new priorities for mutual recognition of qualifications between different countries in an age of globalization. The turbulent high tide of government-led reforms to underperforming teacher education would seem to have passed, and with it the more ardent desires of politicians and bureaucrats to remake teachers as foot-soldiers of a free-market credo. This is not to say that it has unequivocally dawned on decision-makers in such quarters that educational practice has an inherent integrity that deserves acknowledgement and respect. Rather, the rise of new policy priorities such as 'the knowledge society', and the appearance in new attire of older ones such as 'lifelong learning', has altered both the stakes and the rules. Fresh opportunities are thus presented for teacher education to join debate with policy-makers on a more favourable footing.[13]

Competences in a new context

In 2005, an OECD report was published with the lengthy title *Teachers Matter: Attracting, Developing and Retaining Effective Teachers*. This international report was based on extensive preparatory reports from 25 of the 30 OECD countries, and it highlighted the difficulties being experienced in most of these countries in attracting high-quality candidates to teaching. Among its strategies for remedy were measures to improve the image and status of teaching, to better the salaries and conditions of teachers, to provide more access routes to teaching and a more flexible career structure. It also favoured incentives, allowances and other rewards for more specialized or demanding kinds of teaching work.[14] Its diagnosis of the underlying necessity for such measures is revealing:

> A key part of any general strategy must involve reminding teachers that they are highly skilled professionals doing important work. Surveys from a number of countries report that teachers' self-image is relatively low, and indeed lower than wider public opinion of the value of their work.[15]

The finding that, in many economically developed countries, teachers' self-image is lower than the public's overall estimation of the value of their work betokens some malady in the self-understanding of teachers – evidently a chronic one. George Steiner might regard this as evidence for his 'gravediggers' remark about teachers, but one must look more searchingly for a context in which such a finding makes sense. That context has to be one where attitudes of servility and compliance are deeply ingrained in aspects of the professional cultures of teaching. Some ancestral reasons for such attitudes were investigated in Chapter 1 above, especially ones associated with the long history of hierarchical control in education in Western civilization. The important point to consider here, however, is that the compliance enforced by the international reforms of the 1990s marked a resurgence of such hierarchical control, although in more secular forms. *Teachers Matter* does not probe the reasons for the reported low self-image. But it makes the telling point that 'unless teachers are actively involved in policy formulation, and feel a sense of "ownership" of reform, it is unlikely that successful changes will be implemented'.[16]

In addition to its general strategies for pursuing the goals mentioned in its title, the *Teachers Matter* report also proposes specific measures, among which the following three are pertinent to teacher education: (a) providing a continuum of professional development opportunities for teachers within a lifelong learning perspective; (b) 'transforming teaching into a knowledge rich profession'; (c) introducing 'profiles of teacher competencies' derived from 'the objectives for student learning'. This last point catches the eye in a particular way. At first, it looks like a continuation of the controversial reforms of the nineties. This would be a misreading, however, despite the kind of official language that introduces the recommendation: 'There is widespread recognition that countries need to have clear and concise statements of what teachers are expected to know and be able to do, and these teacher profiles need to be embedded throughout the school and teacher education system.'[17] 'Competencies' in such profiles carry different connotations than the 'competence' central to earlier reforms (The word 'competences' is not used by OECD). *Teachers Matter* states that these profiles need to be widely supported by the teaching profession and that they might 'provide profession-wide standards and a shared understanding of what counts as accomplished teaching'. In essence, the necessities being stressed – for concise statements, for wide support for the profiles and for a shared understanding of what constitutes accomplished teaching – mark a clear shift from the behaviourist rationale informing the competences of the 1990s.

This shift is further in evidence when the other two recommendations are examined. In relation to a continuum of professional development opportunities, a framework of different standards for different stages of the teaching career is proposed. Teachers' own responsibilities for their continuing professional development would be accommodated in this framework, together with a system to support teachers' professional expectations beyond the initial preparation and induction phases of their careers. Similarly, the recommendation to transform teaching into a 'knowledge-rich profession' also seeks to involve teachers themselves in new ways. It places a particular emphasis on teachers as active analysts of their own practice and of their students' learning. This would mean a practical research dimension within teachers' everyday actions, and also keeping in touch with ongoing research on teaching and learning in order to enrich the 'evidence base for improved practice'.[18] Other professions, the report points out, are being continually changed by research activities, but teaching has not yet been affected on any large scale.

The new context into which the *Teachers Matter Report* places teacher competencies is similar in major respects to that being developed by bodies such as the European Commission. The educational priorities of the European Commission and European Council of Ministers are regularly reaffirmed as those of the 'Lisbon Strategy', more formally known as 'Education and Training 2010'. In this strategy, education and training are seen as vehicles for the EU's major goal 'to become the most competitive and dynamic knowledge-based economy in the world, capable of sustainable economic growth with more and better jobs and greater social cohesion'.[19] The European Commission has produced a number of documents to monitor the pursuit of these goals and to urge greater efforts by national governments to achieve them. The most important of these is the publication *Common European Principles for Teacher Competences and Qualifications*, issued in 2005. This concise document (five pages) provides the clearest evidence that the international policy context for the reform and development of teacher education is now populated by new concerns. These spring from the Lisbon strategy, although less conspicuously so than in previous EU policy documents. For instance, 'the cultural dimensions of education' are explicitly acknowledged on this occasion, and there is a reference to the teaching profession being 'inspired by values of inclusiveness and the need to nurture the potential of all learners'.[20] Just four 'common principles' are contained in this document and these are followed by just three 'key competences'. The document concludes with four 'recommendations to national and regional policy-makers' linked to each of the four principles.

The four Common European Principles are: 'a well qualified profession'; 'a profession placed within the context of lifelong learning'; 'a mobile profession'; and 'a profession based on partnerships'.[21] The three 'key competences' are then introduced chiefly as the capabilities needed to make the principles work in practice. These competences are: 'Teachers should be able to: work with others; work with knowledge, technology and information; work with and in society.'[22] A brief exploration of the substance of these principles and competences should reveal just how significant the change of context has become. Taking the four principles first, the 'well qualified profession' principle refers not only to the necessity for all teachers to be graduates from higher-education institutions, but also that they should be afforded opportunities to continue their studies to the highest level 'to develop their teaching competences and to increase their opportunities for progression within the profession'. This dovetails naturally with the second principle – 'lifelong learning' – that can be seen as regular opportunities for teachers 'to continue their professional development throughout their careers' and to innovate and use research evidence to inform their work.[23] The third principle – 'a mobile profession' – emphasizes the importance of student-exchange schemes to enable teachers and student teachers to spend time studying and working in countries other than their own. It also calls attention to the merits of a common framework for professional qualifications. The final principle – 'a profession based on partnerships' – high-lights the necessity for active collaboration between teacher education centres in universities and the schools, colleges and other learning environments where the students' teaching practice is carried out. On the European Commission's view, such collaboration should seek not only to ensure a mutual strengthening of the learning undertaken by student teachers on campus and on teaching practice; it should also seek to 'provide teachers with the competence and confidence to reflect on their own and others' practice'.[24]

Taking the three competences next, the first of these – 'teachers should be able to work with others' – begins by mentioning 'the values of social inclusion and nurturing the potential of every learner'. Other necessities included under this competence are: knowledge of human growth and development; self-confidence when engaging with others; being able to work with learners as individuals; being able to support learners to develop as active members of society; being able to work in ways that increase the collective intelligence of learners; being able to collaborate with colleagues to enhance their learning and teaching.[25] The second competence states that teachers should 'be able to work with knowledge, technology and information'. Under this heading, the particulars mentioned include: having a good understanding of subject knowledge and viewing learning as a lifelong journey; being able to access, analyse, validate, reflect on and transmit knowledge, making effective use of technology where appropriate; being able to build and manage learning environments; being able to retain 'the intellectual freedom to make choices over the delivery of education'; being able to integrate ICT effectively into learning and teaching; being able to learn from their own experience and to match a wide range of teaching strategies to the needs of learners.[26] The final competence stresses a requirement for teachers 'to work with and in society'. This mentions things such as: preparing learners as globally responsible EU citizens; promoting 'mobility and cooperation and encouraging intercultural respect and understanding'; 'understanding the factors that create social cohesion and inclusion'; 'being aware of the ethical dimensions of the knowledge society'; being able to work effectively with the local community and 'with parents, teacher education institutions, and representative groups'.[27]

From this brief overview of the 'common principles and competences', a few important conclusions can be drawn. The first of these is that the official disquiet that led to the sweeping reforms of the 1990s has yielded to a quite different outlook. The urgency to do something dramatic about an alleged failure of schools has been replaced by a more strategic concern – in fact, one marked more by a diplomatic than a penalizing stance towards teachers. This is the pan-European effort to mobilize energies at national levels to draw teachers into the mainstream promotion of the European Union's social and economic priorities. Of course, the frequent references to social exclusion, social cohesion, mobility of students and teachers, are reminders that the driving forces of this new generation of policy development are socio-economic policy goals, more so than educational ones. When viewed from an educational practitioner's standpoint, nevertheless, such forces are clearly more benign than the doctrines of the free market that gained an international ascendancy in educational policy quarters during the 1990s. Following the global economic downturn of 2008–2009, moreover, there has been an acceleration in the decline of ideas for social policy originating in such doctrines.

A second conclusion is that the references to partnership in the more recent policy discourse on teacher education carry more conviction than those in the reform measures of the 1990s. Those earlier references to partnership were effectively undermined by the tenor of reform policy itself. The more recent references have their political home in the European Union's efforts to build social cohesion, which themselves date back to the 1990s and have been backed by substantial 'structural' and 'cohesion' funding programmes since then.[28]

A third conclusion is related to this concern for partnership, although how important a factor it will be remains to be seen. In essence, it is a new recognition of the voice of educational practitioners as influential agents. This recognition is evident in the European Commission's observation on teachers having 'the intellectual freedom to make choices over the delivery of the curriculum'. It is also evident in the recurring references to teachers as innovators and teachers as researchers, as it is in viewing lifelong learning as the context for teacher education. Whatever about the infelicity of phrases like 'delivery of the curriculum,' there is a substantial degree of influential agency envisaged here for teachers. Among its more important possibilities is the opportunity for teachers to become key agents in shaping their own professional development; for instance, through working with universities and other agencies to promote workshops and learning networks, thus placing teacher education centrally in a lifelong learning context. This emphasis on partnership contrasts in all key respects with the downgrading occasioned by the elaborate checklists of competences in the first waves of reform, and with the inspection systems devised to police these reforms.

Finally, in proposing the measures they do, it is significant that neither the *Teachers Matter* report nor the Common European Principles make any prescriptions about the curriculum to be followed in programmes of teacher education. Unlike the first wave of reforms that intervened directly in such matters, the more recent policy discourse refrains from this and identifies, instead, important new challenges worthy of the efforts of teacher educators. The new context also provides opportunities for teacher educators to work with other agencies in tackling these challenges. The final section of the chapter will sketch some promising approaches to this work – approaches, moreover, that allow the integrity of educational practice itself to be advanced.

The quality of learning experiences in teacher education

Throughout this book, there has been a recurring emphasis on the experienced quality of learning. This contrasts both with the emphasis placed by quality assurance systems on procedures and policies and that placed by earlier 'competences' approaches on the listing and assessment of behaviours. Whatever the merits of such systems and approaches, something vital is bypassed if explorations of quality in educational practice fail to get inside the actions of teaching and learning themselves. It should also be clear that things such as performance indicators, because of their captivity to indexed measures, are ill-suited to discerning the experienced quality of learning. A growing awareness of points such as these has been evident in the international policy literature on teacher education in recent years, such as the OECD and European Commission reports that we considered in the previous section. The establishment or development of statutory Teaching Councils (e.g. Scotland, Northern Ireland, Wales, Ireland) or similar bodies (e.g. Ontario College of Teachers, New South Wales Institute of Teachers) has recently brought historic changes to the ethos of teacher education itself. Prominent among the changes is that powers formerly claimed by politicians and Ministries of Education are increasingly being exercised by the Councils (with the notable exception of England, where power continues to lie with the Teacher Training Agency). Typically, membership of the Councils includes a strong representation of teacher practitioners (sometimes over 50%), but also includes representatives from teacher educators, managerial bodies, parents, industry, trade unions and Ministries of Education. In recent years, the Councils have progressively shifted the focus of attention from the indexing of performance to the experienced quality of learning, both in initial teacher education and in continuing professional development.

To illustrate this point, it is worth looking again at the example of Northern Ireland, where, as we have seen, a performance system comprising a set of 92 competences was imposed in the late 1990s. By 2005, however, the Council, established in 1998, had effectively replaced this with a different rationale and a new set of foundations for the teaching profession in a pluralist Northern Ireland. The new rationale was set out in a major policy statement, titled *Teaching: The Reflective Profession*. The Introduction affirmed clearly a distinct 'sense of identity of teachers' and stressed this as 'an essential requirement for the exercise of professional autonomy'.[29] Claims for such recognition and autonomy had been officially silenced for more than a decade previously. The new self-assurance in *Teaching: The Reflective Profession* is also evident in its recasting of a competence approach. This recasting shows a keen awareness of the main directions of the European Commission's thinking and also of the OECD's, but it is bolder than either in its explicit rejection of the behaviourist logic underlying the earlier competence regimes:

> Teaching can never be reduced to a set of discrete skills to be mastered in some mechanical process of assimilation. To adopt such a reductionist approach would be to deny the intellectual basis of our work and the richness of the ongoing dialogue and learning that enhances our professional practice.[30]

It also becomes clear as one reads the document that the 'ongoing dialogue' mentioned here, and particularly dialogue with practitioners, is a regular feature of the Council's approach. A further feature is its placing of the newer European-style competence model within a rationale that stresses the inter-personal character of educational practice and the moral purposes of teaching. Accordingly, the Northern Ireland Council's 'Code of Values and Practice' is set out under the three following headings: 'Commitment to Learners', 'Commitment to Colleagues and Others' and 'Commitment to the Profession'.[31] These three sections of *The Reflective Profession* illustrate the Council's thinking on the expectations that should properly inform the conduct of teaching and learning. They also seek to relate such expectations to what the document has to say in its section on competences. In introducing this latter section, it points out that 'the Council rejects a restricted view of competences',[32] and stresses that their real value lies in providing a clearly recognized repertoire of teaching strategies on which the 'acquired professional judgement' of teachers would be exercised. A further merit of this approach, it argues, is that such a repertoire can be categorized into those that are appropriate to four identified phases of teacher education: initial, induction, early professional development and continuing professional development.[33] *The Reflective Profession* includes a total of 27 competences, reduced from the 92 in the 1998 *Handbook*, and now grouped under three main headings: 'Professional Values and Practice' (one entry – namely, the code itself); 'Professional Knowledge and Understanding' (12 entries); 'Professional Skills and Application' (14 entries). Exemplars of each of the competences are then provided for each of the four phases of teacher education, ranging from a basic proficiency in the beginning phases to sophisticated levels of accomplishment and co-operation in the later phases.

This review of the Northern Ireland example shows evidence of some pioneering work in the development of new approaches to teacher education – approaches that are also under way or being considered in other countries. The review has not focused specifically, however, on the actions of teacher educators themselves (as distinct from practitioners, Teaching Councils or other agencies) in these developments, and this issue now calls for attention before concluding this chapter.

The more recent contexts of teacher education that we have just been examining carry some strong parallels to the explorations of personal qualities and relationships of learning in Chapter 3 above. For instance, notwithstanding some differences between one Teaching Council and another, the newer contexts envisage three main dimensions in programmes of teacher education: (a) professional knowledge and understanding; (b) professional skills and attitudes; and (c) professional values and commitment. Retaining the sequence just outlined, this threefold division maps quite closely onto three of the relationships of learning that we considered in Chapter 3: the teacher's relationship to the subject(s) he or she is teaching; the teacher's relationship to learners; and the teacher's relationship to herself/himself (i.e. the teacher's self-understanding and occupational convictions). The fourth set of relationships that we considered in Chapter 3 – namely, the teachers' relationships to colleagues, parents and the public more widely – would most likely feature under (b) above. But it might also be distributed between categories, or might feature as a fourth category.

The critical point, however, is to understand *how* the categories established by statutory Teaching Councils relate to the relationships of learning as described in Chapter 3. To illustrate this, it is worth recalling in summary a few points from that chapter. The first of these concerns the flatness of any characterization of teaching that confines itself to an identification of skills, competences and human qualities, initially useful although such identification might be. In Chapter 3, it was argued that what captures the distinctiveness of teaching is how such skills and competences *get embodied in the relationships* that give instances of learning their experienced quality and flavour. The heart of teacher education is concerned with the *bringing about* of such embodiment. It is concerned with learning experiences – on campus and in school – that *cultivate* a high quality of relationship between the student teacher and the subject, between the student teacher and students, between the student teacher and parents, colleagues and others. In such learning experiences, skills and competences are not studied as theory and then applied in practice. On the contrary, the unpredictable challenges thrown up by experiences of teaching call the student teacher's attitudes and emotions – i.e. predispositions – into play in powerful ways. In other words, the experienced quality of learning-to-become-a-teacher involves a recurring turbulence – excitement, disappointment, anticipation, achievement, frustration and so on. This highly charged learning environment influences how and to what extent competences of any kind find a home in the teacher's self-understanding. Without an incisive appreciation of this point, what is called 'reflective practice' can become mainly a technique for the continual alignment of performances to competences conceived as performance indicators.

Competences, in short, can now take fertile root in experiences of learning that are themselves relationships of learning. Educational endeavours in such contexts are concerned less with the making of teachers to this or that design than with a certain kind of birth, or bringing-to-life. This is not to be confused with a 'born again' experience that accompanies certain religious conversions. Rather, it involves, on the part of teacher educators and their students, a commitment to proficiency in the imaginative work of the heart that has been a central theme of these chapters.

11 The new significance of learning

A different starting point

The opening chapter explored how education in Western civilizations lost its original identity as a practice in its own right and became largely subordinated to the more institutionalized interests in society. These were church interests at first, and for many centuries, but later more secular ones. The most recent turns in this story of colonization have been the international waves of educational reform of the last two decades. These have sought to realign education on a grand scale to the demands of a globalized economic order. As the twentieth century yielded to the twenty-first, this order had become fuelled by a profit motive quite shorn of the restraints previously placed on it by the Keynesian economic policies of most Western governments. Some might claim that this international realignment grants a historically new significance to learning, tailoring it now to a new range of strategic priorities. As the first decade of the twenty-first century draws to a close, they might also add that the new order of things has itself landed monumental economic and social crises at the feet of national governments and international agencies. But, in any case, where education is concerned, the realignment movement is more correctly seen as a new version of an already old picture. It does not grant a new significance to anything educational, although it may well do so to already colonized forms of learning.

By contrast, to speak of the new significance of learning *in educational terms* is to view education from a different perspective than any version of the colonization picture does. It is to start from the premise that educational undertakings, properly so called, constitute a coherent family of practices, and to pursue faithfully the consequences of that premise. This is chiefly what has been underway in this book so far. In summary, these consequences might be put as follows. First, the family of practices that constitute education has a distinct and distinguished ancestry, but a largely eclipsed one, in Western civilization. Second, the sustenance and renewal of such practices draw upon a distinctive tradition. In keeping with its Socratic origins, this is a tradition that is conversational rather than partisan in its self-understanding. Third, this tradition itself contributes best to human welfare when it is accorded public recognition and trust, enabling its benefits to the public to be the fruits of its own best inspirations. Fourth, the public's trust in education is best advanced where educational practitioners remain regularly accountable to the public, but for benefits that are born of educational practice itself. To put all of this concisely, learning attains a significance that is historically new to the extent that education is clearly acknowledged and carried out as a practice in its own right.

In the explorations of earlier chapters, we have already seen what this means for things such as the quality of relationships in teaching and learning, the experienced quality of learning itself and the kinds of care and love that teaching calls for. We have also reviewed, from this perspective, the uses of communications technology in learning environments, the self-understanding of teachers and, not least, the educational import of cultural tradition. In this chapter, the focus shifts to a range of concerns that affect the public as much as the teachers and students who are the insiders of educational practice. These concerns comprise such a long list – e.g. the aims of school curricula, policies for assessment and certification, education and the economy, education as a force for equality and justice, provision for special educational needs, parental rights in education, the purposes of higher research just to start with – that an exhaustive treatment is not possible. A few salient themes might be selected, however, as examples. Reviewing these in the light of our earlier investigations will provide practical illustrations of the different significance these investigations give, not just to the selected themes, but to educational thought and action more widely. The themes I propose to select are the following three, which include some grouping of the items just mentioned: curriculum development and the assessment of learning; equality and justice in education; and the relationship of higher research to economic policy.

Curriculum development and the appraisal of learning

Scarcely a more telling example can be shown of the subordination of education to external forces than where a Minister of Education can make changes at will to a school curriculum. Yet in more than a few Western countries, the first wave of reforms of the late 1980s and early 1990s saw Ministers of Education assume such powers in sometimes dramatic ways.[1] It is in the nature of school and college curricula, of course, that they must develop, not merely to reflect advances in knowledge, but also advances in pedagogy. It is also likely that that the development of curricula will always be an arena of some disagreement, even if the influence of those with proprietorial designs on the minds and hearts of learners can largely be kept at bay. And it is here that a more discerning kind of educational reform can prove crucial. In some countries, for instance, national curriculum councils have been instituted to place the task of curriculum development at a remove from politicians and ministry officials.[2] The work of such councils seeks to ensure that the curricula adopted will promote, insofar as possible, the identification of learners' best attributes and the cultivation of their best potentials. Although this sounds like a fairly straightforward brief, it is enormously difficult to accomplish in practice. The sub-committees, or boards, through which the brief is carried out, usually include representatives from different occupations. Most boards, however, have either a majority of teachers, or include teachers as the most strongly represented occupation. In the deliberations of such boards (usually a board per school subject), competing claims are regularly made on behalf of different material to be included in the curriculum. These competing demands can be more readily negotiated when the thinking of the board members is focused mainly on the learners for whom the curriculum in question is intended. More precisely, this is the case when it is focused on *the experienced quality* of the learning that this curriculum might yield. But when this focus on learning and the learner recedes to the background, as has often been the case in deliberations on subjects at secondary school level, other considerations take the centre stage. These include anxieties over the need to make the curriculum look a decent representative of the subject in question; or over a 'dumbing down' of the curriculum if topic X, or theorem Y or author Z is left out. Loyalties to a subject's standing in a cultural tradition, as distinct from a keen educational understanding of cultural tradition itself, hinders the clear-sightedness of deliberations here. It also tends to overload the syllabus in the different subjects and to curtail the fruitfulness of the curriculum when it comes to be experienced by teachers and students.

Such deliberations have a different character, however, when viewed from the perspective of the fourfold relationships of learning explored in Chapter 4. Carrying out this shift of perspective means that proposed material for inclusion in a curriculum must now be appraised on different grounds. These include its capacity: (a) to provoke original reflections in teachers' minds; (b) to encourage vibrant encounters between teachers and the students for whom the curriculum is intended; and (c) to disclose imaginative possibilities in teachers' discussions with each other. In short, such material must engage energetically with the thoughts and actions of teachers, as distinct from residing as inert matter in textbooks, curriculum packs and syllabus documents. Where the deliberations of curriculum councils are carried on in this more focused way, they also serve an important function of public accountability. Far from giving prominence to territorial battles among subject specialists with cherished likes and dislikes, they reveal what a key dimension of educational planning looks like when properly addressed. This means, moreover, that there is no reason in principle why the proceedings of curriculum councils shouldn't be open to the public; or more practicably perhaps, why they shouldn't be recorded for the public record.

Turning now to the assessment of the benefits of learning, this goes hand-in-hand with the recurring work of curriculum development and renewal. Far too often, however, it has become divorced from it, or has been tied to a flawed conception of curriculum development itself. Assessment regimes that have been sponsored by the international educational reforms of recent decades frequently reveal such deficiencies. For the most part, they are mechanisms of testing, capable of capturing what is readily measurable, but falling far short when it comes to making valid appraisals of the enduring benefits that students have gained from their learning. A machinery of testing can produce, on a regular basis, the kind of quantitative data that facilitates the ranking of performances and thus the comparison of individuals, class groups or schools. But it fails to ask if the educational heart of the matter may have dropped out of its reckonings. The oversight here, moreover, tends to be a habit-forming one. In the name of 'quality assurance', regular publication of league tables engenders a curious illusion among large sections of the public. This is the belief that the quality of a schools' efforts to promote learning can be adequately evaluated on the same basis that performance is measured in sport or industry: the number of wins and goals scored in a football league, or the percentage increase in profits or market share in a business enterprise. Yet, on sober reflection, few parents, or students, or members of the public more widely, would seriously want to hold with the underlying assumption of this belief.

By contrast, how might the appraisal of learning look from a perspective that is educational before being anything else? In response to this question, it is first important to stress the legitimate purposes of assessment itself. These seek to provide a valid, coherent and adequate account of the lasting benefits that students gain from their educational experiences. Assessment here must not be understood in a restricted way. It includes assessment for certification purposes and assessment for feedback purposes to students. The former is usually called 'assessment *of* learning' and the latter 'assessment *for* learning'. Taking assessment for certification purposes first, to make assessment procedures equal to the demands of validity, coherence and adequacy requires one to focus on something more substantial than what can be most easily measured. Efforts must concentrate instead on those benefits or accomplishments that are the most important in the case of the learning experience in question or, more accurately, the series of learning experiences. This is a concern with enduring benefits, and it views examinations and tests in that context. It involves the continual development and modification of criteria, ranging from ones that capture rudimentary skills (e.g. comprehension, accurate recall, sequential ordering) to ones that encompass advanced fluencies and higher-order attributes (e.g. discernment, analysis, judgement, originality).

The pooling of advanced expertise by practitioners in the development and refinement of such criteria marks one of the most important contributions that teachers can make to this difficult work. Workshops involving cross-moderation exercises between colleagues play a decisive part not only in the development, but also in the proper application, of these criteria. This also draws on the best insights of international educational research. And where such efforts are pursued hand-in-hand with the development of curricula by councils with a statutory remit, they can advance educational practice itself in a number of crucial ways. Prominent among these are the following two. First, where such actions become an established feature of educational practice in any particular country or state, a recognizable tradition develops. Of course, an emergent tradition of this kind can draw strength from the statutory base on which a curriculum council operates. More importantly, however, its acknowledged competence in maintaining major dimensions of educational practice in healthy order enhances the tradition itself in the eyes of the public. And a failure to do so can have the reverse effect. Second, where the development of assessment criteria (no less than of new curricula) springs from the best insights of accomplished practitioners and of relevant research, a strong fund of ideas is provided for the professional development of teachers. Recalling a point made in the last chapter, these ideas are likely to prove most productive where professional development opportunities are available regularly and take the form of participatory workshops and seminars.

Where assessment for feedback purposes is concerned (i.e. 'assessment for learning'), many of the points just made are relevant here also. To begin with, the practice of giving constructive feedback to students on a regular basis makes it clear – to parents as well as to students – that students are expected to act in a progressive way on that feedback. Research studies have shown that this tends to work best when grades are recorded but withheld for the time being; in other words, where 'comment-only' marking is used.[3] This is because when both marks and comments are supplied, most students focus on the mark and ignore the comments. In the comment-only approach, asking students to record the comments before they act on them also provides more precise guidelines for the work that needs to be undertaken. Constructive feedback here means, in each instance, a small number of carefully focused comments that contain suggestions for corrective work or further probing by students. Where related practices such as the use of learning criteria, peer assessment, self-assessment and 'wait time' in questioning, are employed, these serve to introduce further significant changes into environments of learning. Mounting research evidence suggests that such practices remove many of the distractions arising from preoccupation with grades. It also reveals that students gain better satisfaction and understanding from their work, and that their achievements in examinations improve as a result.[4]

As the character of learning environments is altered incrementally by these means, so also is that of the learning relationships between students and teachers. From the students' side of the experience, it becomes increasingly clear that their proper role is not that of recipients who are expected to comply and conform. On the contrary, the feedback practices promote a shared awareness that they are active and responsible participants in their own learning. It becomes natural for them to ask questions of their own, not just for clarification purposes, but also more searching questions. They engage now in a range of diverse learning activities: contributing productive suggestions to collective classroom explorations of particular topics or themes; participating in group-work where each group member has specific responsibilities; carrying out experiments requiring increasing degrees of responsibility and capability; becoming practised in research skills that involve a variety of print and electronic media.[5]

From the teacher's side of the experience, the changes are no less significant. The burden of teaching previously shouldered by the teacher now begins to become a more shared one as students become, in more than one sense, teachers of one another. Involving the students in more active ways also allows the students to reveal to themselves, and to the teacher, a wider range of their own potentials than would previously have been evident. This provides essential information to the teacher in designing further learning challenges and in perceptively assigning learning tasks and responsibilities. In the case of each student, it also gives the teacher a fuller picture over time of where, to use Dewey's phrase, the educational experience is heading.[6] The shift in self-understanding for the teacher is at least as significant as for the students, if not more so. Without such a shift on the teacher's part, a conformist emphasis is likely to remain decisive and things will remain much the same as before for both students and teacher. The teacher must be prepared to let go of traditional images and stereotypes that are still alive in the professional cultures of teaching. Otherwise it is not possible to make way for the quality of learning relationships here that recalls the more detailed explorations of Chapters 4, 5 and 6.

In conclusion, it should be noted that learning environments built up in this way promote their own air of industry and their own sense of order and restraint. Although this building work can be greatly encouraged by school-wide expectations and procedures, it is unlikely to result from any kind of imposition from above. Such learning environments are more communities of learning sustained by the efforts of their participants than arenas of compliance sustained through enforcement. They are in contrast with all forms of education as a colonization of experience.

Justice and equality in education

In reviewing this topic, two distinct but related dimensions need to be identified. The first is the promotion of justice and equality within educational practice itself and the second is the promotion of justice and equality in society more widely through education systems. The first is a concern of educational practice, properly so called. The second is a legitimate concern of government social policy, but one in which educational practice plays its own proper part. This second concern provokes widespread debate and controversy, and often tends to eclipse qualitative issues associated with the first. For instance, equality of educational opportunity is an issue that has exercised policy-makers, students and parents for many decades, and continues to do so. Yet most of this debate has focused on the widening of access to educational institutions themselves, with a comparative neglect of the equality of opportunity that needs to be attended to once students have arrived in the institutions.

This neglect is likely to persist while the inherited conventional views of education reviewed in the opening chapter above remain dominant. Recall that such views regard education as a subordinate part of the machinery available to the powers-that-be, as distinct from a practice in its own right. At their best, and most democratic, they maintain a macro perspective that is keenly conscious of persistent inequalities and that takes pains to update itself with the latest available socio-economic statistics. Yet it is a perspective that sees education more as an arena to be controlled than as a practice to be regulated in co-operation with its practitioners. Such a perspective is largely a stranger to what constitutes equality of educational opportunity when this is viewed from the standpoint of the quality of educational provision within schools and colleges. It is more remote still from the inequalities and injustices in the *experienced quality of learning* in schools and colleges. The macro perspective is at its worst, however – that is to say, most self-deluding – when it sponsors populist moves that catch the public imagination but fails to pay much attention to the practical measures needed for the success of such moves. One of the more prominent examples of this is the 'No child left behind' policy in the USA, introduced by statute in 2002. The reforms that have sprung from this movement have built a vast apparatus of testing, with severe consequences for funding in the case of underperformance.[7] These reforms have not, however, highlighted the kinds of initiatives that are most conducive to making learning environments themselves more healthy. Nor have they concentrated resources on the cultivation among teachers and educational leaders of assessment practices such as those considered in the previous paragraphs.

By contrast, things look much brighter where core aspects of government educational policy are themselves informed by the more encouraging insights of research on educational practice, and by the better inroads made within innovative practice itself. In this connection, moves in recent years to look to evidence-based research as a source of promising educational policies represent, in principle, a significant advance. The advance is largely cancelled, however, even reversed, if what counts as evidence is effectively confined to what testing regimes produce. Many educational researchers are cannily aware of this. In order to remain in receipt of research funding from official sources, they are accordingly willing to tailor their investigations to concentrate on the kind of data that the testing regimes are seeking. Such action pushes issues of equality and justice to the margins of research, or else deals with them from a methodological standpoint that doesn't allow them to emerge in their proper dimensions. Where the consequences for educational practice are concerned, findings furnished by a restrictive methodological stance are akin to the incomplete or slanted perspectives yielded by the discrete forms of ethical theory that we examined in Chapter 6. Such theories, as we saw there, give a special standing to one or other important feature; for instance, ethics of justice, of duty, of care and so on. But they tend to neglect the interplay of different features in the experiences of practice itself, including conflicts between justice and care, or justice and equality, that mark the predicaments experienced daily by teachers, school leaders and others.

Less likely to fall prey to such neglect is the kind of thinking that keeps the experienced quality of educational practice continually in its sights when reviewing issues of justice and equality. Far from being confined to research activities, such thinking needs to be nurtured and widely articulated by educational practitioners, including teachers, leaders and researchers. This is in keeping with a view of education as a practice in its own right. But as an inherent part of that practice, educational research has a central part to play in the promotion of such thinking. That part involves incisive studies by teachers and educational leaders of their own actions and their effects. But it also requires the regular inclusion in research of critical perspective from students and former students, from professional colleagues, and from parents and guardians. Different strands of this kind of research have been making piecemeal, but significant, advances since the 1980s. To mention just a few examples, they include, first, the many forms of action research now widespread in education, springing from pioneering approaches of John Elliott and others. Also productive are the approaches to justice in education developed by Morwenna Griffiths and colleagues, highlighting different voices of educational experience and drawing on autobiographical perspectives from diverse participants in education. Most recently, there are the many studies being carried out in the United Kingdom by Richard Pring and a large team of associates in the Nuffield Review of 14–19 Education and Training. Approaches such as these provide telling accounts of what the more customary research approaches have missed, or inadequately grasped, and especially where matters of justice and equality in education are concerned.[8]

Of course, the evidence produced by such research approaches is not scientific in the sense that evidence from the natural sciences is. If it had to be evidence of this sort, it would have to deal with education as a phenomenon, or at best as a biological process, rather than as a human practice. It could tell little that is really illuminating about equality and justice in education. The warrant of research approaches such as those just mentioned lies, rather, in the gradual accumulation of a body of insights that is capable of bearing up well under critical scrutiny, and is worthy of the commitments and efforts of practitioners. These insights might regularly draw on quantitative data. But they arise mainly from sources such as the critical analysis of commentaries by teachers, students and former students on the shorter- and longer-term effects of established policies and practices in schools. They also arise from a close study of the consequences of new initiatives in schools, including intended and unintended consequences. Such efforts require the involvement of significant numbers of practitioners in research activity, either as researchers in their own right or as practitioners who are regularly consulted by researchers. Thus, a continuing yield of fresh data is provided on how new departures – for instance, in special educational needs, in geography fieldwork, in web-assisted learning – advance or diminish the quality of educational experience for students. Attention to unintended outcomes, in particular, sheds a revealing light on equality and justice issues, serving to enlighten decisions as to the best allocation of resources and to inform also the reliable lore of professional practice itself.

Where educational policy and practice are mindful of the demands of justice and equality, the shift of emphasis we have just been considering discloses a few important practical features of the new significance of learning. I shall briefly mention three of these. First, educational policy-making finds here sources that produce richer insights than those produced by elaborate testing machinery and its associated payment-by-results mentality. This is especially so where initiatives to promote equality of educational opportunity can get intelligently to grips with the pedagogical practices through which quality in educational experience is cultivated and sustained. Second, where the discourse of policy-makers is thus enriched, opportunities grow for some real meeting of minds between practitioners (including researchers) and themselves. A policy-making culture informed by the best insights of research and innovative practice is not, of course, without its own tensions. It would be unhealthy if it were. But such a culture marks a historic advance, as it does a clear reversal of one of the most damaging consequences of the international reforms from the late 1980s onwards: namely, ingrained stances of mutual incomprehension and distrust. Third, by nurturing education as a practice in healthy order, these shifts of perspective promote a society's mature appreciations of how this practice makes its own best contributions to equality and justice in the society at large. This broader issue will be taken up in the final chapter, but for now the third main theme of this chapter calls for attention. That is the question of higher research and its new significance, including its priorities and conduct, its funding and applications.

Higher research

The phrase 'research and innovation' is more commonly heard today than the word 'research' on its own. This is hardly surprising in view of the enormous technological changes that have made life as lived now so different from that lived a century ago. A quick reminder of the extent of these changes is provided by considering the effects of an electricity power failure on hospitals, on schools, on transport, on manufacturing and service industries, or on leisure activities and pastimes. Innovation, in brief, has become commonplace. A view of research that fuses it with innovation, however, promotes the standing of certain forms of research while relegating others. It privileges technological research, or research that has prompt commercial applications. But it neglects research that doesn't have such features, including most research in the humanities and much research in the social and natural sciences. That is not to jump to the facile conclusion that some research is carried out for the sake of the applications it yields, while other research is carried out for its own sake. Recalling the point made in Chapter 3 about the problematic phrase 'education for its own sake', a similar point can now be made about research. All research is pursued for the benefits it brings, and it is through a critical appraisal of such benefits – inherent and extrinsic – that the worthiness of any form of research is to be evaluated.

A few brief historical examples – away from the heat of today's controversies but yet shedding light on them – will help to clarify this point and underline its significance. In 1481, Leonardo da Vinci wrote to Ludovico Sforza, ruler of Milan, seeking a patron for his diverse investigations. Leonardo's letter stressed the advantages to Ludovico of the various kinds of military technology he had already invented, or was in the course of developing. These devices included guns, mortars, catapults, chariots, portable bridges, and something suggesting a battleship or submarine: 'And if the fight should be at sea I have many kinds of machines most efficient for offence and defence; and vessels which will resist the attacks of the largest guns and powder and fumes.'[9] Leonardo's time at the turbulent Sforza Court was to last almost two decades, until Ludovico was deposed in 1499. Despite frequent interruptions to his work, this period was one of the most creative of Leonardo's life. The patronage his researches enjoyed enabled him to enquire into matters close to his heart that had no military or commercial application, as well as producing a wealth of designs and artefacts that had. The former included riches that remain the most celebrated accomplishments of the Renaissance: Leonardo's remarkable discoveries in anatomy and his artistic probings of the passions of the human soul that were to produce paintings such as the Last Supper and, later, the Mona Lisa.

Other striking examples include figures such as Galileo and Newton. While both made contributions to the development and refinement of scientific implements, their researches were concerned mainly with something other than applied science. These researches were made possible, moreover, through circumstances that were more hospitable than Leonardo's: Galileo's through renewed appointments at the University of Padua and Newton's through a succession of posts that offered him the leisure to pursue his investigations largely unhindered. In both cases, the distinctness of their investigations from those guided by the imperatives of innovation can be ascertained by asking about what guided their research interests. And, in both cases, the answer lies in a passionate commitment to pursuing the truth of the matter, whatever that might be, or wherever that might lead thinking. The disclosures of research here not only advance human understanding. Equally important, they furnish inheritances of learning with an abundance of possibilities for transforming human *self*-understanding. Yet research of this kind, which is not itself technological, can have enormous consequences for technological innovations, including military, medical and commercial applications. This can be seen, for instance, from the researches of major scientists such as Charles Darwin, Marie Curie and Albert Einstein – figures whose enquiries were primarily scientific rather than technological.

These historical examples reveal the character of an interest that is, at heart, a research interest, and help to distinguish it from a research interest that is primarily technological. This distinction becomes stronger in more recent writings. For instance, in some of his later works, Martin Heidegger makes an incisive case that it is mistaken to regard technology as neutral – that is, as a realm of scientific discoveries available for subsequent harnessing to this purpose or that.[10] At first sight, his argument looks odd, because countless examples can be given to show that an understanding of technology as a neutral instrument in itself is correct. But Heidegger correctly reveals that this understanding doesn't take us to the heart of the matter, and may often conceal it. Technology, he maintains, particularly as it advances from basic to more sophisticated forms, grants priority to a particular kind of relationship – one that is anything but neutral. This is a relationship between humans and the world of nature that embodies a technological attitude – one that seeks, *from the start*, to disclose nature as something to be harnessed and set to work. As the products of this relationship become more impressive and more numerous, the attitude embodied in the relationship advances in self-assurance and influence. Thus, a mentality that Heidegger calls 'enframing' (*Gestell*) achieves an enhanced standing in social and cultural outlooks, as well as in research circles. 'Enframing', he explains, 'means that way of revealing that holds sway in the essence of modern technology and that is itself nothing technological.'[11] In other words, at the heart of technology as a human endeavour lies not neutrality but an assertive stance. This is a stance that challenges nature to yield up its mysteries to a calculative kind of probing. Arguments with some resonances of Heidegger's critique have also been advanced by Jacques Ellul in his 1964 book *The Technological Society*, which documents the penetration of efficient technique into all fields of human action. Both critiques point to a similar conclusion: the thinking that informs the public conduct of human affairs has become largely technologized. In fact, evidence on a global scale today suggests that the institutional standing gained by technologized forms of thinking parallels that held by authoritative forms of theological thinking in earlier centuries of Western learning. It should not be surprising in such circumstances to see research fused not only with innovation, but also with strategic planning, in today's debates about educational policy. This holds true both within states and nations, and internationally.

We return here to a theme first touched on in the opening chapter. Despite springing from secular as distinct from ecclesiastical authorities, todays' dominant policies on higher research constitute no less a colonization than did earlier ones of purposes that are properly educational. These policies work in ways that are more subtle, although scarcely less coercive, than the custodianship of thought in medieval academies. Lyotard's analyses of the reign of 'performativity' in today's cultures of bureaucratic management are revealing here, not least in connection with the control and steering of research efforts. 'The decision makers' arrogance', Lyotard concludes, 'consists in the exercise of terror: "Adapt your aspirations to our ends – or else."'[12] Such decision-makers include not only politicians and ministry officials who determine the shaping and funding of national research policies. They also include business interests on research funding bodies and more than a few office holders within centres of higher learning. Among the latter are those who have given their professional commitments to technologized forms of research and scholarship; also those who haven't, but who sense that their own best future depends on aligning their research purposes with their paymasters' orthodoxies.

Critically viewed, this effective conquest of research energies can be seen as an anxious, lopsided preoccupation – an absence of intellectual maturity. It is easier to identify forms of this immaturity in the orthodoxies of previous eras, as in the Vatican's efforts of the sixteenth and seventeenth century to align the researches of astronomers to its own authorized view. But the kind of rationale that couples research with innovation, and then regards the offspring of this coupling as the heart of research itself, is no less an immaturity. And the historical, or longer-term, perspective that allows this immaturity to be disclosed as such, reveals a few more points as well. Two of these are particularly relevant to the theme of research. First, far from finding its fulfilment through being coupled to economic, or political, or religious interests, research is an inherent feature, indeed a defining one, of education as a practice in its own right. To put this more precisely in the context of advanced research, consider practices such as medicine, engineering, teaching and nursing. In these arenas, the purposes served by research are educational in the first instance. These are to better the conduct of the practice in question through the provision of new insights that practitioners recognize as enriching the practice. Such insights inform – sometimes transform – the continuing education of experienced practitioners and the initial education of new students of the practice.

Second, a historical perspective also discloses the faulty sources of the post-modern reluctance to envisage constructive alternatives to the practices criticized by post-modern analysis itself. This reticence has evident roots in a tendency to see the 'grand narrative' and its oppressive effects in even the best ideals of the past. A clear instance lies in the criticisms of Lyotard and Bill Readings of the liberal research university – in particular, their criticisms of the seminal ideals guiding Wilhelm von Humboldt's founding of the University of Berlin in 1810.[13] Lyotard perceives in Humboldt a clash between the university as an institution that 'lives and continually renews itself on its own' and one that orients itself to 'the spiritual and moral training of the nation'. Many of Readings' criticisms of the 'University of Culture' proceed from a similar perception. Humboldt's reference, in fact, is not to spiritual and moral training – a notion with a strong doctrinal flavour – but to the 'moral culture of the nation' (*die moralische Cultur der Nation*). Granted, his references to 'nation', especially in a German connection, may carry connotations today that are quite different to those suggested by their first utterance in a Berlin occupied by Napoleon. Yet, there is something lost, but also added, in the translations of Lyotard and Readings here, as in their critiques of Humboldt's work more generally. Humboldt appears in their writings more as a disciple of a suspect philosophical idealism than as an untypical policy-maker with a brief opportunity to lay lasting foundations for academic freedom in Prussia. Both authors attribute correctly to Humboldt a conception of higher education and research that was to become historically influential far beyond the borders of Prussia. Incorrectly, however, they also perceive this as a conception that is in thrall to a 'grand narrative', and on that account unaware of its own doctrinaire dangers. But, for all Humboldt's concessions to his founding colleagues – the nationalist philosopher Fichte and theologian Schleiermacher

– the practical goal of his proposals has its heart in neither's philosophy. Under critical scrutiny, that goal remains primarily educational: 'the combination of objective scientific-scholarly knowledge (*Wissenschaft*) with the development of the person (*Bildung*)'.[14] Post-modernist readings tend to bypass this, or to see Bildung more as a metaphysical programme than as a personal venture. They tend to disregard, moreover, the radical character of Humboldt's central concerns. These latter include: the freedom of research from control by the state or other agencies; the open-ended nature of research as an 'unceasing process of enquiry'; the importance of 'wholly uncoerced and disinterested collaboration' among researchers old and young.[15]

Post-modernist criticisms also overlook a further crucial point – namely, Humboldt's concern to make secure, in Prussia, the foundations for educational institutions where the free pursuit of research might *thus* best serve the welfare of a society and its citizens.[16] It would be difficult to articulate such concerns, as it would anything resembling a freedom charter, without invoking ideals of liberty *and* community that hearten courageous action. Fallible though such ideals may be, they become dangerous only where a lack of self-critical perspective allows them to combine with something else – especially with institutionalized power and its self-expansion. The critiques of Readings and Lyotard – like those of Derrida, Foucault and other writers in a post-modern vein – are especially sensitive to, and sceptical of, such power. Readings' analysis rightly highlights the vacuity of the concept of 'research excellence' canvassed alike by many of today's university administrations and their corporate superiors. That of Lyotard reveals the coercive nature of performance requirements designed to enforce such 'excellence'. Yet the studied hesitancy of both critiques on matters of constructive action disables their own best inspirations. In effect, this leaves the initiative to other hands that are unhesitant to harness research to their own designs, and it also beclouds the many possibilities of a more adequate understanding of research itself.

This review of three central themes – curriculum and assessment, justice and equality in education, higher research – could be extended to many others. It would essentially involve applying to a further range of issues the kind of thinking that gives pride of place to educational, as distinct from extrinsic, concerns in the conduct of educational practice. Rather than following this long route, which would require another chapter like the present one, I will conclude with a few summary observations. The new significance of learning we have been reviewing here is not neglectful of the requirements in today's economy and society for a plenitude of human capability. But it does not start from a standpoint that sees education chiefly as the supplier of resources for the macro concerns of strategic planning. To do so would be to engage in a secular version of the medieval preoccupation with reproducing an active, yet compliant, clerical intelligentsia, while neglecting to look properly to the diverse educational possibilities of the population at large. A mature educational practice pays close attention to the ever-changing nature of occupational opportunities, including a wide range of leadership opportunities.

It concentrates its best efforts, however, on identifying and cultivating each learner's own potentials and on nurturing a durable sense of identity and community in harmony with these potentials. By these means, it promotes the best balance between the realized capabilities of a population and the kinds of economic activity that are likely to be most productive for that population. In thus committing itself, a mature educational practice keeps a perceptive eye on lessons from history and also understands the necessity to keep its own heart in the right place.

12 Imagination's heartwork

Important lessons

This final chapter provides an opportunity to bring together many of the central themes of the book. In doing this, however, I'm keen to retain the focus of the previous chapter on the wider public arena in which education as a practice is situated. So, here the heartwork that was earlier explored – specifically in contexts of teaching and learning – will also be considered in the contexts of educational debate and policy-making at both local and international levels. If that heartwork is now seen to have a more pragmatic emphasis than in earlier pages, this should not be regarded as detracting from its merits. On the contrary, it should underline the point that an educational tradition confident of its own distinct merits must also be at home in policy-making quarters, and be well-versed in speaking its mind convincingly in such quarters.

We have noted the importance given by post-modern currents of thinking to the destabilizing of emergent hegemonies (influences that hold sway over others). We have also noted, most recently in relation to research, the debilitating consequences of a reluctance to press beyond critique; to elucidate constructive actions, in the absence of which the question 'critique for the sake of what?' remains unaddressed. And in the absence of sustained practical efforts to shape and to realize worthy alternatives, the political hegemonies of the day – neo-liberalism in recent decades – find for themselves a better place in the sun. The fact that critique in its scholarly aloofness refrains from getting its hands dirty in engaging with policy-makers compounds the difficulties. It intensifies the cultural gap between an academic intelligentsia and the holders of political power. More precisely, whatever influence academics might have on policy-makers gets concentrated in the hands of those, usually in faculties of business studies and technological sciences, who are happy to gain the ear of a policy-maker on any occasion.

The integrity of education as a practice cannot be safeguarded by forms of critique that seek to remain untainted by the forces at play in economic and social policy, either nationally or internationally. The recent international experience of educational reform reveals this clearly. The historical evidence is compelling, moreover, to show that dominant interests in society – nowadays those of state and commercial bodies rather than of the churches – will repeatedly look to education as a vehicle to advance their own designs. Unless they are to fall victim to recurrent waves of conquest and colonization, schools and colleges must speak distinctly and decisively for themselves. More particularly, educational practitioners and their leaders must build and clearly articulate a tradition of self-critical practice. Such a tradition has, at its heart, a commitment to informed and critical dialogue, rather than anything more partisan. Accordingly, it is always prepared to give a cogent account of itself and to join debate with whoever would wish educational practice to do things differently, or to do different things. Putting this more frankly, if educational practitioners and their leaders care sufficiently about the distinctiveness of their own traditions, these traditions themselves will include active initiatives to influence the tenor of educational policy at both national and international levels. For instance, the voices of school leadership should be at least as central in EU deliberations on 'education and training' as have those of bodies such as the European Roundtable of Industrialists or the European University Association.[1] This point applies also to national and more local quarters of policy-making.

None of this is to suggest that the voices that speak on behalf of educational practice should have everything their own way. As we have seen from the investigations of Chapter 7, every tradition, in addition to having its own internal tensions, is partial in both senses of that word. A tradition's best understandings are incomplete, and are also burdened by biases. In the case of any and every tradition, such incompleteness and bias need to be addressed in debates with contrasting perspectives. These include perspectives on what the tradition stands for, and on how its own affairs are conceived, organized and carried out. What an *educational* tradition, properly so-called, can bring to such debates is a disposition that exemplifies some central virtues of educational practice itself. Drawing centrally now on our earlier explorations, hallmarks of such a disposition include: a willingness to grant that a contrasting standpoint might have something valuable and unexpected to contribute; a capacity to listen attentively to such contrasting standpoint; a capability to discern the most salient issues in a contrasting standpoint and to note these for discussion; a capacity to bring one's own insights energetically into play in exploring such issues; a keen eye for new insights and possibilities that such explorations might yield; and, not least, the courage to put the claims to truth in one's own standpoint at risk, with a view to gaining a better understanding. A tradition that is distinguished by being accomplished in the ways of learning should bring with it exemplary instances of such ways in its encounters with other traditions. Availing of the institutions of democracy to do so regularly and publicly is probably the best means of winning the kind of respect for the integrity of educational practice that has all too frequently been disregarded or denied.

Two important lessons in this connection can be drawn from a study of the first and second waves of international educational reforms since the early 1990s. The first of these is the failure of the marriage between a newly assertive political control of education and a scientific machinery of perform-ance management. The sidelining of practitioners' voices by this machinery, and the alignment of teaching and learning to what the machinery could police and index, had some embarrassing consequences for those controlling the reforms. In particular, such failures now cast a poor light on the controllers more than on practitioners, who in most cases had no choice but to comply with what was being enforced. In addition, it became increasingly difficult in many countries to stem an exodus from teaching, or to attract candidates with imagination and originality to its ranks, or to leadership positions in schools and colleges. The OECD report *Teachers Matter* (2005), and some of the *Country Background Reports* from participating countries, provide some revealing data here.[2] The second lesson is one that has been quietly learned by the more discerning among policy-makers from the many unhappy consequences of the first wave of reforms. It is notably evident in the abandonment of 'scientific' approaches to assessing the quality of teaching and teacher education. This abandonment also means dropping the decisive differences of rank required by such approaches, between practitioners on the one hand and agents of official policy on the other. Increasingly replacing such approaches is a policy discourse that emphasizes educational development rather than educational reform. The developmental push is provided largely by a new awareness of the strategic importance of education in a globalized setting. A perusal of the reports just referred to also discloses that the prominence of punitive language has yielded to more buoyant terms in policy discourse: 'knowledge society', 'social inclu-sion' and 'lifelong learning'. Policy-makers, while not granting to educational practice an unencumbered autonomy, are apparently taking more seriously the 'partnership' that was principally significant in the early reforms as a rhetorical device to give a semblance of democratic participation.

A third lesson, this one more for practitioners and educational leaders, is a pragmatic and hopeful one, but also a circumspect one. The pragmatic dimen-sion starts with an awareness that the new contexts for the development of educational policy have arisen less from considerations that are inherently edu-cational than from socio-economic considerations. It underlines, nevertheless, that these new contexts have yielded some historic opportunities for practition-ers' voices to have a lasting influence in arenas of educational policy-making. This is a lesson that those who are dutiful in their commitment to critique may be inclined to dismiss. But it is one that should be embraced by those who care wholeheartedly about the integrity of education as a practice, and who are keenly aware of its recurring vulnerability in the history of Western education. To care wholeheartedly about something – a tradition, a community, a practice with its own history – is to cultivate earnest hopes for its advancement and enrichment. History is sometimes cruel to such hopes, and sometimes shines fondly on them. Even when the tide of human affairs runs against them, such hopes must be kept alive. Hope keeps a discerning eye on developments, with the belief that advantage lies with those who take the initiative, and who do so in a judicious and timely way. The circumspection central to this third lesson is closely related to this judiciousness and timeliness. For instance, it casts both a cold and an expectant eye on the tenor of recent reforms in higher education internationally, particularly in the domain of research and post-graduate studies. As we have seen in the previous chapter, historic rises in funding from both public and private sources have largely recast advanced research as a quest for discoveries that have profitable commercial application. The interests being served by this are often less those of students and researchers in the service of unfettered enquiry than those of socio-economic policy in a context of global competitiveness. In this connection, a commitment to the integrity of education as a practice reveals itself in the integrity of its practitioners, and in a particular way its leading practitioners. This means being vigilant of the often colonizing character of those interests with which the exercise of educational leadership brings one into contact. It also means cultivating an imaginative pragmatism that can secure a meaningful share of resources that are on offer. But, crucially, it means doing so without acquiescing in a rationality that is uncomprehending of the integrity of either educational practice or its practitioners.

Lessons like these mean that educational practitioners, and particularly those in leadership positions in education, need to be committed and active in ways that have not been common in the past. In addition to cultivating among practitioners the heartwork that we have been exploring in these pages, this means advancing such heartwork in more public arenas. Examples of such heartwork in public arenas include: being thoroughly and courageously fluent in what the integrity of education stands for; being able to articulate and show the fruits of what is most defensible and promising in educational practice; being able to illustrate cogently what benefits might be gained – that would not be gained otherwise – from recognizing education as a distinct office with its own purposes; being actively answerable to the public for education's pursuit of these benefits, and for the resources and trust required for that pursuit.

In the concluding sections of the chapter, we might now survey how such features might be embodied in promising ways in the educational traditions and practices of our own day. More particularly, we might review how such embodiments might advance humanity's more worthy aspirations amid radical forms of pluralism on the one hand and militant fundamentalisms on the other.

Educational experience and the profusion of difference

'To understand at all is to understand differently.' So writes Gadamer in *Truth and Method*. Without the 'at all', this would be more a truism than a keen philosophical insight. For we all know that even among groups marked by wide agreement on major points, there are still tensions and disagreements. Different individuals have 'a different take' on things, as the colloquial expression puts it; even on things on which they substantially agree. Far from being a truism, Gadamer's remark contains the important insight that people can *hardly fail* to understand differently from one another if interpretation is, from the start, a built-in feature of every experience of human understanding. A common understanding is thus not something produced by a communiqué, edict or decree. Rather, it is something reached only through renewed actions of attentive and disciplined dialogue; something, moreover, that remains vulnerable to new differences that are ever-emergent in human experience. On this account, expecting people to understand something (e.g. a historical event, a scientific theory, a religious teaching) with one mind, in the first instance, is a mistaken expectation. Such mistakes are common, not only in education, but also in politics and religion, in workplaces and homes. They are aggravated by blaming the 'subsequent interpretations' of individuals for introducing misleading or biased perspectives into what was already clearly announced on authoritative grounds.

The claim that interpretation is built into each experience of understanding from the start has been advanced, as we have seen, by thinkers such as Heidegger, Gadamer and others. We have also seen that it holds up well under criticism and that it provides insights for an incisive understanding of human understanding itself. Finally, we have seen that such insights furnish the basis for an *educational* conception of understanding. Exploring the nature and scope of such a conception of understanding is crucial to elucidating education as a practice in its own right. This book has been largely such an exploration. The fruits of the exploration can now be summarized by highlighting the ethical tenor of teaching and learning efforts that are particularly worthy of education as a practice in the twenty-first century.

Despite any initial appearances to the contrary, the case that human understanding is inherently interpretative is a robust one. Its educational strength lies in its ability to provide invitational, as distinct from coercive or partisan, conceptions of learning – ones, moreover, that withstand the charge of relativism on the one hand and objectivism on the other. Against relativism, an educational conception of human understanding holds that those standpoints which invite refutation, but have so far withstood it, provide *better* grounds for acceptance than do contrasting standpoints. It adds, however, that while all grounds might be parochial to a greater or lesser degree, a disciplined dialogue with contrasting standpoints can make the parochialism less parochial, and open to further inclusiveness. But there is also a recognition here that the aspiration to universality in an educational conception of understanding, while something to be pursued and cherished, will probably never reach final fulfilment. To make this kind of acknowledgement is to perceive the overlooked significance of the declaration of Socrates in the *Apology*, that 'real wisdom is the property of God'. It is also to add the more recent insight – which is already implicit in Socrates' life and work – that the best that human wisdom can do is to advance an educated sense of its own ignorance. But it is no less to affirm that both the achievements and the continual renewal of this advance are among the most worthy of human undertakings.

To objectivism, an educational conception of understanding addresses an argument such as the following. It would be splendid if human understanding could lay secure hold of the kinds of truth criteria that are free of cultural and historical influences, and of all the other biases to which human experience is prone. But achieving this would require one to be able to step outside of history and culture and to take a 'God's-eye' view of human thinking and its accomplishments. The many mistaken pathways in the history of epistemology reveal the misconceived nature of attempting to do so where the various fields of human enquiry are concerned. In the fields that come nearest to achieving such criteria – mathematics and formal logic – something like a human counterpart of such stepping-out is attempted. But the presuppositions that are at work in these fields are accordingly restricted to axioms (e.g. a triangle is a figure bounded by three straight lines), or to premises that effectively count as axioms (e.g. 'all humans are mortal'). Arguments of medieval philosophers such as Thomas Aquinas that 'our faith is founded on infallible truth',[3] sought to make religious beliefs axiomatic in this sense. Notwithstanding the abundance of perceptive insights in Thomas's writings, this recasting of items of faith as axioms laid the basis for scholasticism as one of the more enduring forms of objectivism in Western learning. Such objectivism moved well beyond the borders of religion. It sought to make its own view of 'absolute truth' universally applicable and various forms of it featured prominently in the history of education. Historical examples, as we have seen, include some institutionalized forms of Christianity in the West, and institutionalized forms of Marxism in the former Eastern Block countries. Today's examples include fundamentalist forms of Islam, chiefly in parts of the Middle East, and of Christianity in certain pockets of Western countries.

Not surprisingly then, the conceptions of cultural tradition that inform educational thought and action carry high stakes. The discussion of conversational and combative forms of tradition in Chapter 8 has already investigated the import of this distinction and has argued for a conversational orientation for educational thought and action. The practical consequences of such an orientation can be illustrated more directly now, by focusing on how a conversational orientation might handle the topical, but frequently vexed question of cultural differences, and more specifically, religious differences in education. Far from removing any religious tradition from places of learning, or from giving an evangelizing role to one or other confessional faith, a conversational orientation in education explores religious traditions in an educational way. Religious traditions now become experienced as inheritances that disclose plural pathways of belief. For *educational* purposes then, no tradition is treated as if faith could be identified with fact, or be regarded as absolute truth. This means that religious traditions are to be encountered on different grounds in public educational settings than they are in homes, Sunday schools and other places of upbringing; or in churches, mosques, synagogues and other places of worship.

An educational conception of human understanding enables the voices of religious tradition to speak by revealing the contrasting vistas that they provide for religious faith. On this kind of account, to become educated in religion stands in contrast with becoming exclusively nurtured in the beliefs of a particular faith. It means becoming progressively familiar with the teachings of more than one tradition of belief. In this anthropological vein, it also means learning how commanding and deeply rooted such belief can be within different cultures. This latter point is an important one, especially if the experienced quality of learning is to yield something more than a bland tolerance of other religions, or even of religion as such. Such learning gains a greater depth and significance as one's educational experiences advance from childhood through adolescence to adulthood. Accordingly, it involves regularly venturing far from one's own habitual assumptions. Far from anything coerced, this venturing is a response to an invitation: to dwell awhile, with heart as well as mind, amid religious outlooks, practices and experiences utterly different from all that was previously familiar. For Western learners, the literature that unfolds such outlooks, practices and experiences from the inside – memorably, poignantly, festively, despairingly – is ever more widely available in English and other Western languages. It includes novels from the Middle East, China, India, Africa and elsewhere that now feature prominently in Western media, not least in the shortlists for international literary prizes. Where such texts are read more in a conversational than a partisan way, environments of learning become more hospitable to appreciating humanity as an inescapable cultural profusion, as distinct from a totality of opposed conceptions of the truth. In case this reference to profusion is taken as too sanguine or florid, I hasten to add that it is not an unequivocal commendation. It includes the minor duplicities, the major treacheries, the odious thraldoms to which humanity is prone, just as it does the inspiring accomplishments and measureless compassion of which humanity is capable.

Where educational practice is in a reasonably healthy order, opportunities for some sustained explorations of this kind can be created, in age-appropriate ways, at various stages of formal and more informal education. For the kinds of venturing mentioned in the previous paragraph, the senior of years of secondary education, as well as the undergraduate years of higher education, provide particular opportunities. The teacher in such instances, contrary to MacIntyre's view, does not act as a figure who provides the students with a final authoritative reading from the standpoint of a particular faith, or a particular culture. But neither does the teacher stand aside, or act in a neutral capacity. Rather, the teacher here is purposefully attentive to the responses emerging from the different readings of the students. The teacher seeks to build a community of enquiry, properly so-called, where the students' thoughts learn to 'take wing' and where each student learns to contribute and receive in a responsible way to a collective exploration. Thus, the teacher re-considers with the students the fruits of their various readings. Under the teacher's guidance, the students elicit from their imaginative, yet wholehearted, encounters with people's experiences in other countries a wealth of thought-provoking reflections from different regions of the earth. Such collective exploration of these reflections – on how life is differently experienced and ordered, constrained and celebrated, emancipated and imprisoned, cherished and wasted – seeks to evoke and engage each learner's distinctive voice. But it gives no one the last word. Instead, it provides fertile ground on which education as a distinct human practice might cultivate a compassionate and mature humanity. This does not detract from the earnestness with which one's own religious convictions or cultural practices may be held, although it may shift one's understanding of religion and cultural difference in a lasting way. The dispositions it fosters make it more likely that religious teachings will be held as matters of sincere faith rather than as ones of established knowledge. Such dispositions are likely to be interested in rather than dismissive of the convictions of others. Far from granting a mistaken tolerance to any and every cultural practice, however, they are likely to appraise all religious teachings and cultural practices for the quality of their humanity, or lack of it.[4]

Humanity's maturity

Resistance to the idea that education is a practice in its own right is not easily dissolved. The contrary idea that education is a subordinate undertaking, controlled by the powers-that-be in a particular society, is deeply rooted even in some of the world's most democratic societies. The idea that education must receive its aims and contents from a body deemed to be superior to its own practitioners and leaders is widely taken as part of the natural order of things. In its present-day forms, this idea represents a secular form of dominion, long after most forms of religious dominion have been consigned to the past. There is something quite curious about this, and it requires explanation if the main arguments advanced by this book are not themselves to look curious. The forms of dominion (lordship, hierarchical control) that were most prominent in Western history grew with the rise of Christianity, the major religion of Western civilization. Yet, Christianity in its origins was anything but a religion of dominion or hegemony. Equally curious is the fact that the decline of religion as a political force in the wake of the Enlightenment and Revolutionary period did not bring a comparable decline in dominion, least of all in education.

To unravel these issues, it is necessary to revisit briefly the main theme of the opening chapter: the takeover and harnessing of learning. Surveying this theme a bit further in the light of the arguments of the intervening pages will show that it is the notion of education as a practice in its own right that is the more natural and promising one. Particular attention needs to be paid to how an imperial impulse to control and rule advanced itself by becoming attached to a major momentum provided by controversial developments in Christian doctrine. It will also be necessary to show how education became drawn into this confluence of religious and political forces and, in doing so, lost its identity as a distinct practice.

We have traced, in the opening chapter, the decisive consequences of the decree of Emperor Theodosius I in AD 381. This had banned all non-Christian religions and made a Christianity based on the Nicene Creed the only religion to be tolerated in the Roman Empire. It also paved the way for the rise of an even stronger dominion by the Vatican, which inherited many of the features of imperial rule. No less than the orthodoxy that followed Theodosius' decree, that lengthy Vatican ascendancy was fuelled by a series of highly charged, theological doctrines that brooked no dissent. In the early Middle Ages, these carried an Augustinian–Platonist stamp, with its sharp distinction between a sublime City of God and a earthly city of sinners. In the centuries following the work of Thomas Aquinas, this earlier emphasis was supplemented by scholasticism, which focused its attentions in a particular way on teaching and learning. From its institutionalized home in the Vatican, this philosophical–theological worldview understood itself as providing comprehensive and authoritative answers on all-important questions that could be asked.

In Chapter 3, we examined the eclipse of a Socratic orientation in education by the more authoritarian outlooks that later generations mined from Plato's metaphysics. That eclipse finds strong parallels in the eclipse of earlier forms of religion, including different variants of Christianity, by the decree of Theodosius I. A suggestive indication of how different things might have been if the eclipsed traditions had become the more influential ones is provided by the tenor of remarkable speech made by the court orator Themestius to the Emperor Jovian in AD 364, 17 years before the Decree of Theodosius I. On the question of religious differences, Themestius spoke as follows:

> God made the favourable disposition towards piety a common attribute of nature, but lets the manner of worship depend on individual inclination. … It is as if all the competitors in a race are hastening towards the same prize giver but not all on the same course, some going by this route, others by that … there is no one road … one is more difficult to travel, another more direct, one steep and another level. All however tend alike towards that one goal, and our competition and our zealousness arise from no other reason that that we do not all travel by the same route.[5]

Although couched in the language of political diplomacy, Themestius' words carry distinct echoes of the speech of Socrates in which he cautioned that human wisdom should not assume pretensions to a God-like omniscience. Where the insights that yield warnings like this are ignored, the way lies open for such pretensions to associate themselves with whatever movements for human betterment emerge in a particular society. Thus, the advance of an urge to dominate becomes masked by motives of a more laudable kind, and there is little reluctance to invoke God, or freedom, as inspirations for actions and practices that are divisive at heart. Where education is concerned, this urge for control is often less overtly political. It is characteristically evident, however, in the quest for certainty, and in the corresponding belief that anything less than certainty is a deficiency to be remedied.

What's most worthy of educational efforts lies in a different direction than

where such pretensions lead. This is why it is necessary from the start to separate what is properly educational from the politics of power and control. Far
from denying that educational practice has its own politics, what is important
here is to acknowledge that education as a practice disavows proprietorial or
partisan designs on the minds and hearts of learners. That practice is centrally
concerned with the purposeful interplay of influences. But that interplay
becomes itself properly intelligible only when illuminated by what has been
called, in these pages, an educational understanding of human understanding
itself; or more broadly, an educational conception of tradition.

Although the heart of this conception is associated with an appreciation
of the predisposed and partial character of understanding – as revealed, for
instance, by researches of Heidegger, Gadamer and others – its ancestry is more
ancient. As noted on a few occasions, that ancestry lies in a special way in the
life and work of Socrates of Athens, suggestive examples of which feature in the
earlier of Plato's dialogues – *Gorgias, Protagoras, Euthyphro, Apology*, and *Republic
Bk.I*. As distinct from Plato's middle and later works, these early dialogues
can be seen as original works in a tradition that began to develop, but which
then became eclipsed. The irony is that this eclipse was hugely contributed to
by the power of Platonist metaphysics to provide justifications for the most
ambitious exercise of power itself.

The fact remains, however, that perceptive insights into the limitations of
human understanding's best efforts are already to be discerned in the educational encounters of Socrates, as described in the early Platonic dialogues.
These insights become more explicit when the dialogues are considered from
an educational point of view, to be distinguished here from the more theoretical standpoints of philosophical scholarship. In effect, the insights of the
early dialogues provide an emergent counsel of wisdom to educational efforts.
Here, human learning, including its deliberate promotion, is disclosed as a
distinctive field of action or practice. That practice, or range of practices, can
clearly be seen to be concerned with the interplays of influence, but in ways
that are different in key respects from practices such as evangelization, politics
or commercial dealing. Learning here is experienced as a questioning, but a
questioning that is at the same time a beckoning of heart and imagination,
not merely of intellect. At its more advanced levels, such learning includes a
disciplined self-criticism, mindful of the necessity to seek and attend carefully
to perspectives and judgements that differ from one's own.

At recurring stages of the history of Western civilization, different echoes
of such insights, or further articulations that bear some family resemblance to
them, broke through the more dominant orthodoxies. Notable examples can
be found in a widely contrasting range: in the letters of Heloise to her former
teacher and lover Peter Abelard, especially in Heloise's retrospective attempts
to establish truthfully the nature of their relationship; in the erudite writings of
Erasmus, including his educational works and the summons to a more authentic Christianity in *Praise of Folly*; in the satires of Rabelais that poked fun at
the more rigid practices of institutionalized religion; not least in the inclusive

and urbane humanity of Montaigne's essays. Examples can also be found in a research vein, such as the ceaseless investigations of Galileo and Newton. In more recent times, one can point to investigations revealing the combination of intellectual modesty and acuity of a Marie Curie or an Albert Einstein.

Examples such as these capture something of the venturesome, yet unassuming, character of an educational conception of understanding, or more precisely of its enduring fruits. The philosophical researches of recent decades that have highlighted the play of predisposing influences in human understanding itself have added a decisive further dimension here. They have done much to bring to explicit awareness the suggestive insights of the eclipsed Socratic legacy. Extending the fruits of these researches into twenty-first century environments of teaching and learning means giving greater definition and strength to a tradition that can itself be called educational before it is anything else. This is work that mostly remains to be done, much of it in new arenas, or in older arenas newly reconstituted. It means availing of all opportunities afforded by ongoing developments in educational discourse to bring about a greater public awareness of the distinctiveness and integrity of educational practice. It also means working to create such opportunities, not only in policy discourse circles, but also within the centres where educational practice itself, and the education of its practitioners, is carried on. As the paths we have travelled in this book have sought to show, the energies that sustain this kind of action are joint ones: of open heart and of lively, disciplined imagination.

Notes

Introduction

1 There was a Byzantine Christendom, with Constantinople as its chief centre of influence, as well as a Western Christendom centred on Rome. The former was already fragmenting before the fall of Constantinople in 1453. My own references to Christendom in this book are to Western Christendom, unless otherwise stated.

2 For older and modern versions of the Hippocratic Oath, see www.pbs.org/wgbh/nova/doctors/oath_today.html (accessed on 9 April 2009).

3 This is particularly clear from the writings of Plato and Aristotle. But so also is their dissatisfaction with the inherited order that granted control of schooling to private hands – usually the hands of the sophists.

1 The harnessing of learning

1 Quoted by S. J. Curtis and M. E. A. Boultwood in *A Short History of Educational Ideas*, Slough: University Tutorial Press, 1977, p. 101.

2 Quoted in *The Letters of Abelard and Heloise*, translated with an Introduction by B. Radice, London: Penguin, 2004, p. 36.

3 Quoted by J. Bronowski and B. Mazlish in *The Western Intellectual Tradition*, Harmondsworth: Penguin, 1970, p. 110.

4 *The New Testament, English Standard Version*, Dublin: Talbot Press, 1970, Matthew, 28:19; Mark, 16:15.

5 Ibid., Romans, Chapters 7 and 8.

6 For a detailed study of Augustine's life and influence, see P. Brown, *Augustine of Hippo: A Biography* (new edition with Epilogue), London: Faber and Faber, 2000.

7 I have explored these issues in greater detail in *The Custody and Courtship of Experience*, Dublin: Columba Press, 1995, pp. 47–53.

8 Aristotle, *Politics*, translated by H. Rackham, Cambridge MA: Harvard University Press – Loeb Classical Library, Bk. VIII, 1337a29–30.

9 The Stalinist and Nazi regimes spring to mind, as does the Cultural Revolution in China. But other examples include the Francoist regime in Spain, the Apartheid regime in South Africa and the Pinochet regime in Chile.

10 Numerous sources, including empirical studies, bear out this point. For evidence from the United States and Canada, see A. Hargreaves, *Teaching in the Knowledge Society*, Maidenhead and New York: Open University Press / McGraw-Hill

Education, 2003, Chapters 3 and 4. From England, arguably the most telling evidence is the admission in a *Sunday Times* article of 3 August 2008 by the former Chief Inspector, Chris Woodhead, that the reforms in which he had played such a central part had failed. See www.timesonline.co.uk/tol/news/uk/education/article4448440.ece (accessed on 8 April 2009).

11 European Commission White Paper, *Teaching and Learning: Towards the Learning Society*, Brussels: Commission of the European Communities, 1996.

12 The first three of these are included as goals in the 1996 EU White Paper. These and the others I have mentioned have become quite commonplace not only in official publications but in the discourse of educational policy-making internationally and in news media coverage of educational matters.

2 Overcoming a post-modern debility

1 An illuminating critical review of the lifelong education movement of the 1970s and 1980s, with extensive bibliographical sources, is provided by K. Wain in Chapter 1 of his book, *The Learning Society in a Postmodern World*, New York: Peter Lang, 2004. The other publications mentioned in this paragraph are included in the bibliography.

2 I. Illich, *Deschooling Society*, Harmondsworth: Penguin, 1973, p. 34.

3 J. F. Lyotard, *The Postmodern Condition: A Report on Knowledge*, translated by G. Bennington and B. Massumi, with Foreword by F. Jameson, Manchester: Manchester University Press, 1984, p.xxiv.

4 The three categories here are my own, not Lyotard's. The style of *The Postmodern Condition* is particularly terse, not least in those infrequent instances where it gives concrete examples.

5 Ibid., pp. 4–5.

6 Ibid., p. 11.

7 Ibid., p. 63.

8 Ibid., pp. 63–64.

9 Ibid., p. 27.

10 Ibid., p. 12.

11 Ibid., p. 66.

12 Ibid., p. 16.

13 J. Derrida, *Of Grammatology*, translated by G. C. Spivak, Baltimore: Johns Hopkins University Press, 1976, p. 10.

14 Derrida cites this criticism, but does not identify the critic, in a 1994 interview on the 'Cambridge Affair' in *Points ... Interviews 1974–1994*, by Jacques Derrida, edited by E. Weber, Stanford: Stanford University Press, 1995, p. 405.

15 'The Principle of Reason: The University in the Eyes of its Pupils', in *Diacritics*, Fall, 1983, p. 15.

16 J. Derrida, *Specters of Marx: The State of the Debt, the Work of Mourning, and the New International*, translated by P. Kamuf, with Introduction by B. Magnus and S. Cullenberg, New York: Routledge, 1994, p. 59.

17 Ibid.

18 J. Derrida, 'Force of Law: The "Mystical Foundation of Authority"', in D. Cornell, M. Rosenfeld and D. G. Carlson (eds), *Deconstruction and the Possibility of Justice*, New York and London: Routledge, 1992, pp. 14ff.

19 Ibid., p. 92.

20 M. Foucault, 'Truth and Power' in P. Rabinow, ed. *The Foucault Reader*, Harmondsworth: Penguin, 1986, p. 73.

21 Ibid., p. 89.

22 Ibid., pp. 76–77.

23 M. Foucault, *Discipline and Punish: The Birth of the Prison*, translated by A. Sheridan, Harmondsworth: Penguin, 1979, pp. 27–28.

24 Such critics include prominent philosophers such as Charles Taylor, Nancy Fraser, Richard Bernstein, Jürgen Habermas and others.

25 C. Taylor, 'Foucault on Freedom and Truth', in D. C. Hoy, *Foucault: A Critical Reader*, Oxford: Blackwell, 1991, p. 93.

26 In the 'Introductory note' to their jointly edited book, *The Final Foucault*, Cambridge Mass. The MIT Press, 1994, J. Bernauer and D. Rasmussen provide a revealing comment on this issue. Among the characteristics of Foucault, they write, was 'a personal pleasure in being different, in not appearing with the face his commentators predicted on the basis of his earlier writings. As Foucault once put it: "No, no, I'm not where you are lying in wait for me, but over here, laughing at you."' (p.vii).

27 M. Foucault, 'What is Enlightenment?', in P. Rabinow, ed. *The Foucault Reader*, pp. 46–47.

28 M. Foucault, 'Polemics, Politics and Problemizations', in P. Rabinow (ed), *The Foucault Reader*, p. 381.

29 See 'On the Genealogy of Ethics: An Overview of Work in Progress', in *The Foucault Reader*, pp. 361–362.

30 At the time of writing, Foucault's last course in the College de France on *Parrhesia* is not published in English, but is available (in French) at the Foucault archives at the Institut Mémoires de L'Edition Contemporaine (IMEC). A detailed account and review of the course, however, are presented in Thomas Flynn's essay 'Foucault as Parrhesiast: his last course at the Collège de France (1984)' in *The Final Foucault*. Transcripts in English of recordings of a similar course, presented in six lectures at the University of California at Berkeley in October – November 1983, were published as *Fearless Speech*, edited by J. Pearson, Los Angeles: Semiotext(E), 2001. An investigation of some educational implications of the California lectures can be found in 'Truth-Telling as an Educational Practice of the Self: Foucault, Parrhesia and the Ethics of Subjectivity', by M. A. Peters, *Oxford Review of Education*, vol. 29, no. 2, 2003, pp. 207–223.

31 M. Foucault, 'Politics and Ethics: An Interview', in *The Foucault Reader*, pp. 378–379.

32 M. Foucault, 'On the Genealogy of Ethics', in *The Foucault Reader*, p. 343.

33 M. Foucault, 'What is Enlightenment?', in *The Foucault Reader*, p. 47.

34 The following quotation is a good example of this indistinctness. Derrida is getting at something he regards as particularly important, but what it could mean in practice remains rather obscure: 'This abstract messianicity belongs from the very beginning to the experience of faith, of believing, of a credit that is irreducible to knowledge and of a trust that "founds" all relation to the other in testimony. This justice, which I distinguish from right, alone allows the hope, beyond all "messianisms", of a universalizable culture of singularities, a culture in which the abstract possibility of the impossible translation could nevertheless be announced.' J. Derrida, 'Faith and Knowledge: The Two Sources of "Religion" at the Limits of Reason Alone', in J. Derrida and G. Vattimo (eds), *Religion*, Cambridge: Polity

Press in association with Basil Blackwell Ltd. Oxford, 1998, p. 18.

35 A. MacIntyre, *After Virtue, A Study in Moral Theory*, 2nd edn, London: Duckworth, 1985, p. 187.

36 *After Virtue*, p. 188.

37 In an essay that builds insightfully on MacIntyre's analysis of a practice, Joseph Dunne explores in detail the distinction between internal and external goods in education: J. Dunne, 'What's the Good of Education?', in W. Carr (ed.), *The RoutledgeFalmer Reader in Philosophy of Education*, London and New York: Routledge, 2005, pp. 145–160.

3 The integrity of educational practice

1 See the collection of Carr's papers published under the title *For Education: Towards Critical Educational Inquiry*, Buckingham and Philadelphia: Open University Press, 1995; also his article 'Philosophy and Education', in W. Carr (ed), *The RoutledgeFalmer Reader in Philosophy of Education*, pp. 34–49.

2 J. Wilson 'Philosophy and Education: Retrospect and Prospect', in *Oxford Review of Education*, 1980, vol.6, no.1, p.43.

3 J. Wilson, 'Concepts, Contestability and the Philosophy of Education', in *Journal of Philosophy of Education*, 1981, vol. 15, no.1, p. 8.

4 Plato, *The Republic*, translated with Introduction by D. Lee, Harmondsworth: Penguin, 1974, 501a.

5 When viewed from an educational perspective, the differences between the early and later dialogues of Plato emerge as striking. The Socrates of early dialogues such as *Protagoras, Gorgias, Euthyphro, Apology, Republic* Bk. I, is quite different from the Socrates of later works such as *Timaeus, Sophist, Laws*. The Socrates of the early dialogues probably resembles the historical Socrates, with a philosophical stance quite different to that of Plato's works. In the later works, Socrates tends to play a minor role (*Timaeus, Sophist*) or no role (*Laws*). In dialogues of Plato's middle period, like *Republic* Bks. II–X, Socrates frequently features as a literary device for voicing Plato's increasingly un-Socratic philosophy. For instance, Plato's elaborate educational scheme, outlined from Bk II–X of *Republic*, included a major role for females. Socrates had no such scheme, and didn't seem to question the absence of females from public life. The differences between the early, middle and later dialogues of Plato are explored in searching detail by G. Vlastos in *Socrates: Ironist and Moral Philosopher*, Cambridge: Cambridge University Press, 1991.

6 Plato, *Republic*, 336c-d.

7 Ibid., 336e.

8 Ibid., 338c.

9 Plato, *Apology*, included in *The Last Days of Socrates*, (Euthyphro, Apology, Crito, Phaedo) translated by H. Trendennick, and H. Tarrant, with Introduction by H. Tarrant, London: Penguin, 2003, 22c.

10 Ibid, 29e.

11 Instances of good practice in primary schools are recorded in official reports (e.g. Ireland, Scotland, Finland, Denmark) as occasions where the spontaneous playfulness of children becomes, through the insightful actions of a teacher, a more structured interplay that guides learning to fresh discoveries. Where practice is faulted by inspectors, this is mainly for shortcomings in imaginative planning and for failing to involve learners sufficiently as active participants in their own

learning. For instance, a 2005 report by the Inspectorate of the government Department of Education on the implementation of a new primary curriculum (1999) in Ireland commented that, where early mathematics education was concerned, 'Good or very good practice was widespread'. The Mathematics *Teacher Guidelines*, issued by the same Department in 1999, stated: 'It is through play that young children learn to share and co-operate, to share toys and express ideas. This differs greatly from child to child. Play in the classroom develops these skills by providing structured situations for the child to explore.' (p.9) Similar themes are stressed in the Scottish report *The Child at the Centre* (2007) by Her Majesty's Inspectorate of Education. Further examples from Finland and Denmark can be found in *The Education of Six Year Olds in England, Denmark and Finland: An International Comparative Study* (London: OFSTED, 2003), which contrasts the more participatory learning environments that are common in these countries with more formal and rigid ones in England.

12 See K. Popper's *The Open Society and its Enemies* (vol. 1 Plato; vol.2 Hegel and Marx) London: Routledge 1945/2003; also, 'The Villanova Roundtable: A Conversation with Jacques Derrida', in J. D. Caputo (ed.), *Deconstruction in a Nutshell*, New York: Fordham University Press, 1997.

13 It is important to point out here that there are forms of epistemology that are not in thrall to rationalism. Where educational thought is concerned, the work of H. Siegel provides some good examples: *Educating Reason: Rationality, Critical Thinking, and Education*, New York and London: Routledge, 1988; *Rationality Redeemed?: Further Dialogues on an Educational Ideal*, New York and London: Routledge, 1997.

4   Disclosing educational practice from the inside

1 'Alasdair MacIntyre on Education: In Dialogue with Joseph Dunne'. The dialogue was originally published in the *Journal of Philosophy of Education* vol. 36, no. 1, 2003. A collection of articles responding to the issues raised in it was published as a special issue of this journal, vol. 37, no. 2, 2003. This special issue and the MacIntyre–Dunne dialogue were published together as a book in 2004: *Education and Practice: Upholding the Integrity of Teaching and Learning*, Joseph Dunne and Pádraig Hogan (eds), Oxford, UK and Malden: USA: Blackwell, 2004.

2 'Alasdair MacIntyre on Education: In Dialogue with Joseph Dunne', in *Education and Practice*, p. 5.

3 Ibid.

4 Ibid., p. 6, 8.

5 Ibid., p. 9.

6 B. Russell, *On Education*, London: George Allen and Unwin, 1926, p. 24.

7 J. Dewey, *Experience and Education*, New York: Collier Macmillan, 1938, 1975, p. 48.

8 This is the thrust of MacIntyre's argument on p. 5 of the dialogue with Dunne, not only in relation to mathematics, but also in relation to some other subjects he instances, such as science, history and imaginative literature.

9 Paulo Freire uses this phrase to explain what he means by humankind's 'ontological and historical vocation'. See Freire's *Pedagogy of the Oppressed*, translated by M. Bergman Ramos, Harmondsworth: Penguin, 1972, p. 48, 56. The macropolitical connotations that are to the forefront in Freire's use of the phrase are not absent

from my own thinking, but they are secondary to something else: the emergent quality of relationships of learning, to be explored in this chapter.

10 I have explored different aspects of the courtship conception in a number of research papers, but it received its first full elucidation in Chapter 7 of *The Custody and Courtship of Experience*. The word 'heartwork' is not to be found in a dictionary. It occurs in a line of Rilke's poem 'Turning' (*Wendung*): 'Work of sight is achieved, / Now for some heart-work / on all those images, prisoned within you.' *The Selected Poetry of Rainer Maria Rilke*, edited and translated by S. Mitchell, with Introduction by R. Hass, New York: Random House, 1982.

11 See Lyotard's *The Postmodern Condition*, section 12, p. 47, and 'Alasdair MacIntyre On Education: In Dialogue with Joseph Dunne', p. 5.

12 Michael Oakeshott, The Voice of Poetry in the Conversation of Mankind', in *Rationalism in Politics and Other Essays*, London: Methuen, 1962. Oakeshott's thinking on education appears in a range of articles and papers rather than in a single work. A searching review of the educational richness of this thinking, as well as of its unintentional elitist aspects, is provided by K. Williams in *Education and the Voice of Michael Oakeshott*, Exeter: Imprint Academic, 2007.

13 M. Oakeshott, 'The Voice of Poetry', p. 197.

14 Ibid., pp. 199–200.

5 Opening Delphi

1 George Steiner, *Lessons of the Masters*, Cambridge, MA and London: Harvard University Press, 2003. A range of contrasting appraisals of the book can be found at http://www.complete-review.com/reviews/steinerg/lessons.htm (accessed on 9 April 2009).

2 Ibid., pp. 16–17.

3 Ibid., p. 17.

4 Ibid. It is hard to say how seriously Steiner takes these affinities. He introduces them with a rather ambiguous remark: 'There are affinities, always to be questioned, even ironized, to the oracular: *sequar ora moventum / Rite deum Delphosque meus ipsumque recludam.*'

5 Ibid.

6 Ibid., p. 18.

7 Ibid.

8 Ibid.

9 Except in quoting passages from Steiner, I will use a small 'm' for 'master'.

10 Ibid., p. 14.

11 Ibid., pp. 15–16.

12 Ibid., p. 14.

13 Ibid., p. 31.

14 Ibid., p. 34.

15 Ibid.

16 Ibid., p. 36.

17 Ibid., p. 35.

18 Ibid., p. 26.

19 Ibid.

20 Ibid., p. 28.

21 Ibid.

22 Ibid., p. 140.

23 Ibid., p. 141.
24 Ibid., p. 181.
25 Ibid., p. 2.
26 Ibid., p. 184.
27 Ibid.
28 Dramatic accounts of these events can be found in Plato's *Apology* (for Socrates), and in the autobiographical 'Historia calamitatum' written by Peter Abelard. The latter is included in *The Letters of Abelard and Heloise*, translated with an Introduction by B. Radice, London: Penguin, 1974.
29 It is important to point out here that the teaching of religion could also be approached in this way. The teacher, for instance, may take a reverent stance to the body of teaching in question, but one where 'the dogmatic principle' – notably stressed by John Henry Newman – is partnered by a 'critical principle' that is appropriate to the students' level of understanding and development.
30 Ibid., p.183.
31 Ibid.
32 National initiatives promoting such approaches are now becoming more common in many countries. In the case of Ireland, for instance, see www.projectmaths.ie (accessed on 9 April 2009).
33 M. Heidegger, 'The Origin of the Work of Art', in *Poetry, Language Thought*, translated by A. Hofstadter, New York: Harper and Row, 1971, p. 76.

6 *Eros*, inclusion, and care in teaching and learning

1 Except when used in quotations drawn from other authors, the word *eros* will be written in italics, to emphasize its Greek origins.
2 J. Garrison, *Dewey and Eros*, New York and London: Teachers College Press, 1977, p. xix.
3 Ibid., p. 3.
4 Ibid.
5 Plato gives different accounts of this ascent, and its educational significance, all of which involve a memorable use of drama; for instance, in *Republic*, in *Phaedrus* and in *Symposium*. The last of these provides a particular focus for Garrison's analysis.
6 The passage is from Dewey's book *Art as Experience* (1934), and is quoted by Garrison on p. 15 of *Dewey and Eros*.
7 One of the more telling examples of this lies in the enduring challenge that Plato's writings present for a 'post-modern' writer such as Jacques Derrida. See Derrida's remarks at 'The Villanova Roundtable: A Conversation with Jacques Derrida', in J. D. Caputo (ed.), *Deconstruction in a Nutshell*, New York, Fordham University Press, 1997.
8 Garrison, *Dewey and Eros*, p. 21.
9 Ibid, pp. xx, 25.
10 Ibid., p. 28.
11 D. H. Lawrence, *The Rainbow*, (first published 1915) New York: Alfred A. Knopf, 1993, p. 341.
12 Ibid., p. 355.
13 Ibid., p.367, 377.
14 These explorations are mainly in Ch. 2 of *Dewey and Eros*, and the examples are in Ch. 4, pp. 115–25 and Ch. 6, pp. 178–200.

15 Ibid., p. 40.
16 M. Buber, 'Education', in *Between Man and Man*, translated with an Introduction by R. G. Smith, London: Kegan Paul, Trench, Trubner and Co. Ltd., 1947/1969, p. 121.
17 Ibid., pp. 121–122.
18 Replacing the word *eros* with *agape* or *philia*, has its own difficulties, however. *Agape* carries connotations of Christian love, associated in a particular way with the writings of St. Paul. *Philia* has connotations of friendship between adults, which might also be misleading for describing relations in education.
19 S. Todd, *Learning from the Other: Levinas, Psychoanalysis, and Ethical Possibilities in Education*, Albany: State University of New York Press, 2003, p. 52 and 53.
20 P. Standish, 'Ethics Before Equality', in W. Carr (ed.), *The RoutledgeFalmer Reader in Philosophy of Education*, p. 233.
21 J. Rawls, *A Theory of Justice*, Oxford: Oxford University Press, 1973, pp. 12ff.
22 N. Noddings, *The Challenge to Care in Schools*, New York: Teachers College Press, 1992, p. 18.
23 Ibid., pp. 15–16.
24 Ibid., p. 16.
25 Ibid., pp. 16–17.
26 Ibid., p. 22.
27 Ibid.
28 Ibid., p. 23.
29 Ibid., pp. 23–24.
30 Ibid., p. 25.
31 Ibid., p. 26.
32 Ibid., p. 28.
33 M. J. Alder, *The Paideia Proposal: An Educational Manifesto*, New York and London: Macmillan, 1982.
34 Ibid., p. 70.

7 Understanding in human experience and in learning

1 J. Dewey, *Experience and Education*, p. 38.
2 H.-G. Gadamer, 'The Universality of the Hermeneutical Problem', in *Philosophical Hermeneutics*, translated and edited by D. E. Linge, Berkeley: University of California Press, 1976, p. 9. See also the following references to this by Gadamer: *Truth and Method*, translated from the second German edition by G. Barden and J. Cumming, London: Sheed and Ward, 1975, p. 245; 'Hermeneutics as Practical Philosophy', in *Reason in the Age of Science*, translated by F. G. Lawrence, Cambridge, MA: The MIT Press, 1981, p. 111.
3 'The Universality of the Hermeneutical Problem', p. 9.
4 *Truth and Method*, p. 238.
5 Ibid., p. 239.
6 M. Heidegger, *Being and Time*, translated by J. Macquarrie and E. Robinson, Oxford: Basil Blackwell, 1973, Section 32, p. 192.
7 Ibid.
8 Ibid., p. 195.
9 *Truth and Method*, p. 245.
10 Ibid.

8 Cultural tradition and educational experience

1 There are many website articles that address such Western fears. For the most part, these conclude that the role played by madrassas in Islamic countries is quite small, compared to other kinds of schools, and that very many madrassas function more like ordinary schools than schools for extremists. See for instance, www.uvm.edu/~envprog/madrassah.html, http://www.nytimes.com/2005/06/14/opinion/14bergen.html, http://en.wikipedia.org/wiki/Madrassa. For the views of a former US ambassador to the UN on madrassas in Pakistan, see www.pbs.org/wgbh/pages/frontline/shows/saudi/analyses/madrassas.htm. (All accessed on 9 April 2009).

2 *Truth and Method*, p. 249.

3 T. Eagleton, *Literary Theory*, quoted in G. Bruns, *Hermeneutics Ancient and Modern*, New Haven: Yale University Press, 1992, p. 195.

4 Ibid.

5 *Truth and Method*, Foreword to the Second Edition p.xvi ff.

6 The German word '*Überlieferung*', which appears more frequently than '*Tradition*' in *Truth and Method*, is less misleading, as it calls attention to the totality of that which 'lies over' our efforts to understand, or that which is 'delivered over' to such efforts. This avoids the distracting, or more highly charged, connotations that 'tradition' can have; viz. as a paternalistic or conservative force.

7 See, for instance, Gadamer's essay 'Reflections on my philosophical journey', in L. E. Hahn (ed.), *The Philosophy of Hans-Georg Gadamer*, Chicago: Open Court Publishing, 1997, p. 35.

8 *After Virtue* (Second Edition, 1985), p. 220.

9 See, for instance, *After Virtue*, p. 44. To say that MacIntyre argues suggestively is not quite the same as saying that his arguments are fully compelling, or inescapable. A strong case can be made that the arguments of Heidegger (early) and of Gadamer fare better in this regard.

10 Ibid., p. 221.

11 Ibid., pp. 121–122.

12 Ibid., p. 222.

13 *Whose Virtue? Which Rationality?*, p. 367.

14 'Reflections on my Philosophical Journey' p. 29.

15 *Whose Virtue? Which Rationality?*, p. 367.

16 In his later book *Dependent Rational Animals*, London: Duckworth, 1999, MacIntyre's exploration of the 'virtues of acknowledged dependence' emphasizes human vulnerability over the more combative qualities stressed in the three books of his that we have been considering. He leaves implicit, however, the educational import of this new line of argument.

17 'The Idea of an Educated Public', in G. Haydon (ed.), *Education and Values: The Richard Peters Lectures*, London: University of London Institute of Education, 1987, pp. 18–19.

18 It might plausibly be charged that this puts the 'educated public' back within 'local precedent and custom'. In any case, MacIntyre illustrates that the rise of this 'Scottish Enlightenment' was associated chiefly by the intellectual climate created by the works of Thomas Reid and Dugald Stewart. Its prominent figures included Adam Ferguson, Adam Smith, John Millar, Thomas Brown and Alexander Carlyle. MacIntyre points out that there were many issues of conflict in this educated public, but that the conflict was yet contained within the standards set by a

'widespread shared philosophical education'. (The Idea of an Educated Public', p. 22.)

19 *Whose Justice? Which Rationality?*, p. 400.

20 Letter from Thomas Jefferson to William Roscoe, 20 December 1820, quoted at http://www.monticello.org/reports/quotes/uva.html (accessed on 9 April 2009).

21 W. Von Humboldt, 'On the Spirit and the Organizational Framework of Intellectual Institutions in Berlin (1809/1810)', reproduced in *Minerva: A Review of Science, Learning and Policy*, 1970, vol. 8, no.2.

22 *Whose Justice? Which Rationality?*, 399.

23 *Three Rival Versions of Moral Enquiry*, p. 233.

24 Ibid., p. 228.

25 Ibid., p. 231.

26 Ibid. In the final chapter of *Three Rival Versions of Moral Enquiry*, MacIntyre makes frequent references to 'the curriculum'. The discussion introduces it as if it were the humanities, broadly understood, that are under consideration (for instance the text of pp. 227–230). In the later pages, however, although the theme of reform of university teaching remains unchanged, his remarks seem to have theology and moral philosophy chiefly in mind.

27 A word such as 'respondee' comes to mind, but this is too contrived, and it also distracts attention from the point that this person plays a number of different roles, as one does in any genuine conversation: attentive listening, active speaking, calling on the participation of others, joining together what one has just heard with some ideas of one's own, and so on. 'Learner' is a bit formal, but if the term can apply to the experiences of everyday life as well as to those of education and training, perhaps it isn't such a bad choice.

28 On this point, Gadamer writes, 'The hermeneutic task consists in not covering up this tension by attempting a naive assimilation, but consciously bringing it out.' *Truth and Method*, p. 273.

29 Ibid., p. 340.

30 The phrase is introduced in the closing paragraphs of Part II of *Truth and Method* (p. 340) and announces the theme of Part III: 'The Ontological Shift of Hermeneutics Guided by Language.'

31 Michael Oakeshott, 'The Voice of Poetry in the Conversation of Mankind', p. 200.

32 Ibid., p. 198.

33 Ibid., p. 199.

34 *Truth and Method*, p. 340.

35 Ibid.

9 Giving voice to the text

1 I. Kant, 'An Answer to the Question: What Is Enlightenment?' (1784). Available at http://www.english.upenn.edu/~mgamer/Etexts/kant.html (accessed on 9 April 2009).

2 Kant's own short work, *Über Pädagogik* (1803), takes up some of these challenges in an initial way. For instance, he speaks of cultivating 'positive obedience' among children, always with a view to combining this with 'free will'. An English translation by A. Churton, titled *On Education*, was published in 1900. This is available at http://files.libertyfund.org/files/356/Kant_0235_EBk_v4.pdf (accessed on 9 April 2009).

3 Apart from hermeneutic and pragmatist philosophers, this conclusion can also be discerned in the works of authors such as the later Wittgenstein and Karl Popper, and also in the writings of analytic philosophers such as Donald Davidson and John McDowell.

4 For instance, the teaching of topics such as graphs, bar charts, pie charts and statistics can use commonplace data (e.g. the number of cars sold in a country each month), or more stimulating data (e.g. comparative figures from sources such as the World Health Organization, United Nations, or Jubilee Research; or data on one's own country comparing successive decades).

5 It might be objected that 'diversity' puts the matter too strongly, especially where the more commonplace experiences of life are concerned. This kind of objection overlooks the critical point that in any few hours of one's life there is likely to be a diversity of influences at play – for instance, even within each of the following experiences: reading a newspaper, working with others, watching a television drama, talking to friends, listening to a radio phone-in programme, watching a match.

6 *Whose Justice? Which Rationality?*, p. 367.

7 In the literature of educational research, the term 'curriculum' refers not just to a syllabus, but to the experienced quality of learning. In the current description, however, what is intended is the narrower, or dictionary definition: 'a course of study'.

8 S. Heaney, *The Burial at Thebes: Sophocles' Antigone*, London: Faber and Faber, 2005.

9 *Whose Justice? Which Rationality?* p. 373.

10 Ibid. p. 382 ff.

11 W. Shakespeare, *The Tragedy of Hamlet, Prince of Denmark* in *The Tragedies of Shakespeare*, London: Marshall Cavendish, 1988, Act 1, Sc.i.

12 *Whose Justice? Which Rationality?*, p. 385.

13 Ibid., p. 400.

14 Ibid., p. 399.

15 Where the continuing professional development of teachers has reached advanced levels, part of such preparatory readings might be undertaken in workshop settings, largely organized by teachers themselves, but supported by national educational support agencies.

16 This is not to say that other kinds of environments – for instance, electronic learning environments – are morally neutral. The moral dimension associated with the 'good influence' of a teacher may not be a feature of such environments, but it may be present in other ways: in the attitudes evoked, cultivated or discouraged in learners through their relations with the pre-packaged learning materials.

17 *Experience and Education*, p. 48.

18 Of course, some denominational schools can be quite divisive in this sense, where pronounced theological differences are strengthened by cultural features. See, for instance, the study by D. Murray, *Worlds Apart: Segregated Schools in Northern Ireland*, Belfast: Appletree Press, 1985.

19 *Three Rival Versions of Moral Enquiry*, p. 231.

20 Some, although by no means all, of the teaching in the Irish Hedge Schools of the eighteenth and early nineteenth centuries seems to have been characterized by an open-ended relationship with inheritances of learning. The Hedge Schools were clandestine schools during the Penal Laws period of Irish history (1695 to

the late 1700s). Their teachers were laymen whose actions frequently invoked the displeasure of both secular and religious authorities. See, for instance, P. J. Dowling, *The Hedge Schools of Ireland*, Cork: Mercier Press, 1968; and A. McManus, *The Irish Hedge School and Its Books, 1695–1831*, Dublin: Four Courts Press, 2006. The opening scene of Brian Friel's play *Translations*, is set in a Donegal Hedge School in the year 1830: B. Friel, *Translations*, London: Faber,1981.

21 *Whose Justice? Which Rationality?* p. 367.

22 S. Benhabib, *Situating the Self: Gender, Community and Postmodernism in Contemporary Ethics*, New York: Routledge, 1992, p. 30, 227.

10 Neither born nor made: the education of teachers

1 J. Dewey, *Experience and Education*, pp. 19–20.

2 Ibid., p. 6.

3 For a good overview and analysis, see the following two articles: M. Cochran-Smith and M. K. Fries, 'Sticks, Stones, and Ideology: The Discourse of Reform in Teacher Education' in *Educational Researcher*, 2001, vol. 30, no.8; also J. Furlong, 'Ideology and Reform in Teacher Education in England: Some Reflections on Cochran-Smith and Fries' in *Educational Researcher*, 2002, vol. 31, no. 6.

4 J. Coolahan, *Irish Education: History and Structure*, Dublin: Institute of Public Administration, 1981, p. 32.

5 Hillgate Group, *Learning to Teach*, London: The Claridge Press, 1989; S. Lawlor, *Teachers Mistaught: Training in Theories or Education in Subjects*, London: Centre for Policy Studies, 1990.

6 *The Northern Ireland Teacher Education Partnership Handbook*, Department of Education Northern Ireland, 1998, available at http://www.deni.gov.uk/teacher_education_partnership_handbook-3.pdf (accessed on 9 April 2009).

7 The 92 competences are presented under these five headings on pp. 11–16 of the *Handbook*.

8 The long-term damage occasioned by such policy measures – not least a lasting technicism that has infected educational thinking – has been thoughtfully explored by R. Smith in various writings; for instance: 'Paths of Judgement: The revival of practical wisdom', in W. Carr (ed.), *The RoutledgeFalmer Reader in Philosophy of Education*, pp. 206–18; 'The Long Slide to Happiness', in *Journal of Philosophy of Education*, 2008, vol. 42, no. 3–4, pp. 559–573.

9 See, for instance, P. Gilroy, 'Inspecting the Inspecting of Teacher Education', in *Journal of Education for Teaching*, 1999, vol. 25, no. 3.

10 See P. Gilroy, 'The Political Rape of Initial Teacher Education in England and Wales', in *Journal of Education for Teaching*, 1992, vol.18, no. 1.

11 See E. Stones, 'Directions for the Future', in *Journal of Education for Teaching*, 2002, vol. 28, no. 3.

12 See E. C. Wragg, 'State-approved Knowledge: Ten Steps Down a Slippery Slope', in *The Art and Science of Teaching and Learning: The selected writings of Ted Wragg*, London: Routledge, 2005; also E. Stones, 'Apocalypse Imposed', in *Journal of Education for Teaching*, 1999, vol. 25, no. 3.

13 On this theme, see J. Coolahan 'The Operational Environment for Future Planning in Teacher Education' in R. Dolan and J. Gleeson (eds), *The Competences Approach to Teacher Professional Development: Current Practices and Future Prospects*, Armagh: SCoTENS, 2007, pp. 7–14.

14 OECD *Teachers Matter: Attracting, Developing and Retaining Effective Teachers*, Paris: OECD, 2005, pp. 86–90.

15 Ibid., p. 87.

16 Ibid., p. 15.

17 Ibid., pp. 13–14.

18 Ibid., p. 14.

19 The Introduction to the EU policy document of 2004 titled *Education and Training 2010: The Success Of The Lisbon Strategy Hinges On Urgent Reforms*, provided a fuller statement as follows: 'At the Lisbon European Council held in March 2000, the Heads of State and Government acknowledged that *"the European Union is confronted with a quantum shift resulting from globalisation and the challenges of a new knowledge-driven economy"* and set the EU a major strategic goal for 2010 *"to become the most competitive and dynamic knowledge-based economy in the world, capable of sustainable economic growth with more and better jobs and greater social cohesion."* It stressed that this would require not only a *"radical transformation of the European economy"*, but also a *"challenging programme for modernising social welfare and education systems."'* The text is available at http://ec.europa.eu/education/policies/2010/doc/jir_council_final.pdf (accessed on 9 April 2009).

20 European Commission (2005) *Common European Principles for Teacher Competences and Qualifications*, http://ec.europa.eu/education/policies/2010/doc/principles_en.pdf, pp. 1–2 (accessed on 9 April 2009).

21 Ibid., pp. 2–3.

22 Ibid., pp. 4–5.

23 Ibid.

24 Ibid., p. 3.

25 Ibid.

26 Ibid., pp. 3–4.

27 Ibid., p. 4.

28 For details of EU work in social cohesion, see http://europa.eu/pol/reg/index_en.htm (accessed on 9 April 2009).

29 General Teaching Council for Northern Ireland (2005) *Teaching: The Reflective Profession*, p. 5 (available at www.gtcni.org.uk (accessed on 9April 2009).

30 Ibid.

31 Ibid., pp. 45–46.

32 Ibid., p. 11.

33 Ibid.

11 The new significance of learning

1 In the case of England and Wales, a retrospective account of such dramatic changes is provided in an essay by S. Maclure 'Through the Revolution and Out the Other Side', in *Oxford Review of Education*, 1998, vol. 24, no. 1, pp. 5–24.

2 In different jurisdictions, the degree of independence of such councils varies. In all cases, unsurprisingly, Ministers seem to retain the final authority. In Ireland, for instance, the Minister for Education approved in 1999 the new curriculum for primary schools developed by the National Council for Curriculum and Assessment. But, in 2005, the Minister declined to approve, on grounds of cost, reform proposals for the senior cycle post-primary curriculum prepared by the NCCA. By contrast, in England, the Qualifications and Curriculum Agency seems

to operate from the start as a subordinate arm of the government. The following extract from the QCA website is revealing: 'During 2009–2010, QCA will evolve into the Qualifications and Curriculum Development Agency (QCDA), a new agency which will create, develop and deliver the Government's programmes for the management and reform of qualifications, curriculum and assessment.' http:// www.qca.org.uk/qca (accessed on 9 April 2009).

3 P. Black, C. Harrison, C. Lee, B. Marshall, D. Wiliam, *Assessment for Learning: Putting it Into Practice*, Maidenhead: Open University Press/McGraw-Hill Education, 2003.

4 Ibid., pp. 2–3.

5 Much of this material is based on findings from a research and development project in a number of Irish post-primary schools in which my colleagues and I were involved in recent years. See P. Hogan, A. Brosnan, B. de Róiste, A. MacAlister, A. Malone, N. Quirke-Bolt, G. Smith, *Learning Anew: Final Report of the Research and Development Project Teaching and Learning for the 21st Century, 2003–2007*, Maynooth: National University of Ireland, Maynooth, 2008. Also available at www.nuim.ie/TL21 (accessed on 9 April 2009).

6 *Experience and Education*, p. 38.

7 For critical appraisals of this reform movement by some prominent American educators, see D. Meier and G. Harrison Wood (eds), *Many Children Left Behind*, Boston: Beacon Press, 2004.

8 Sources here include J. Elliott, *Reflecting Where the Action Is: The Selected Works of John Elliott*, London and New York: Routledge, 2007; M. Griffiths, *Action for Social Justice in Education*, Maidenhead: Open University Press/ McGraw-Hill Education, 2003; M. Griffiths and C. Davies, *In Fairness to Children*, London: David Fulton Publishers, 1995; R. Pring, G. Hayward, A. Hodgson, J. Johnson, G. Rees, K. Spours, E. Keep, A. Oancea, S. Wilde, *Education for All: The Future of Education and Training for 14–19 year-olds*, London: Routledge, 2009. The website publications of The Nuffield Review of 14–19 Education and Training at: http://www. nuffield14-19review.org.uk (accessed on 9 April 2009).

9 Quoted by J. Bronowski and B. Mazlish, *The Western Intellectual Tradition*, Harmondsworth: Penguin, 1970, p. 28.

10 M. Heidegger, 'The Question Concerning Technology', in *Martin Heidegger: Basic Writings*, D. Farrell Krell (ed.), London: Routledge and Kegan Paul, 1978, p. 288.

11 Ibid., p. 302.

12 *The Postmodern Condition*, p. 64.

13 Ibid., pp. 32–33; also B. Readings, *The University in Ruins*, Cambridge MA: Harvard University Press, 1996, Ch. 5.

14 W. von Humboldt, 'On the Spirit and the Organizational Framework of Intellectual Institutions in Berlin', pp. 242–243.

15 Ibid., p. 243.

16 This concern is evident in Humboldt's remarks on universities, already quoted in chapter 8, p.114. It is treated in detail in Humboldt's posthumously published book (1854), *The Limits of State Action*, J. W. Burrow (ed.), Indianapolis: Liberty Fund, 1991.

12 Imagination's heartwork

1 Since the European Commission's White Paper of 1996, *Teaching and Learning: Towards the Learning Society*, the word 'education' in EU policy documents has been

replaced by the phrase 'education and training'. The full text is available at http://
europa.eu/documents/comm/white_papers/pdf/com95_590_en.pdf (accessed on
9 April 2009). The EU White Paper reveals many similarities to a report of the
previous year published by the European Round Table of Industrialists, *Education
for Europeans: Towards the Learning Society*. The full text of this is available at http://
www.ert.be/doc/0061.pdf (accessed on 9 April 2009).

2 An extended summary of the *Teachers Matter* report, as well as the texts of the
Country Background Reports, can be found at www.oecd.org/edu/teacherpolicy
(accessed on 9 April 2009).

3 Thomas Aquinas, *Summa Theologiae*, translated by the English Dominican Fathers,
London: Blackfriars, in association with Eyre and Spottiswoode, 1963–74, Ia, q.1,
a8.

4 Important issues of cultural differences that I have touched on only lightly here are
insightfully explored by M. Papastephanou in her recent paper 'The Cosmopolitan
Self Does Her Homework'; forthcoming, but available at http://www.philosophy-
of-education.org/conferences/pdfs/Papastephanou.pdf (accessed 9 April 2009).

5 Quoted by C. Freeman in AD *381: Heretics, Pagans and the Christian State*, London:
Pimlico, 2008, pp. 27–28.

Bibliography

Books

Adler, M. J. *The Paideia Proposal: An Educational Manifesto*, New York and London: Macmillan, 1982.

Aquinas, T. *Summa Theologiae*, translated by the English Dominican Fathers, London: Blackfriars, in association with Eyre and Spottiswoode, 1963–1974.

Aristotle, *Politics*, translated by H. Rackham, Cambridge MA: Harvard University Press – Loeb Classical Library, 1998.

Benhabib, S. *Situating the Self: Gender, Community and Postmodernism in Contemporary Ethics*, New York: Routledge, 1992.

Bernauer, J. and D. Rasmussen. *The Final Foucault*, Cambridge MA: The MIT Press, 1994.

Black, P., C. Harrison, C. Lee, B. Marshall and D. Wiliam. *Assessment for Learning: Putting it into Practice*, Maidenhead: Open University Press/McGraw-Hill Education, 2003.

Bronowski, J. and B. Mazlish. *The Western Intellectual Tradition*, Harmondsworth: Penguin, 1970.

Brown, P. *Augustine of Hippo: A Biography* (new edition with Epilogue), London: Faber and Faber, 2000.

Bruns, G. *Hermeneutics Ancient and Modern*, New Haven: Yale University Press, 1992.

Burbules, N. C. *Dialogue in Teaching: Theory and Practice*, New York: Teachers College Press, 1993.

Caputo, J. D. (ed.). *Deconstruction in a Nutshell*, New York: Fordham University Press, 1997.

Carr, W. (ed.). *The RoutledgeFalmer Reader in Philosophy of Education*, London and New York: Routledge, 2005.

Carr, W. *For Education: Towards Critical Educational Inquiry*, Buckingham and Philadelphia: Open University Press, 1995.

Coolahan, J. *Irish Education: History and Structure*, Dublin: Institute of Public Administration, 1981.

Curtis, S. J. and M. E. A. Boultwood. *A Short History of Educational Ideas*, Slough: University Tutorial Press, 1977.

Derrida, J. *Specters of Marx: The State of the Debt, the Work of Mourning, and the New International*, translated by P. Kamuf, with Introduction by B. Magnus and S. Cullenberg, New York: Routledge, 1994.

Derrida, J. *Of Grammatology*, translated by G. C. Spivak, Baltimore: Johns Hopkins University Press, 1976.

Derrida, J. *Points ... Interviews 1974–1994*, E. Weber (ed.), Stanford: Stanford University Press, 1995.

Dewey, J. *Art as Experience*, New York: Penguin Putnam, 1934, 2005.

Dewey, J. *Experience and Education*, New York: Collier Macmillan, 1938, 1975.

Dolan, R. and J. Gleeson (eds). *The Competences Approach to Teacher Professional Development: Current Practices and Future Prospects*, Armagh: SCoTENS, 2007.

Dowling, P. J. *The Hedge Schools of Ireland*, Cork: Mercier Press, 1968.

Dunne, J. and P. Hogan. *Education and Practice: Upholding the Integrity of Teaching and Learning*, J. Dunne and P. Hogan (eds), Oxford, UK and Malden: USA: Blackwell, 2004.

Elliott, J. *Reflecting Where the Action Is: The Selected Works of John Elliott*, London and New York: Routledge, 2007.

Foucault, M. *Discipline and Punish: The Birth of the Prison*, translated by A. Sheridan, Harmondsworth: Penguin, 1979.

Foucault, M. *Fearless Speech*, edited by J. Pearson, Los Angeles: Semiotext(E), 2001.

Freeman, C. *AD 381: Heretics, Pagans and the Christian State*, London: Pimlico, 2008.

Freire, P. *Pedagogy of the Oppressed*, translated by M. Bergman Ramos, Harmondsworth: Penguin, 1972.

Friel, B. *Translations*, London: Faber, 1981.

Gadamer, H.-G. *Truth and Method*, translated from the second German edition by G. Barden and J. Cumming, London: Sheed and Ward, 1975.

Garrison, J. *Dewey and Eros*, New York and London: Teachers College Press, 1977.

Griffiths, M. *Action for Social Justice in Education*, Maidenhead: Open University Press / McGraw-Hill Education, 2003.

Griffiths, M. and C. Davies, *In Fairness to Children*, London: David Fulton Publishers, 1995.

Hargreaves, A. *Teaching in the Knowledge Society*, Maidenhead and New York: Open University Press / McGraw-Hill Education, 2003.

Heaney, S. *The Burial at Thebes: Sophocles' Antigone*, London: Faber and Faber, 2005.

Heidegger, M. *Being and Time*, translated by J. Macquarrie and E. Robinson, Oxford: Basil Blackwell, 1973.

Hillgate Group, *Learning to Teach*, London: The Claridge Press, 1989.

Hogan, P. *The Custody and Courtship of Experience*, Dublin: Columba Press, 1995.

Hogan, P, A. Brosnan, B. de Róiste, A. MacAlister, A. Malone, N. Quirke-Bolt and G. Smith. *Learning Anew: Final Report of the Research and Development Project Teaching and Learning for the 21st Century, 2003–2007*, Maynooth: National University of Ireland, Maynooth, 2007. Also available at www.nuim.ie/TL21 (accessed on 9 April 2009).

Hoy, D. C. *Foucault: A Critical Reader*, Oxford: Blackwell, 1991.

Illich, I. *Deschooling Society*, Harmondsworth: Penguin, 1973.

Kant, I. *Über Pädagogik* (1803) translated as *On Education*, by A. Churtin, available at http://files.libertyfund.org/files/356/Kant_0235_EBk_v4.pdf (accessed on 9 April 2009).

Lawlor, S. *Teachers Mistaught: Training in Theories or Education in Subjects*, London: Centre for Policy Studies, 1990.

Lawrence, D. H. *The Rainbow*, New York: Alfred A. Knopf, 1993.

Lyotard, J. F. *The Postmodern Condition: A Report on Knowledge*, translated by G. Bennington and B. Massumi, with Foreword by F. Jameson, Manchester: Manchester University Press, 1984.

MacIntyre, A. *After Virtue, A Study in Moral Theory*, Second Edition, London: Duckworth, 1985.

MacIntyre, A. *Whose Virtue? Which Rationality?*, London: Duckworth, 1988.

MacIntyre, A. *Three Rival Versions of Moral Enquiry*, London: Duckworth, 1990.

MacIntyre, A. *Dependent Rational Animals*, London: Duckworth, 1999.

McManus, A. *The Irish Hedge School and Its Books, 1695–1831*, Dublin: Four Courts Press, 2006.

Meier, D. and G. Harrison Wood (eds). *Many Children Left Behind*, Boston: Beacon Press, 2004.

Murray, D. *Worlds Apart: Segregated Schools in Northern Ireland*, Belfast: Appletree Press, 1985.

The New Testament, English Standard Version, Dublin: Talbot Press, 1970.

Noddings, N. *The Challenge to Care in Schools*, New York: Teachers College Press, 1992.

Oakeshott, M. *Rationalism in Politics and Other Essays*, London: Methuen, 1981.

Ovid, *Metamorphoses*, translated by Rolfe Humphries, Bloomington: Indiana University Press, 1955.

Plato, *The Dialogues of Plato* (in two volumes) translated by B. Jowett, with Introduction by R. Demos, New York: Random House, 1937.

Plato, *The Republic*, translated with Introduction by D. Lee, Harmondsworth: Penguin, 1974.

Popper. K. *The Open Society and its Enemies* (Vol. 1 Plato; Vol. 2 Hegel and Marx), London: Routledge 1945, 2003.

Pring, R., G. Hayward, A. Hodgson, J. Johnson, G. Rees, K. Spours, E. Keep, A. Oancea and S. Wilde. *Education for All: The Future of Education and Training for 14–19 year-olds*, London: Routledge, 2009.

Radice, B. (ed.). *The Letters of Abelard and Heloise*, London: Penguin, 2004.

Rawls, J. *A Theory of Justice*, Oxford: Oxford University Press, 1973.

Readings, B. *The University in Ruins*, Cambridge MA: Harvard University Press, 1996.

Rilke, R. M. *The Selected Poetry of Rainer Maria Rilke*, edited and translated by S. Mitchell, with Introduction by R. Hass, New York: Random House, 1982.

Russell, B. *On Education*, London: George Allen and Unwin, 1926.

Shakespeare, W. *The Tragedies of Shakespeare*, London: Marshall Cavendish, 1988.

Siegel, H. *Educating Reason: Rationality, Critical Thinking, and Education*, New York and London: Routledge, 1988.

Siegel, H. *Rationality Redeemed?: Further Dialogues on an Educational Ideal*, New York and London: Routledge, 1997.

Steiner, G. *Lessons of the Masters*, Cambridge, MA and London: Harvard University Press, 2003.

Todd, S. *Learning from the Other: Levinas, Psychoanalysis, and Ethical Possibilities in Education*, Albany: State University of New York Press, 2003.

Toulmin, S. *Cosmopolis: The Hidden Agenda of Modernity*, Chicago: University of Chicago Press, 1990.

Trendennick, H. and Tarrant, H. (eds). *The Last Days of Socrates*, London: Penguin, 2003.

Vlastos, G. *Socrates: Ironist and Moral Philosopher*, Cambridge: Cambridge University Press, 1991.

von Humboldt, W. *The Limits of State Action* (1854), J. W. Burrow (ed.), Indianapolis: Liberty Fund, 1991.

Wain, K. *The Learning Society in a Postmodern World*, New York: Peter Lang, 2004.

Williams, K. *Education and the Voice of Michael Oakeshott*, Exeter: Imprint Academic, 2007.

Wittgenstein, L. *Philosophical Investigations,* translated by G. E. M. Anscombe, Oxford: Basil Blackwell, 1953, 1978.

Wragg, E. C. (ed.). *The Art and Science of Teaching and Learning: The Selected Writings of Ted Wragg*, London: Routledge, 2005.

Articles, book chapters and reports

Buber, M. 'Education', in *Between Man and Man*, translated with an Introduction by R. G. Smith, London: Kegan Paul, Trench, Trubner and Co. Ltd., 1947/1969, pp. 109–131.

Carr, W. 'Philosophy and Education', in Carr, W. (ed.), *The RoutledgeFalmer Reader in Philosophy of Education*, London and New York: Routledge, 2005, pp. 34–49.

Cochran-Smith M. and Fries, M. K. 'Sticks, Stones, and Ideology: The Discourse of Reform in Teacher Education', in *Educational Researcher*, 2001, vol. 30, no. 8, pp. 3–15.

Commission of the European Communities, *Common European Principles for Teacher Competences and Qualifications*, Brussels: EU Commission, 2005, http://ec.europa.eu/education/policies/2010/doc/principles_en.pdf, pp. 1–2 (accessed on 9 April 2009).

Coolahan, J. 'The Operational Environment for Future Planning in Teacher Education', in R. Dolan and J. Gleeson (eds), *The Competences Approach to Teacher Professional Development: Current Practices and Future Prospects*, Armagh: SCoTENS, 2007, pp. 7–14.

Department of Education Northern Ireland, *The Northern Ireland Teacher Education Partnership Handbook*, 1998, available at http://www.deni.gov.uk/teacher_education_partnership_handbook-3.pdf (accessed on 9 April 2009).

Derrida, J. 'Force of Law: The "Mystical Foundation of Authority"', in D. Cornell, M. Rosenfeld and D. G. Carlson (eds), *Deconstruction and the Possibility of Justice*, New York and London: Routledge, 1992, pp. 3–67.

Derrida, J. 'The Principle of Reason: The University in the Eyes of its Pupils', translated by C. Porter and E. P. Morris, in *Diacritics*, Fall, 1983, pp. 3–20.

Derrida, J. 'The Villanova Roundtable: A Conversation with Jacques Derrida', in J. D.Caputo (ed.), *Deconstruction in a Nutshell*, New York: Fordham University Press, 1997, pp. 3–28.

Derrida, J. 'Faith and Knowledge: The Two Sources of "Religion" at the Limits of Reason Alone', in J. Derrida and G. Vattimo (eds), *Religion*, Cambridge: Polity Press in association with Basil Blackwell Ltd. Oxford, 1998, pp. 1–78.

Dunne, J. 'What's the Good of Education?', in W. Carr (ed.), *The RoutledgeFalmer Reader in Philosophy of Education*, London: Routledge, 2005, pp. 145–160.

European Commission, White Paper, *Teaching and Learning: Towards the Learning Society*, Brussels: Commission of the European Communities, 1996.

Flynn, T. 'Foucault as Parrhesiast: his last course at the Collège de France (1984)', in *The Final Foucault*, pp. 102–118.

Foucault, M. 'Truth and Power', in P. Rabinow (ed.), *The Foucault Reader*, Harmondsworth: Penguin, 1984, pp. 51–75.

Foucault, M. 'Polemics, Politics and Problemizations: An Interview with Michel Foucault', in Rabinow, P. (ed.), *The Foucault Reader*, pp. 381–390.

Foucault, M. 'Politics and Ethics: An Interview', in P. Rabinow (ed.), *The Foucault Reader*, pp. 370–379.

Foucault, M. 'What is Enlightenment?', in P. Rabinow (ed.), *The Foucault Reader*, London: Penguin, 1984, pp. 32–50.

Foucault, M. 'On the Genealogy of Ethics: An Overview of Work in Progress', in P. Rabinow (ed.), *The Foucault Reader*, pp. 381–389.

Foucault, M. *Fearless Speech*, J. Pearson (ed.), Los Angeles: Semiotext(E), 2001.

Furlong, J. 'Ideology and Reform in Teacher Education in England: Some Reflections on Cochran-Smith and Fries', in *Educational Researcher*, 2002, vol. 31, no. 6, pp. 23–35.

Gadamer, H.-G. 'Hermeneutics as Practical Philosophy', in *Reason in the Age of Science*, translated with Introduction by F. G. Lawrence, Cambridge, MA: The MIT Press, 1981, pp. 88–112.

Gadamer, H.-G. 'Reflections on my Philosophical Journey', in L. E. Hahn (ed.), *The Philosophy of Hans-Georg Gadamer*, Chicago: Open Court Publishing, 1997, pp. 3–63.

Gadamer, H.-G. 'The Universality of the Hermeneutical Problem', in *Philosophical Hermeneutics*, translated and edited by D. E. Linge, Berkeley: University of California Press, 1976, pp. 3–17.

General Teaching Council for Northern Ireland. *Teaching: The Reflective Profession*, Belfast: GTCNI, 2005 (available at www.gtcni.org.uk (accessed on 9 April 2009).

Gilroy, P. 'Inspecting the Inspecting of Teacher Education', in *Journal of Education for Teaching*, 1999, vol. 25, no. 3, pp. 215–219.

Gilroy, P. 'The Political Rape of Initial Teacher Education in England and Wales', in *Journal of Education for Teaching*, 1992, vol. 18, no. 1, pp. 5–22.

Heidegger, M. 'The Origin of the Work of Art', in *Poetry, Language Thought*, translated with Introduction by A. Hofstadter, New York: Harper and Row, 1971, pp. 17–87.

Heidegger, M. 'The Question Concerning Technology', in *Martin Heidegger: Basic Writings*, D. Farrell Krell (ed.), London: Routledge and Kegan Paul, 1978, pp. 287–318.

Her Majesty's Inspectorate of Education. *The Child at the Centre*, Edinburgh, HMIE, 2007.

Kant, I. 'An Answer to the Question: What Is Enlightenment?' (1784) available at http://www.english.upenn.edu/~mgamer/Etexts/kant.html (accessed on 9 April 2009).

MacIntyre, A. 'The Idea of an Educated Public', in G. Haydon (ed.), *Education and Values: The Richard Peters Lectures*, London: University of London Institute of Education, 1987, pp. 15–36.

MacIntyre, A. and J. Dunne. 'Alasdair MacIntyre on Education: In Dialogue with Joseph Dunne', in *Education and Practice: Upholding the Integrity of Teaching and Learning*, J. Dunne and P. Hogan (eds), Oxford, UK and Malden: USA: Blackwell, 2004, pp. 1–17.

Maclure, S. 'Through the Revolution and Out the Other Side', in *Oxford Review of Education*, 1998, vol. 24, no. 1, pp. 5–24.

Oakeshott, M. 'The Voice of Poetry in the Conversation of Mankind', in *Rationalism in Politics and Other Essays*, London: Methuen, 1981, pp. 197–247.

Office for Standards in Education, *The Education of Six Year Olds in England, Denmark and Finland: An International Comparative Study*, London: OFSTED, 2003.

Organization for Economic Co-operation and Development. *Teachers Matter: Attracting, Developing and Retaining Effective Teachers*, Paris: OECD, 2005.

Peters, M. A. 'Truth-Telling as an Educational Practice of the Self: Foucault, Parrhesia and the Ethics of Subjectivity', in *Oxford Review of Education*, vol. 29, no. 2, 2003, pp. 207–223.

Smith, R. 'Paths of Judgement: The Revival of Practical Wisdom', in W. Carr (ed.), *The RoutledgeFalmer Reader in Philosophy of Education*, pp. 206–218.

Smith, R. 'The Long Slide to Happiness', in *Journal of Philosophy of Education*, 2008, vol. 42, no. 3–4, pp. 559–573.

Standish, P. 'Ethics Before Equality', in W. Carr (ed.), *The RoutledgeFalmer Reader in Philosophy of Education*, pp. 230–237.

Stones, E. 'Apocalypse Imposed', in *Journal of Education for Teaching*, 1999, vol. 25, no. 3, pp. 189–190.

Stones, E. 'Directions for the Future', in *Journal of Education for Teaching*, 2002, vol. 28, no. 3, pp. 207–210.

Taylor, C. 'Foucault on Freedom and Truth', in D. C. Hoy, *Foucault: A Critical Reader*, Oxford: Blackwell, 1991, pp. 69–102.

von Humboldt, W. 'On the Spirit and the Organisational Framework of Intellectual Institutions in Berlin' (1809/1810), reproduced in *Minerva: A Review of Science, Learning and Policy*, 1970, vol. 8, no. 2. pp. 242–267.

Wilson, J. 'Concepts, Contestability and the Philosophy of Education', in *Journal of Philosophy of Education*, 1981, vol. 15, no. 1, pp. 3–15.

Wilson, J. 'Philosophy and Education: Retrospect and Prospect', in *Oxford Review of Education*, 1980, vol. 6, no. 1, pp. 41–52.

Wragg, E. C. 'State-approved Knowledge: Ten Steps Down a Slippery Slope', in E. C. Wragg (ed.), *The Art and Science of Teaching and Learning: The Selected Writings of Ted Wragg*, London: Routledge, 2005, pp. 197–202.

Index